Media and Religion

This is the first text to examine the history, theory, cultural context, and professional aspects of media and religion. While religion has been explored more fully in psychology, sociology, anthropology, and the humanities, there is no clear bridge of understanding to the communication discipline. Daniel A. Stout tackles this issue by providing a roadmap for examining this understudied area so that discussions about media and religion can more easily proceed. Offering great breadth, this text covers key concepts and historical highlights; world religions, denominations, and cultural religion; and religion and specific media genres. The text also includes key terms and questions to ponder for every chapter, and concludes with an in-class learning activity that can be used to encourage students to explore the media–religion interface and review the essential ideas presented in the book.

Media and Religion is an ideal introduction for undergraduate students in need of a foundation for this emerging field.

Daniel A. Stout is a Professor in the Greenspun School of Journalism and Media Studies at the University of Nevada Las Vegas.

Media and Religion

Foundations of an Emerging Field

Daniel A. Stout

Routledge
Taylor & Francis Group

NEW YORK AND LONDON

First published 2012
by Routledge
711 Third Avenue, New York, NY 10017

Simultaneously published in the UK
by Routledge
2 Park Square, Milton Park, Abingdon, Oxon OX14 4RN

Routledge is an imprint of the Taylor & Francis Group, an informa business

Library of Congress Cataloging in Publication Data
Stout, Daniel A.
Media and religion : foundations of an emerging field / Daniel A. Stout.
    p. cm.
    Includes bibliographical references.
    1. Mass media—Religious aspects—Textbooks. I. Title.
    BL638.S76 2011
    201'.630223—dc23
    2011027521

ISBN: 978-0-8058-6383-3 (hbk)
ISBN: 978-0-8058-6384-0 (pbk)
ISBN: 978-0-203-14811-2 (ebk)

Typeset in Minion
by EvS Communication Networx, Inc.

Printed and bound in the United States of America on acid-free paper
by Edwards Brothers, Inc.

To Kayna

Contents

Preface   ix

Chapter 1   Introduction   1

Chapter 2   Key Concepts   9

Chapter 3   Physiology and Mental States   25

Chapter 4   World Religions and Denominations   33

Chapter 5   Cultural Religion   47

Chapter 6   Media Criticism   61

Chapter 7   The Internet   73

Chapter 8   Entertainment Media   85

Chapter 9   The News   97

Chapter 10   Strategic Communication   113

Chapter 11   In the Classroom: A Learning Activity   123

Epilogue   165
Notes   169
References   177
Index   197

Preface

In contemplating media and religion, I'm reminded of the months I lived in Manhattan. On the subway one spring morning, I found myself in the same car with a Hasidic Jew, Catholic school children in uniform, and two Mormon missionaries. Walking uptown, I marveled at St. John the Divine, the Riverside Church, and the Jewish Theological Seminary. On other occasions, the architecture of the Islamic Cultural Center and the coned roof of the Metropolitan Baptist Church provided visual delight and a sense of the city's religious diversity. Only now do I realize how narrow my survey of New York religion was. I had overlooked mediated forms of religion and hadn't realized it. There were the "Rentheads" or devoted fans of the rock musical and subsequent movie *Rent*, who watched the show dozens of times and slept on the sidewalk while they waited for the ticket office to open. Much like a religious congregation, ardent Yankee fans crowded into restaurants and pubs for their ritual of televised baseball. And, invisible to me, were the thousands of New Yorkers pursuing religion online in the privacy of their homes. This expansive view of religion underpins my approach in this book.

Media play a central role in contemporary religion, and conversely, religion is essential to understanding media's place in society. For this reason, a new field of study is emerging that involves the religion–media interface, with research expanding and universities offering courses, and this book is an introduction to the subject; it identifies issues and frameworks so the reader can explore the topic with greater ease. I hope that such a discussion will lend credibility to the new field and encourage deeper and more thoughtful analysis.

The fact that religion has been largely overlooked in media studies is no small matter because it has resulted in inadequate models of mass communication and insufficient theorizing about how individuals experience media today.

Religion is a part of culture and history and students of mass communication should not be afraid to explore it from a scholarly perspective. That's what this book is about: organizing information so that discussion about media and religion can more easily proceed. Such a task cannot be accomplished without identifying relevant ideas, theories, and concepts. This text provides an initial roadmap for examining a divergent and understudied area.

Unfortunately, when students open their mass communication textbooks they see very little about religion. One reason is disciplinary; borders between fields impede the sharing of ideas. While religion has been explored more fully in psychology, sociology, anthropology, and the humanities, there's no clear bridge of understanding that leads to the communication discipline. This book is an effort to synthesize related concepts and create a convenient single source of information.

The media–religion relationship has evolved to the point where it deserves focused systematic study. Online worship, megachurches, and televangelism are just a few examples of media-related religious issues. Secular audiences of popular media also display religionlike behavior and ritual. Despite the fact that religion is expressed in many forms through the media, scholars focus mainly on traditional faith traditions, overlooking new types of worship.

The study of media and religion has value within the media industries; knowledge of comparative religion is a professional asset. News organizations employ religion reporters and editors; some television news programs feature "religion specialists." Within advertising agencies, researchers study how religion influences buying behavior. Public relations practitioners communicate with "religious publics." With the widespread availability of information technology, religious organizations themselves are creating Web sites, producing television programs, and using a wide range of media.

I hope this volume will break down old barriers and facilitate the study of media and religion in an organized fashion. Like most textbooks, it treats the topic in breadth rather than depth; it is impossible to fully cover a subject with so many dimensions and complexities. A basic introduction to a vital subject is the goal.

I would like to thank Judith Buddenbaum for her unequaled contribution to scholarship in this subject, and for her advice and mentoring over the years. Much gratitude also goes to my editor at Taylor & Francis, Linda Bathgate, who supported this project from the beginning with enthusiasm and patience. Finally, I would like to thank Lynn Goeller and her staff for the highly professional work in the editing stage.

CHAPTER 1

Introduction

Few subjects in the last two decades have attracted more attention than the media–religion interface. Examples include: cyberchurches, virtual pilgrimages, online missionaries, megachurches, emergent churches, cybertemples, e-prayer, religious blogs, televangelism, and religious radio. Increasingly popular are media genres such as spiritual rock music, contemporary religious novels, and faith-based video games. Houses of worship have become multimedia environments with big screen projection technology and sophisticated lighting and sound systems. Congregations are no longer confined to physical locales; interactive media create virtual or online churches. These developments beg for closer examination.

How religions are depicted in the media is of vital concern because the media are the source of much of what people know about them. This fact may ultimately determine how groups are perceived and treated. Hence, public relations professionals are often hired by faith groups to prevent misperceptions.

Twenty years ago, the relationship between the media and religion was a topic of growing interest; today it is a developing field of study,[1] a promising area of research that not only provides a fresh perspective on both elements, but contributes to theory-building in the general discipline of mass communication.

In this book, I explore the relationship between the media and religion both inside and outside institutions. Within groups, the media instruct and build community, but organized religion doesn't fully account for the ways that individuals worship today. Religious "questers" seek truth in many places, including the media of popular culture (Roof, 1993, 1999). Consequently, this book is as much about the Oprah Winfrey phenomenon as it is about Radio Islam or the *National Catholic Reporter.*

Two key developments characterize this new age of media and religion: (1) Organized religion is increasingly to be found in a number of different media (i.e., spiritual Web sites, radio sermons, church magazines, etc.), and (2) the elements of religion (i.e., ritual, deep feeling, belief, and community) are experienced through the media of popular culture. In fact, the assumption that any medium is entirely secular is being questioned. In other words, religiosity, broadly defined, helps us better understand the overall media landscape.

It is problematic to assume that the media and religion are distinct phenomena (Carey, 2002; Hoover, 2001); it is more advantageous to understand how they interface in a cultural context of expanding forms of worship.[2] Speaking of contemporary society, Carey (2002) notes that: "Religion has unexpectedly returned to center stage..." (p. 3). In his history of the term *communication,* Peters (1999) points out that religious history teaches us many things about the evolution of the term's meaning. Interest in such subjects is encouraging for media studies. It is time to discuss the contours of the new field and elucidate its importance.

Purpose of the Book

The present work has been conceived as a foundation for the study of the media and religion; it organizes and presents concepts in a way that enables future study and in the process recognizes a major cultural trend in contemporary society. At a basic level, it discusses theory, history, and content. At another level, it presents religion as a useful analytic concept, one that aids our understanding of a full range of media-related experiences, not just those pertaining to denominations. Both traditional and nontraditional religions are examined because people define religion broadly and find it throughout society.

Religion as Broad Analytical Concept

Religion, which has been controversial and not well understood by media researchers in the past, is becoming a useful analytical concept. This approach places religion, previously viewed as a fringe area, in a more central position in media studies by analyzing the media according to their rituals, beliefs, community, and feeling dimensions rather than in terms of validating theology or advocating spiritual worldviews. Only recently have media scholars come to embrace the idea, shared by anthropologists of religion, that these four elements are key ordering concepts of everyday life. According to Sylvan (2005), it is "the notion that religion, in a broader and more fundamental sense, is the underlying substratum for all cultural activity and serves as the foundation for culture in general" (p. 13). A comprehensive approach to a study of the religious aspects of the media is recognized by scholars:

> Anthropological studies of comparative religion and shamanism demonstrate that all cultures possess rites, myths, divine forms, sacred and venerated objects, symbols, consecrated men [sic] and sacred places. Each category is attached to a distinctive morphology that organizes experience and bestows sacred or extraordinary meaning on certain types of conduct and experience. (Rojek, 2007, p. 172)

Such phenomena are ubiquitous in everyday life. As historian of religion Mircea Eliade (1959) notes, religion "may manifest itself no matter how or where in the profane world..." (p. 30). In the same way that culture encompasses ritual, community, and belief, so do media-related behaviors.

Overcoming Barriers to the Study of Media and Religion

If religion is an important analytical concept, why isn't it applied more often in media studies? Why has the subject been approached cautiously in communication programs at secular universities? Carey (2002) attributes this resistance to the Enlightenment when science and empiricism came to dominate educational institutions, which had previously been dominated by the religious groups that founded them. While the separation of the theological and the secular is important, the examination of religion from a cultural perspective became less emphasized in media studies. The sociology of religion, psychology of religion, and anthropology of religion are emerging fields, but for a variety of reasons, a comparable area in media studies is only beginning to take root.

The Problem of Semantics and the Term Religion

Perhaps the biggest impediment to the study of this subject is the term *religion* itself, which is used so widely and loosely that confusion has arisen about what precisely it is we are talking about. If the definition is too restrictive, some quasi-religious media activities will be overlooked. Therefore, Johnstone's (2001) definition is optimal; it defines religion as "a system of beliefs and practices by which a group of people interprets and responds to what they feel is sacred and, usually supernatural as well" (p. 13). Similar to the definition of Cornwall, Albrecht, Cunningham, and Pitcher (1986), it argues that religion is multidimensional, comprised of belief, behavior, community, and feeling. Such a definition sets reasonable criteria for what qualifies as religious, but the definition is broad enough to include wide-ranging media experiences. Furthermore, it emphasizes that belief in the supernatural is usually, but not always present in human culture. This allows us to apply a religious analysis to a broader range of popular media.

Because the term *religion* is used in both theological and academic contexts, its meaning varies. The study of "religion" means something different in a mosque, for example, than it does in a secular college classroom. Unlike theologians who base their work on an assumed deity, academics approach the subject like any other, applying the same analytical methods that they use in the study of history, social science, and the humanities. The media and religion is an academic subject much like political communication or media ethics; its goal is not to advocate spirituality or any particular worldview.

To address the problem of semantics, this book uses the term *religion* as well as the term *numinous* because numinous experiences are similar to religious ones and may occur outside institutions, and such experiences do not necessarily involve the supernatural. For example, some may be more comfortable describing the experience of Elvis fandom as numinous rather than religious. Lohrey (2010) contends that there are religious as well as nonreligious perspectives on the numinous, the latter recently embraced by atheist scholars Richard Dawkins, Christopher Hitchens, and Sam Harris.

The concept is discussed in depth later in the chapter. The point is that alternative terms broaden the discussion, and move us beyond the restrictions of semantic boundaries.

Getting Beyond Dualism

A common assumption is that media and religion are distinct, impermeable phenomena often in perpetual conflict. This idea was particularly prevalent in the late 1980s and early 1990s culture wars (Hunter, 1992). Picketers gathered outside movie theaters to protest *The Last Temptation of Christ* (Scorsese, 2000) and Muslims denounced Salman Rushdie's (1988) novel *Satanic Verses*. Movie critic Michael Medved (1992) declared that Hollywood and religion embraced incompatible worldviews and James Dobson, host of the popular radio program *Focus on the Family* observed a wide gulf between family values and those depicted in the media. The boycott of Disney entertainment products by the Southern Baptist Convention is yet another example of the divide between religion and the media. Sociologists at that time observed considerable *cultural conflict,* or a condition where little agreement existed about which worldviews were most important in a democratic society.[3] Hunter (1992) defined this culture war as a battle between orthodox and progressive impulses.

Today, researchers are expanding their analysis beyond this oppositional framework. The culture wars approach, while useful in some contexts, doesn't capture the myriad ways that media and religion interact; it has considerable limitations as an analytical concept.[4] In today's information society, it is important that students and researchers have considerable latitude in exploring the topic. The fact is, members of denominations both use and criticize the media in diverse ways. Media that are scrutinized one day are used on another day to attract converts and solicit donations. Citizens pray in their houses of worship, but may also view a movie in a theater or online, which can also be religious experiences. This book, then, seeks a broader discussion of the ways religion interacts with the media.

The Lack of Interdisciplinary Study

Analysis is aided by interdisciplinary study.[5] Scholars in other disciplines are making new discoveries about religion and society. Historians, for example, investigate the role of religion in the development of printing and other technologies. In the humanities, the influence of religion on writing and the critique of literature is of interest. Sociologists provide insights about the Internet and religious community. One goal of this book is to make interdisciplinary connections that have not been easy to make in the past.

The Need for Common Terminology

Prior to the 1990s, research on the media and religion was disparate and sporadic.[6] Since the mid-1990s, however, there has been a considerable increase in writing on the subject. Subject areas include religion and cultural studies (Hoover, 2006; Hoover & Clark, 2002; Hoover & Lundby, 1997); religious audiences (Stout & Buddenbaum, 1996, 2001); religion and popular culture (Forbes & Mahan, 2005); critical studies (de Vries & Weber, 2001); and historical perspectives (Sloan, 2000) to name a few. Yet the field remains divergent: There is no common language of analysis, different terminology is being used to describe similar phenomena. The present volume responds to this situation in two ways: First, it identifies foundational concepts for more precise study. Second, it organizes and categorizes information so that it can be accessed with greater ease. Lastly, it discusses frameworks and theories that define the parameters of the new field.

Expanding the Discussion: Religion and the Numinous

Statues in a temple or video in a megachurch are easily categorized as religious media. But, what about the music in the Broadway musical *Rent*? Is there a concept that recognizes ritual, belief, community, and feeling in all of these examples? Is there a term that permits us to study media in both traditional and nontraditional religious settings? While there are many categories of religion (e.g., denominational religion, civil religion, popular religion, cultural religion, etc.), a broad concept is needed in order to examine the quasi-religious dimensions of a broad range of media. Such a concept is the *numinous,* an idea once confined to traditional religion, which is now finding application in sociology, anthropology, psychology, ethnobotany, ethnomusicology, literary studies, museum studies, and other fields.[7]

The numinous is a broadly defined term whose application isn't restricted to the experiences of institutional religion or the supernatural. According to Casement and Tacey (2006), the numinous is not precisely the same thing as religion, "but rather the 'religious attitude' in a variety of disciplinary and experiential contexts" (p. xvi). For example, the numinous concept allows us to study both Catholic audiences of the Catholic Community Television Network as well as teenage players of video games. Members of both groups claim to have religious experiences.

The numinous requires the following elements: deep feeling (affect), belief (cognition), ritual (behavior), and congregation (community). When all four are present in an experience with the media, audience members tend to describe it in religious terms; this is the numinous. It may occur within a church, but doesn't have to; it may happen in a movie theater instead. It is related to psychoanalyst Sigmund Freud's (1919/1953) concept of the "uncanny" and Todorov's (1975) notion of the "fantastic." When an individual declares, "That movie was a spiritual experience," she or he is describing numinous aspects of a medium. In today's media landscape, such experiences abound. Casement and Tacey (2006) explain it this way:

> The numinous means something like "awesome" and ... has gained currency in the postmodern world, and even materialists and atheists are able to affirm a "numinous" quality in nature and human experience, whereas before our time, the numinous (from *numen,* Latin for deity or divine will) would have been confined to religious discourses. Along with the concept of spirituality, which also exists outside formal religion, the numinous has been transformed,

and is now included in humanist, secular and scientific views of the world. (p. xvi)

The most thorough study of the numinous was by philosopher and theologian Rudolf Otto, who sought to describe religious experience across cultures. In his seminal book *The Idea of the Holy* (1958), he defines the numinous as something "awakened in the mind" (Otto, 1958, p. 7) that creates a sense of awe, fear, and fascination. These experiences are not confined to traditional religions, but are also associated with the media of popular culture as well. By using both the terms *religion* and *numinous*, a wider net is cast in our analysis. The purpose is not to advocate a religious worldview, but to explore media studies from a multifaceted perspective.

This book is a reflection of a shifting religious culture. Wuthnow (2003) observes that paintings, sculpture, film, dance, and other art forms are playing an increasing role within faith traditions. Perry and Wolfe (2001) argue that listening to contemporary religious music is a form of worship. Similarly, consumers of religious products (e.g., books, CDs, clothing, jewelry) engage in "witnessing," and express "excitement about one's beliefs" (Haley, White, & Cunningham, 2001, p. 281).

Individuals describe the numinous inside groups and denominations, but also experience it through media that are usually considered secular. Examples include Elvis worship (Doss, 1999), the Oprah Winfrey phenomenon (Nelson, 2005), UFO enthusiasts (Paradis, 2002), Rentheads[8] (Hymnowitz, 2008), Deadheads[9] (Adams, 2000), Parrotheads[10] (Ingersoll, 2001), dance raves (Sylvan, 2005), and baseball fans (Evans & Herzog, 2002) among others. In order to capture a full range of experiences both inside and outside denominations, it is important to define religion and religious experience in broad terms.

Organization of the Book

This chapter has provided an introduction and explained the concept of the numinous. Chapter 2 lays out key concepts that include historical highlights; it also identifies related fields and what they contribute to the subject. Chapter 3 discusses mental states or the biological and psychological levels of the interplay between the media and religion. Chapter 4 addresses world religions and denominations, while chapter 5 investigates cultural religion and numinous experiences with the media of popular culture. Chapter 6 delves into the area of media criticism. Analytical skills necessary to critique, interpret, and enjoy media that depict religion are teased out.

The next four chapters deal with specific media forms or genres. Chapter 7 explores religion and the Internet, and entertainment media is examined in chapter 8. Religion in the news is the topic of chapter 9. Chapter 10 covers strategic communication such as religious advertising and public relations. Chapter 11 contains a classroom learning activity in the form of a play, *Redeeming Value,* designed to introduce or review essential ideas in the book.

Key Terms

cultural religion: Religious practices that center in media of popular culture (e.g., movies, novels, television programs, etc.).

culture war: Societal discourse that is forever in conflict; argumentation that has no goal of resolution.

denominational religion: Religious practices associated with established institutions such as Christianity, Judaism, Islam, Hinduism, Buddhism, etc.

dualism: The assumption that a phenomenon can only be explained in one of two ways.

mediated religion: Those religious experiences aided by some form of information technology.

paradigm: A dominant or accepted approach to the study of a phenomenon.

ritual: An established patterned set of behaviors in religious worship.

secularization: The theory that religious commitments are gradually eroded through interaction with the larger society.

Questions to Ponder

1. What societal developments led to the present situation where religion is present in all sectors of the culture?
2. What are the limitations of the culture wars model in studying media and religion?
3. What are the differences between religion and the numinous? What are the similarities?
4. How do the media of denominational religion differ from the media of cultural religion?
5. Is religion an important concept in understanding media processes and effects?

CHAPTER 2

Key Concepts

The study of media and religion requires a set of analytical tools. How do we think about it with greater clarity? Where do we begin an examination of this subject? A set of theories and a framework is required. This chapter discusses key concepts from a number of perspectives, including historical insights and relevant fields of study, in order to examine the media and religion. By doing so, we get a sense of the field's importance and complexity. As we shall see, scholars in other disciplines provide useful ideas. Religiosity is expressed in diverse ways today, and the role of the media should be considered thoughtfully and carefully. This is particularly important in an era when numinous experience occurs throughout the culture. Concepts are the tools at our fingertips for assessing the present situation.

Key Concepts: Ideas to Think With

Our goal is to provoke thinking about the media and religion. This book doesn't provide all the answers. It does, however, introduce analytical concepts enabling us to articulate cogent and relevant questions; they help us explore the topic thoroughly and concisely.

Media as Religion

In many cases, religious activity emanates from media events and experiences. Through time, audiences for recorded music, movies, and other media form communities, develop belief systems, and engage in rituals. In other words, a media-related experience can deepen to the point where it takes on religious or numinous characteristics all its own. One example is the Jesus rock music genre among Evangelicals. The music itself is a focal point for worship and community.

Ritual

Media can involve *ritual* behavior, an essential element of culture. Ritual "is a standardized, repetitive activity carried out for the purpose of expressing and communicating basic cultural ideals and symbols" (Arens, 2003, p. 81).

Many religious rituals revolve around media of some kind, such as altars, statuary, or sacred writings. While Durkheim (1912/1954) associates ritual with all sacred actions, our discussion focuses on technologies that extend capacities for religious activity. Although watching television, listening to the radio, and using the Internet seem insignificant on the surface, they have deep meanings for some audience members. A weekly family gathering to watch a DVD could be a sacred activity if it locks out the profane world for a few hours, and stimulates meaningful discussion on a moral topic. Similarly, when individuals annually gather around a television to watch the Super Bowl, it involves more than a football game. Through conversation, friendships are made and neighborhood ties strengthened. This is what Carey (1989) calls the "ritual view of communication" (p. 18). The media facilitate a "sacred ceremony that draws persons together in fellowship and commonality" (p. 18).

EX:

Beyond fellowship, media rituals have a mythic quality, preserving moral beliefs through narratives. When viewers discuss their favorite soap opera over lunch, conversation about appropriate conduct of the characters may ensue. Television presents heroes and villains; it depicts moral dilemmas (Goethals, 1981). Rothenbuhler (1998) observes:

Narrative

> Over and over again, the U.S. media present stories of good versus evil, us versus them, civilization versus chaos, the enduring importance of kinship, claims of primordiality, Christian themes, variations on Oedipus, Horatio Alger, freedom, manifest destiny and so on. (p. 90)

EX

Media rituals provide opportunities for moral engagement. Dichotomies such as sacred media–secular media, religious media–nonreligious media, and Eastern media–Western media, are less useful and compelling today. The point is that virtually any medium can be the focal point of religious or numinous activity. It is important to progress beyond tenuous dualities that limit understanding.

Personalized Religion

A shift toward privatized religious experience is occurring both within and without denominations. Although face-to-face congregations endure, religious experimentation and individualized worship abound (Roof, 1999; Wuthnow, 1988, 1994).[1] In this postmodern era of abundant choice, both structured and unstructured religion is accommodated in many nations.[2] It is a time when religion is no longer captured by stable and static definitions; religion or more broadly, the numinous, can be experienced any time any place through the use of the media.

The rise of personalized religion is the result of many social, political, and economic factors, yet the media play an essential role. Through them, religious information can be stored, accessed, and shared in ways not possible in the past. Counsel from clergy is instantly available online, for example. Participation in religious discussion is immediate through computers and hand-held devices; one doesn't have to drive to a building to hear a sermon or interact with one's fellow parishioners.

Level of Analysis

The media–religion interface occurs at various levels, each deserving attention. It can be examined at the individual, social, and cultural dimensions of everyday life (see Sylvan, 2002). Each level reveals something different about the relationship.

First, there's the basic level of the senses and the electrical–chemical processes of the brain (discussed in more detail in chapter 3). Neuroscience and biology reveal much about trance formation, ecstatic states, and deep listening, and the media are increasingly involved in all three. Such experiences are associated with music, dance, or a combination of media. Examples include dance raves, rock music festivals, and trance films. Given the expanding range of contemplative media genres, brain structure and how it generates emotional responses,[3] is a promising area in the study of media and religion.

At the social level, the relationship between the media and religion is a community matter. Communities are geographical, but they also form around media messages and their interpretation (Fish, 1980; Lindlof, 2002). The phrase "People of the book" describes Judaism and its connection to the Torah, Islam and its connection with the Quran, and Christianity and its connection with the Bible, for example. Among some Evangelical Christians, reading novels with a religious theme is the basis for social interaction and reinforcement of belief (Frykholm, 2005). In

India, discussions about Hinduism and nationalism often follow Hindi language film viewing (Dwyer, 2006a). The Internet provides a home for religious communities in cyberchurches and other social media Web sites (Campbell, 2010a). In the information age, the media play a major role in the social dimension of religion. These "interpretive communities" are discussed further in chapters 4 and 5.

Ritual

Media and religion can also be analyzed at the level of societies and cultures. Norms, values, artifacts, and customs help us understand the media–religion interface for entire nations. Rituals of *civil religion* connect individuals in a common moral cause through media. The November-to-January holiday season in many countries, for example, is accompanied

Ex:

by movies, TV programs, and radio concerts stressing altruism and gratitude. The same is true of patriotic holidays such as the Fourth of July and Memorial Day in the U.S.

The media allow citizens in great numbers to reinforce their beliefs. Pastor Joel Osteen's interdenominational broadcasts from the Lakewood Church in Houston, Texas is one example; they reach over 7 million viewers each week (Duin, 2008, p. 1). While societies are large and complex, the same religious messages are shared through electronic channels. Meyer and Moors (2006) argue that religion is becoming more public in various cultures; it is being presented in new formats and styles through an array of new media. As Mazur and McCarthy (2001) aptly observe, "religion is everywhere" today (p. 2).

Secularization

Secularization—the idea that religious commitment weakens through exposure to the media—is a controversial concept in the study of the media and religion. Berger (1967) argues that in a secularized culture, religion is deemphasized in the arts, philosophy, and literature. The secularization hypothesis assumes that devotion is eroded by competing information systems, cultures, and technologies (Maguire & Weatherby, 1998). This is a heated debate in the sociology of religion.[4] For example, Stout (2004) finds that Mormons devise strategies to remain devout in Las Vegas, despite exposure to media considered deleterious to their beliefs (e.g., sexually explicit advertising, gambling promotion, etc.). Warren's (2001) study of Southern Baptists' criticism of Disney entertainment products ultimately resulted in stronger group cohesion, suggesting that the effects of secular media are difficult to predict.

Researchers agree that the nature of religious commitment is complex. Secularization has to do with the relative strength of group culture. While it is useful to think about the longevity of denominations, secularization is hard to sort out in an age of numinous media and broad definitions of religion. Something like religion occurs in every sector of society; the sacred–secular distinction is increasingly difficult to discern. An individual may leave a particular church only to discover the numinous through the media of popular culture. As Van der Leeuw (1963) puts it, "ultimately, all culture is religious."

Medium vs. Message

The medium must be considered apart from its specific content (McLuhan, 1964; Innis, 1951). Media influence their environments in ways beyond the messages themselves; each medium engages the senses in different ways and encourages certain patterns of behavior.[5] Print media facilitate reflection and contemplation of the sacred according to Postman (1985, 1992), and Campbell (2005) observes the Internet's community-oriented nature. Media genres also emphasize particular elements of religion. Talk shows are about storytelling; guests engage in self-examination and public confession (Primiano, 2001). Communication style, therefore, is as important as what is actually said. In the current age of numinous experience, it's important to ask how media facilitate religious ritual, interaction, and behavior in ways that transcend individual messages.

Historical Insights

History reveals a great deal about the media–religion interface. At various times, the media were particularly prominent in religious worship. These periods yield interesting insights about the numinous, and help us better understand the media today. While a comprehensive history is beyond the scope of this book, highlights in the evolution of media and religion suggest questions for further study.

Prehistory: Media and Ecstatic States

One must return to prehistory to understand media and religion at a fundamental level.[6] Dance, music, and chanting existed 10,000 years ago; we know that such activities had religious elements. It is ironic that one of the most ignored aspects of popular media today was one of the earliest components of ancient cultures. Through the basic medium of the drum, *trance* behaviors or sleeplike states of consciousness have been achieved throughout recorded history. Similar phenomena occur today in dance raves and the trance music genre, for example. According to Rouget (1985) trance has both psychophysiological and cultural dimensions; it is an innate part of human nature. These phenomena are depicted in cave drawings and rock art discovered in Africa, Egypt, Israel, Turkey, and Italy; some argue that trance inducing dance dates back to the Paleolithic era (Ehrenreich, 2006; Garfinkel, 2003; Pickrell, 2004).

Today, anthropologists of religion, neurobiologists, neuropsychologists, and ethnomusicologists are examining the connection between ancient trance behavior and contemporary trancelike experiences associated with a wide range of media from the Internet to film. The study of ancient forms of trance will continue to broaden our understanding of contemporary media experience. Trance behavior helps us grasp the deep feeling dimension of contemporary media, and represents an important area of future research.

Ancient Egypt: All Media Were Essentially Religious

At first glance, one might wonder what ancient Egypt with its majestic pyramids and monuments has to do with contemporary media and religion. Although it is natural to feel disconnected from a civilization that preceded the Roman Empire by 2,000 years, Egypt illustrates how the synthesis of media and religion plays a vital role in the day-to-day lives of citizens. Sacred media were ubiquitous: "As a means of increasing the prestige and power of the king in the response to the demands of a vast increase in territory and of maintaining continuity of dynastic power, provision was made for the development of a state religion with elaborate temple endowments, rituals, and priesthoods, and an increasing emphasis on the dead" (Innis, 1951, p. 93). The pyramids were permanent reminders not only of the centrality of power, but of the omnipresence of the gods and the continuity of the sacred. Because the gods were at the center of life, it was natural that dominant media such as architecture had deep religious significance.

According to Innis (1951), the permanence of stone when used in architecture and art created a bias toward belief in immortality.[7] If a foreigner entered the Egyptian capital of Thebes between 1540 and 1075 BC, she or he would become instantly aware of what Egyptians valued most: life after death. Temples, pyramids, obelisks, sphinxes, and hieroglyphic writings were all testimony to the Egyptians' lasting belief in eternity.

These media did not fade into the background of everyday life; they were interwoven into Egyptian community and ritual. They were sites of sacred ceremonies, feasts, and lively family gatherings. Culturally, they symbolized harmony with the gods and evocation of the divine in daily activities. Art and hieroglyphics advocated devotion to the god who was the pharaoh.

Although ancient Egypt and the present are vastly different in terms of culture and historical context, there is an important similarity. The media today are also ubiquitous. Thompson (1990) observes that millions "share, by virtue of their participation in a mediated culture, a common experience and a collective memory" (p. 163). We share with the Egyptians of long ago the condition of *mediazation* where technology touches so many aspects of life. This situation contributed to religious tradition in ancient Egypt, while today it favors a worldview of religious quest and a search for truth.

Ancient Greece and the Oral Tradition

About 2,000 years after the deterioration of Egyptian civilization, ancient Greece emerged as a world leader. Like the Egyptians, the Greeks used media in worshiping their gods; they built ornate temples, created religious statuary, and held sacred holiday feasts. The Greeks, however, located power not just in the king but also in the individual. The best way to honor the gods was to maximize one's potential and accomplish all that one could with what she or he had been given. This admonition to make the most of one's gifts inspired a matchless oral tradition. Important media of Greek religion, therefore, were epic poetry, lyrical drama, and oratory (i.e., speech and rhetoric). These continue to play a role in religion in some form today.

Orality, according to Gibson (2010b), is the "understanding of oral modes of communication as information technologies for preserving and transmitting history, religion, and other cultural knowledge" (p. 301). This form of communication dominated ancient Greece and subsequently its religion. Homer's *Iliad* and the *Odyssey* were important religious sources not only because they contained expectations of the gods, but because initially they were preserved and conveyed orally in everyday speech. Havelock (1963) goes so far as to say that oral poetry was the central communication form of Greek civilization and that Homer's epics were key educational vehicles for the teaching of religion and ethics. Orality represents a personal type of interaction with a deity that differs from that achieved through literacy.[8] Bowra (1965) underlines the importance of friendship in Greek orality. Through hymns, prayers, dramas, dance, and oratories, love was conveyed by human beings to their gods in hopes that it would be reciprocated in some form of kindness toward the people. Orality is essential to numinous experience; it enabled the expression of religious feelings, preservation of belief, and was the focal point of community gatherings.

Today, orality manifests itself in the media–religion interface in multiple ways. While changes to, and erosion of, the oral tradition were

Orality in media today

attributed to the rise of literacy and printing (McLuhan, 1964), digital technologies create new opportunities for both literate and oral experiences simultaneously. The convergence, for example, of text, audio, and visual elements on the Internet make multiple types of religious experience possible.

The Reformation

MLK and Printing Press

The early modern European period known as the Reformation contributes much to our understanding of numinous media. When Martin Luther nailed his 95 theses to the door of the Wittenberg Church in 1517, and continuing through the mid-1600s, a new era of religious pluralism was in progress (Hankins, 2003). The printing press played a role in this development; it provided access to doctrine once reserved for clergy and scholars. Nine million books were in print in Europe by 1500 compared to the less than 100,000 hand-inscribed manuscripts that existed 50 years earlier (Simon, 1966, p. 13).

Printing emerged as a numinous medium for several reasons. Books, tracts, proclamations, and pamphlets helped new denominations embrace uniform beliefs by transporting texts to distant regions. Religious communities often have a standard work or official source to discuss and reflect upon. Study itself is a ritual of learning and contemplation. The printing press also made possible the reproduction of iconography and art. Sacred symbols and drawings were accessed by greater numbers for personal worship.

Institutions

In this period of emerging literacy, much was demanded from print media. Not only were institutions reformed, but personal reformation also characterized the early 16th century. According to Graf (1995), these programs of improvement included "the reaffirmation of community, the reorganization of lay piety and religion, and the reintegration of the outer and inner self" (p. 125). For the devout, printing enabled religious commitment at several levels; it is difficult to imagine the expansion of Western religious pluralism without it.

Nineteenth-Century Revivalism

Evolution in tech →

Ex:

Favorable conditions for, and experimentation with numinous media was found in revivalism of the mid-19th century. By 1840, America was a land in transition. Bolstered by technology and industry on the one hand (e.g., canal systems, manufacturing, the telegraph, railroads expanding westward, etc.) and social challenges on the other (e.g., transience, uprooted families, rising competition in business), churches became outlets for freedom and creative expression. As new sects and denominations formed, media were necessary to attract followers and maintain existing congregations. *Spiritualism* or communication with disembodied spirits and lost loved ones was practiced at the time, with some considering it "an extension of the revival" (Carroll, 1997, p. 128). According to Leonard (1999) the frontier revival meeting often incorporated "multiple preachers, indigenous hymnody, shouting, glossolalia, shaking, jerking, tears, prayer, and praise" (p. 232). Promoters such as P.T. Barnum connected religion to entertainment, seeking to capitalize on spiritualism as spectacle (Carroll, 1997).

In urban areas, meeting houses took on the appearance of theaters; some preachers saw little difference between the pulpit and the stage. As Halgren-Kilde (1999) notes, the theater was familiar, and the stage was an excellent way to present the new religion to the common person. American revivalism, then, is characterized by willingness in some instances to mix religion and entertainment if it praised God. Religious theater continues within many denominations today.

The Sixties: Peace, Love, and Numinous Media

The 1960s contributed much to our understanding of media and religion. The rock mass was created by Catholics to lure young people back to church. Peace signs were seen on the yarmulkes of boys in Reform Jewish synagogues. In the Broadway musical *Jesus Christ Superstar*, Biblical stories were set to rock music. In *Godspell*, messages from the New Testament were sung by a Christ figure in a Superman t-shirt. The Indian sitar player Ravi Shankar enjoyed widespread popularity. Jim Morrison, lead singer of The Doors, considered himself a shaman. The 1960s also saw a return of the *festival*[9] that provided an outlet for new forms of ecstatic ritual. One example is the 1969 Woodstock music festival in New York, a gathering of over 300,000 people. There, young people meditated, entered trances, and listened to music for 3 days.

No single variable fully explains the rise of numinous media in the 1960s.[10] The period exemplifies the idea that many factors determine how important mediated religion is at any given time, and that certain conditions are more conducive to the numinous than others. First, the 1960s was a period of relative economic prosperity. Middle-class young adults had sufficient time and resources to explore new religious possibilities. It was also a decade when institutions of all types were called into question. The political climate was characterized by the unpopular Vietnam War and corruption in Richard Nixon's government; this mistrust manifested itself in educational, business, and religious institutions.

New Age Religion in the Twentieth Century

New Age religion emphasizes telepathy, clairvoyance, and spiritual healing. While existing outside traditional denominations, it often draws from
and combines elements of Christianity, Eastern philosophy, and other
faith traditions. The transference of spiritual messages from one medium
to another is essential to New Age thought. Such communication may
involve God, extraterrestrials, or spirits of the deceased. Media coverage of
actor Shirley MacLaine's spiritual experiences in Peru as well as her book
Out on a Limb (1983) drew considerable public attention.

New Age religion is important for several reasons. First, it was unbound
by institutional traditions; adherents were free to deviate from the mainstream. Channeling, horoscopes, and tarot readings are a few examples.
For a time, the use of crystals was common; they were worn by followers
as a means of sharing spiritual light and energy. Divine messages were
transmitted by UFOs according to a number of devotees (Albanese, 2007).
Traditional religious media were not abandoned by New Age religion,
however. Teachings from the Bible, Torah, and Quran, for example, were
combined with other sources. Psychic Edgar Cayce claimed to have con-
versed and eaten with Jesus Christ during dreams; he also added to Biblical passages during trance states (Bro, 1989).

The New Age movement is also interesting in terms of media distribution. Given that merchandising was the key source of funding, business
channels were developed to market books and other products. Einstein
(2008) argues that much can be learned about the rise of religious branding as well as contemporary marketing of religious products by studying
the history of New Age religion.

Expansion of Televangelism

Televangelism is a significant milestone in the evolution of media and religion; it is also discussed in chapter 8. Early televangelism came in the form
of televised sermons or church meetings and later adopted several formats
including talk shows and news programs. In the 1950s and 1960s, Catholic
Bishop Fulton J. Sheen engaged millions of TV viewers through "his warm
personality, his somewhat theatrical presentation style, his storytelling
skills, and his always engaging and pleasant manner" (Armstrong, 2010,
p. 426). Billy Graham's specials were aired throughout the United States
and Canada for several decades, demonstrating that live sermons could be
adapted successfully to television.

While many religious groups employ television, use of the medium for
preaching, healing, and prayer is particularly common among some Evan-

gelical Christians. Jimmy Swaggert, Jerry Falwell, and Jim and Tammy Faye Bakker exemplify a demonstrative televangelism emphasizing a charismatic style, personal witnessing, and the solicitation of donations. Pat Robertson combines religious messages with the news show format, and Joel Osteen uses basic sermons to stress prosperity theology, or belief that God rewards good works with financial blessings.

Lippy (1999) comments on the contribution of televangelism to individualized worship:

> Televangelism also buttressed the increasing privatization of vital religiosity, for individuals watched the television preachers in the privacy of their own homes, frequently supplementing what they received from the religious groups with which they remained affiliated with beliefs taken over from the televangelists, to create personal religious worldviews. (p. 52)

This ability to worship within the privacy of the home led to numinous experiences that are still being developed today. Not only does the typical religious program on radio, television, or the Internet offer sermons, but directs viewers to call phone numbers or visit Web sites for prayer, confession, and opportunities for service.

The Age of Information and Networks

In the period of late capitalism, the information society is a unique and robust era for media and religion.[11] Information is a dominant component of contemporary culture, and is often sold as a commodity. Citizens are increasingly dependent on information technology, and many are employed in the information sector. Perhaps the most vital characteristic of this age is interactivity and the ability, through the use of various media, to instantly develop relationships and communities across great distances. Religion has a bold presence in the information society spawned by the rise of autonomous worship as well as a growing affinity for new technologies among the youth culture.

Networks or how media tie people together is key to understanding religion in the information society. Castells (2000) argues that networks are the foundational units of the current age. While the spiritual leader of a congregation observes physical interactions between parishioners at a house of worship, participation in Internet sites such as Facebook may go unnoticed.

We have arrived at the point where virtually any religious phenomenon can be experienced through technology. This isn't to say that praying at a cybertemple is the same experience as visiting a physical building and interacting with one's fellow parishioners face-to-face. Nor are individuals likely to worship entirely through the media. The point is that we live in a time when Wright's (1986) four functions of mass media (i.e., surveillance, correlation, socialization, entertainment) no longer capture the complexity of mediated communication and mediated religion in particular. The current landscape is one where, under the right conditions, any of a vast array of media can reinforce belief, facilitate ritual, and provide outlets for expressions of deep feeling. In this sense, the present age is highly favorable for numinous media.

Media and Religion Today: A Rich Synthesis of Past and Present

History deepens understanding of media and religion today. From the awe-inspiring pyramids of ancient Egypt to the oral culture of the Greeks; from the entrepreneurial spirit of 19th-century revivalism to the rebellious spirit of the 1960s, we live in a time when all of these elements combine in complex ways. Simply put, the media–religion relationship is a common element of everyday life. In other words, we have arrived at an age when numinous media play a key role both inside and outside denominations.

Individuals have many options. Technologically speaking, the access to information and social networks seems limitless. The key strands of modern society have lined up in a way that is conducive to mediated religion and the numinous.

While ritual, community, belief, and deep feeling have characterized the religious experience throughout history, the contexts in which they can be experienced have multiplied. Media are often associated with denominations, but sometimes they're not. Religious media are found in houses of worship, but also in one's own home. Religious conversations can be face-to-face, but they're often mediated through the Internet as well. The lesson learned from history is that traditional media endure, but are now combined with new technologies to create multiple ways of mediating religion today.

A Student of the Media and Religion Wears Many Hats

The study of the media and religion draws on related fields for ideas and theoretical directions (Stout & Buddenbaum, 2002a). Each solves part of the puzzle, and identifies important issues for future study. These include psychology of religion, sociology of religion, anthropology of religion, media ecology, and moral criticism in the humanities. In other words, the media and religion is interdisciplinary, and can be examined from multiple perspectives.

How the Psychologist Sees Media and Religion

Psychologists are interested in mental states and the brain's role in religious behavior. They might study neurological responses to a drumbeat, for example, or ecstatic states at church services that use multimedia. The ways in which the media play a role in identity, personality, and perception are also important issues for psychologists of religion. The numinous has surfaced in psychotherapy; clinicians want to know more about the relationship between religion and mental health. Neuroscientists analyze mental states at festivals and ceremonies; they examine the physical aspects of trance and ecstatic states during religious rituals. Stimulation from multimedia begs for additional study; this includes both houses of worship and online environments. Given that deep feeling is a key element of religion, the psychology of religion is of growing importance.

How the Sociologist Sees Media and Religion

Given sociologists' concerns about community, it is natural that they are curious about media audiences as well. In some cases, religious audiences are religious communities; they are less defined in terms of geographical neighborhoods and more in terms of media use. Evangelical teenagers, for example, might identify more with fans of contemporary religious music than they do with adults in their home congregation. Similarly, a parishioner may attend a house of worship each week, but have a greater affinity for those she or he has come to know on the Internet.

The distinction between congregations and audiences is no longer as clear as it once was. Some audiences are *interpretive communities* or groups that share strategies of interpreting media texts (Fish, 1980; Lindlof, 1988). According to Lindlof (2010, 2002) there are several types of interpretive communities in the religious world. Among them are groups that reject some forms of media, such as Mormons' avoidance of R-rated movies or Muslims' denunciation of gratuitous content in Western films. *Genre communities* are also common. Avid readers of religious novels or devout listeners to religious talk radio are a few examples. The extent to which these audiences turn out to be actual communities is an important question for the future.

How Anthropologists See Media and Religion

Anthropologists offer insights regarding media and religion. Particularly valuable is their study of *ritual*, that range of behaviors at the core of all cultures. While ritual is usually associated with sermons, sacraments, prayers, songs, and sacred feasts, watching the evening news or participating in online discussions can also have moral dimensions. Ritual aspects of mass communication deserve additional study (Carey, 1989; Rothenbuhler, 1998). New forms of mediated ritual have emerged. Why are dance raves, rock concerts, and televised sports important rituals for young audiences? Why is religious radio part of the daily routine for some? Such questions deepen our understanding of contemporary culture, according to anthropologists.

How Media Ecologists See Media and Religion

Media ecologists examine media as environments (Postman, 1992). A general assumption is that technology, symbols, and aesthetic form shape the environments out of which human affairs proceed (Strate, 2006a). Philosophers such as Mumford, Innis, McLuhan, and Postman share the view that technology, particularly communication media, are catalysts for change, while Postman (1985) fears that television erodes sacred environments through its entertainment orientation. McLuhan expressed similar fears about the connection between electronic media and attrition within the Catholic Church, observing that the "TV generation" struggles to tolerate the catechism (quoted in Cooper, 2006). The expansion of media environments through the Internet is likely to enhance the importance of media ecology for years to come.

How Literary Critics See Media and Religion

Some literary critics analyze the ethical and moral dimensions of texts; they determine how well a work cultivates moral character. Silk's (1995) book *Unsecular Media* is a moral analysis of religion news coverage; it argues that journalists embrace similar values as religious institutions. Woods and Patton's (2010) *Prophetically Incorrect: A Christian Introduction to Media Criticism* suggests a theistic perspective on how the media can be used optimally.

While moral critiques of novels, plays, and short stories are common, new media are also being subjected to this type of analysis. Schultze (2002) evaluates the Internet from a moral perspective. With increased use of digital media, moral criticism is likely to expand within public discourse;

its importance is, therefore, likely to grow as a branch within the study of the media and religion.

Foundational Concepts Advance Our Study in a Numinous Age

We find ourselves in a period of religious experimentation and widespread numinous activity. This chapter provides a conceptual foundation for analyzing the current situation; it suggests concepts for better understanding media, religion, and their relationship to society. Key ideas such as media-as-religion, personalized worship, and secularization get us beyond generalities; historical events provide a broader context in which to assess recent developments. By looking at media and religion through the lenses of other fields, we broaden our perspectives on the changing media landscape. These ideas help us think more deeply and cogently as we consider other topics in the book.

Key Terms

anthropology of religion: The study of religion as it relates to culture and civilization.

information society: The postindustrial era where communication technology is an essential element in everyday life and information an important commodity in the economy.

interpretive community theory: The approach that communities can be defined according to shared strategies of interpretation of media messages.

levels of analysis: The recognition that mediated religion can be studied according to its personal, social, and cultural dimensions.

literary criticism: The skills necessary to analyze literature. In the religious context, it concerns how works treat moral issues.

media as religion: A situation where media are involved in virtually all dimensions of religious worship including ritual, deep feeling, community, and belief.

media ecology: The idea that media can be studied as environments. In the case of religion, it's the way sacred places are shaped by technology.

mediazation: The condition where most everyday activities involve technology at some level.

---

personalized religion: The capacity through new media to have individualized religious experiences that aren't necessarily connected to institutions.

psychology of religion: The study of religion from the perspective of mental processes.

secularization theory: Assumption that exposure to competing systems of information, culture, and technology erodes religious commitment over time.

sociology of religion: The study of religion from the perspective of social groups and processes.

Questions to Ponder

1. How important is the study of media and religion? Do you think the subject deserves to be a separate field of study? Why or why not?

2. Do you think that secularization is a useful concept in thinking about media and religion? Why or why not?

3. How is the phenomenon of media and religion seen from the perspectives of different fields?

4. How does the present interplay between media and religion differ from that in earlier historical periods?

5. What is the information society? How has religion evolved in this contemporary period?

CHAPTER 3

Physiology and Mental States

Individuals often describe media-related experiences in terms of euphoria, deep feeling, and reflection. A Muslim may feel inspired while meditating over the Quran. A Lutheran may engage in deep listening during a Bach organ recital. A moviegoer may experience a new level of thought during Mel Gibson's film, *The Passion of Christ*. A participant may describe a dance rave as "not of this world." Such occurrences have social and cultural dimensions, but cannot be fully understood without examining basic psychological and biological processes. This chapter discusses how mediated religion is experienced through mental states of consciousness, a subject that is of great interest to psychologists, neuropsychologists, neurobiologists, and ethnomusicologists.[1]

States of consciousness are those conditions in which normal awareness is changed in some way. Such states range from meditation to the deeper state of trance. An historical example comes from the Shakers in the 1830s, a Christian sect that engaged in ecstatic rituals, shaking their bodies to cast off evil spirits. This culminated in public shouting and possession states. Dance rituals in tribal religions often involve trance and deep states of consciousness. Similar behaviors are emerging in Western cultures in the form of trance music, trance films, dance raves, televised healings, worship video, and multimedia houses of worship such as megachurches. Mental states provide insight into the numinous and reveal much about the expanding uses of information technology.

Some religious behaviors stem from physical arousal (e.g., changes in heart rate, skin conductance, respiration, and even the "chills").

Sociobiologists argue that religion is genetically influenced; it is a mechanism to stimulate hope of survival and perpetuation of the species (Reynolds & Tanner, 1983). Culture, therefore, is inevitably intertwined with nature. It's at this junction that many numinous experiences occur.

Mental States: The Basic Level of Media and Religion

To understand the media–religion interface, one must know something of the human physiological system and the brain. Individuals process the world through the senses. Moving images in a religious video stimulate heightened emotions. Recorded music does the same through sound; priests use incense to evoke feelings of reverence. New opportunities for sensory experience coincide with the proliferation of media in the information age. The megachurch provides a useful illustration. Big screen video systems, sophisticated sound amplification, and aesthetically designed architectural features simultaneously bombard the senses, making possible deep listening, meditation, near-trance, and trance. Attendees close their eyes, sway to the music, and shout messages of praise.

Emotional States and the Brain

Neurophysiologists trace religious behaviors to specific sectors of the brain. Three areas are important in this regard.[2] The *amygdala* and *septum* are associated with emotionality as is the *hypothalamus;* all three are located in the lower brain. Arousal stimulates neurons that release chemicals in the cerebral cortex region thus enabling cognitive activity and voluntary behavior. This chemical dispersion produces the sensation of the mind slowing down and a feeling of removal from normal time (Damasio, 1999). According to Becker (2004) this slowing of the mind is associated with meditation, trance consciousness, and other religious experiences. Increased access to a variety of media will likely create new opportunities for expression of these emotional states.

The connection between brain functioning and religious behavior is a highly speculative area. The intention is not to reduce the discussion to biology alone; it is simply to suggest that mental states should not be overlooked. As Becker (2004) argues, "emotions are basic to survival and adaptation" (p. 132). The media have adaptive benefits; they extend our auditory and visual abilities. If this is the case, why doesn't the subject of mental states surface more in studies of the media and religion? According to Rafferty (2003), researchers deemphasize these phenomena as having "little utility to present-day western concerns" (p. 257). Expressions of the numinous through popular culture, however, suggest that meditation, ecstatic states, and trance are exhibited every day in the expanding media landscape.

Religion and Mental States through Time

Expression of religion through changed mental states has ancient origins. In early Greece, shamans displayed deep emotions through chanting. Such is also the case in the African Aken society and the ancient Ga society of Ghana. The Berava or drummer caste of Sri Lanka and the Indian Bharata Natyam exhibited mental states through dance. Religion played a major role in these rituals. When early humans faced the challenges of changing natural and economic conditions, they engaged in activities of emotional sublimation, designed to relieve such tensions. These rituals were enhanced by musical instruments, costumes, and architectural surroundings.

Mental states and ecstatic rituals are demonstrated today in many denominations; they include speaking in tongues (glossolalia), ritual healings, and demonstrative conversions. They take place through the media of the Internet, television, film, recorded music, and other sources.

Historically, ecstatic states have been looked down upon in Europe and North America.[3] Ritual dancing and trance, for example, did not conform to the expectations of Puritanism and capitalist colonial America. According to Becker (2004), the suppression of mental states coincides with the emergence of a bounded inviolate *Western self* that impedes "the trance experience of the surrender of self and consequently the ability to imagine trance as a reasonable, natural phenotypic kind of consciousness" (p. 89). The rise of the Western self, by the 17th century had created a culturally based barrier to many rituals that involved changed mental states. Cortés had demonstrated this attitude in the 15th century by pronouncing Aztec ritual dances and chants to be undignified. Similarly, the 18th century explorer, James Cook sought to suppress ecstatic rituals during his explorations of the Polynesian islands. Tart (1983) argues that even researchers have overlooked the exhibition of mental states:

> A further reason for the historical neglect of altered states has been western culture's implicit bias that the ordinary state is natural and best, so that all altered states represent various degrees of useless or pathological deviation from the natural form. Realization of the arbitrary and ethnocentric of much of what we take to be natural about our consciousness allows a more open-minded investigation of altered states. (p. 19)

Western suppression of these phenomena was particularly aggressive by the 16th century when the Puritans arrived in North America. Ecstatic displays were considered base and unrefined; congregations sat reverently while clergy conveyed their messages. Puritanism was a religion of the word, and it was feared that certain rituals, if not checked, could displace God's role.

Displays of altered mental states continued in small groups, however. Some combined emotional displays with the rigid structures of modern Christianity. Well underway by the 1740s, the "Great Awakening" validated the expression of ecstatic states in some congregations. Spiritualist groups engaged in spirit possession (e.g., wringing of hands, shouting, weeping, collapsing, dancing, and rolling on the ground; Downey, 1968; Gewehr, 1930; Lovejoy, 1969; Weisberger, 1958). These behaviors, however, failed to gain widespread acceptance in more established churches, falling prey to the "enlightenment ideal" of the "objectified self" (Becker, 2004, p. 100).

Mental states, especially meditation and trance reemerged in the antiestablishment 1960s.[4] Economic stability and dissatisfaction with the Vietnam War characterized a time of questioning and religious experimentation (see chapter 2). Some churches struggled to retain young parishioners by featuring popular music in their services; the Catholic rock mass was such an attempt.

Since then, mental states have manifested themselves through the media in numerous ways. Televangelists Ernest Angley and Benny Hinn televise ritual healings and speaking in tongues. On his Web site, Angley asks viewers to place their hands on the television or computer screen to be healed from physical and mental infirmities. Heightened awareness and trance is associated with recorded music such as the Pentecostal songs *Wonderous Love* and *Holding On* (Becker, 2004). Religious Web sites assist users in meditating, chanting, and singing in the privacy of their own homes.

Types of Mental States

I now discuss three types of mental states as well as how they are facilitated through media. They are: *flow, meditation,* and *trance.*

Flow

Flow describes a state of optimal experience. It is a psychological state during which one feels the satisfaction of forward movement and growth.[5]

In a flow experience the mind is stretched and inspired. According to Csikszentmihalyi (1990), flow is "the state in which people are so involved in an activity that nothing else seems to matter; the experience itself is so enjoyable that people will do it even at great cost, for the sheer sake of doing it" (p. 4). Examples include a pianist who is unaware that hours have passed as a challenging piece of music is mastered, or the tennis player whose mind and body are stretched to the limits in defeating a talented opponent. Csikszentmihalyi (1990) emphasizes the deep sense of enjoyment and exhilaration that is experienced in flow. Flow experiences occur when the activity is worthwhile and challenging. How media contribute to flow has been studied by Kubey and Csikszentmihalyi (1990) who argue that such experiences can be enhanced through education. Mediated religion has created new opportunities for flow both inside and outside denominations.

Given its role in personal growth, literature plays an important role in flow states. The Bible (Christianity), Quran (Islam), Torah (Judaism), and Bhagavad Gita (Hinduism) are not only religious texts, but are also works of literature. Their narrative elements of plot, character, and symbolism make them vehicles for deep thought and flow. Secular works are also sources of religious reflection such as Bunyan's (1678/1984) *Pilgrim's Progress*, Milton's (1674/2000) *Paradise Lost*, and C. S. Lewis's (1952/2001) *Mere Christianity*. As a vehicle of flow, literature compels the reader to deal with difficult moral questions by creating a state of intense mental engagement. Much of this has to do with the complexity and challenge of the text. Some experiences are so deeply meaningful as to result in changes in outlook and behavior.

The question of how religious flow states occur in popular media is only beginning to be addressed. Much has yet to be learned about television, film, the Internet, contemporary music, and popular literature as vehicles of flow. Despite criticism that these media are insufficiently complex to stimulate flow, it is clear that popular media and genres are evolving, and their intellectual dimensions are difficult to assess.

Popular films treat religion from various perspectives today; this may create favorable circumstances for flow states. Aesthetic, technical, and narrative elements combine to facilitate deep contemplation about difficult religious questions.

The Internet is evolving as a medium of flow. Yet while there is considerable online religious activity, flow demands complexity and challenge. Much is yet to be learned about the Internet and these states. Online games seem particularly suited for this, however. In fact, the religious video game is emerging as a new genre. "Video play is highly challenging, requires skill, and offers rapid feedback and thus possesses all the key structural elements necessary to experiencing flow" (Kubey & Csikszentmihalyi, 1990, p. 144). These trends indicate that outlets for flow are expanding. Religious reflection, contemplation, and learning occur through a variety of new media.

Meditation

If the media are creating new opportunities for flow experiences, the same can be said of meditation. While flow implies that the mind is challenged, concentrating, and mastering some task or problem, meditation is a self-induced state of relaxation. According to Juss (2006) meditation involves "stopping the normal flow of thought" and achieving a state of mind that "would not otherwise have emerged in the human consciousness" (p. 252). It has both elements of relaxation and the loss of self-identity awareness. Meditation has ancient origins and is often associated with religious worship, particularly with Eastern religious philosophy. Hindus, Buddhists, Sufis, Jews, Christians, and Muslims meditate, but in varying forms. Meditation has also become popular outside denominations and has been associated with a number of New Age and alternative religions.

Through television, film, the Internet, and other media, information about Eastern religious philosophy and meditation is increasingly available. Web sites, books, and CDs offer instruction on meditative practices, and certain genres of recorded music are created to aid meditation (e.g., chant, New Age, technomusic). Entire television and radio programs are now dedicated to the art of meditation and learning its techniques. In the 1990s, the recording *Chant*, a collection of prayer music pieces by Benedictine monks sold 6 million CDs (Thigpen, 1995). The New Age music genre also illustrates the popularity of music to meditate by. The genre features flute, harp, acoustic guitar, as well as electronically generated sound.

Trance

Trance is a more intense and deeper state of consciousness than flow and meditation; it is characterized by a suspension of consciousness and mental absorption. While trance is traditionally associated with primitive religion in the form of dance, religious singing, and ritual drumming, it is also achieved through contemporary media.[6] Trance TV, trance film, trance video, trance Internet, and trance radio are a few examples. These can be experienced independently of denominations, but some religious organizations create Internet sites and videos to facilitate this type of worship.

Trance is associated with electronic music and rave culture. These events, usually attended by young adults, combine a deeply religious state with secular recreational experiences of entertainment and "partying" (Sylvan, 2005). Major rave events are held in San Francisco and other major U.S. cities; they are also common in a number of European countries.

At the heart of the rave is the concept of the event, which combines elements of personal interaction, visual media, and sound to produce a sense of awe. In the annual Burning Man festival in Nevada, the combination of visual and aural stimuli through multiple sound stages and art installations is so intense that it creates an environment for trance states.[7] The event is also an essential element of the megachurch experience; it keeps things moving through multimedia such as sound systems, spotlights, and big-screen projection of images. Raves, festivals, and megachurches have something else in common: the emphasis of experience over content. As Sylvan (2005) explains, it is the experiential dimension of these events, not necessarily the content that defines them as religious phenomena.

Mental States Today: Numinous Media

Religiously speaking, media play a key role in mental states. This chapter discusses how flow, meditation, and trance are mediated by technology in new ways. Yet numinous media are not merely conduits to heightened emotions; they involve other elements of religiosity as well. This is why the most compelling examples of mediated religion are those in which mental states function along with the relational, cognitive, and behavioral dimensions of religion. A church that provides an ecstatic experience at its services, but doesn't offer community and a system of beliefs to go with it, is likely to find its members only temporarily engaged. But, today's media create possibilities for a more holistic experience, one where mental states connect with all the levels of religion.

The Internet provides an example. One can watch an engaging well-crafted sermon online and experience flow. But, when a community emerges around the sermon in the form of discussion groups, the experience is taken to another level. Furthermore, when sermon watching becomes ritualized by the community and eventually attached to a set of beliefs, the media experience becomes a numinous one. In the future it is important to not only identify how flow, meditation, or trance is experienced through the media, but to place them in the context of a more complex religious milieu, and try to understand how they work as part of a larger whole. Only then can we better understand the role of altered mental states in the multidimensional dynamic of mediated religion.

Key Terms

deep listening: Processing sounds such as drumming or music in a way that achieves a reflective, meditative, or trance state.

flow: An optimal feeling associated with progressing and learning; it is often accompanied by positive feedback.

glossolalia: The religious practice of speaking in tongues.

hypothalamus: A part of the lower brain system that is associated with emotionality.

media convergence: When existing technologies are combined to create new forms of media.

meditation: Deep contemplation or religious introspection.

mental states: Varying levels of awareness or consciousness. Can include conditions of disconnection from immediate surroundings.

neurophysiology: The subfield of physiology concerned with the nervous system.

personal media environments: Exposure to multiple media in one's home.

trance: A temporary state of suspended consciousness and a lack of awareness of physical surroundings.

Questions to Ponder

1. How do mental states and the brain help explain audience members' religious experience with media?
2. Which parts of the brain are associated with emotionality?
3. Historically, why has the public display of ecstatic states been discouraged in Western cultures?
4. The author argues that trance, while commonly associated with primitive religion, has emerged through contemporary media. Do you agree? Why or why not?
5. Do you agree that the experiential element of religion can be just as important as content? Explain your answer.

CHAPTER 4

World Religions and Denominations

Today, religious groups are increasingly defined as media audiences; they operate within expanding information spheres and mediated networks. That is, the media play an important role in religious organizations. The knowledge culture of Judaism, for example, has expanded into the Internet. A genre of Mormon film has recently emerged. Televangelism is common in many conservative Protestant denominations. Listening to recorded sermons is a daily activity for many Muslims, and reading the *vani* or published messages of gurus is an important ritual in the Hindu diaspora. Along with doctrine and dogma, the media are at the center of worship.

From Congregation to Interpretive Community

The congregation has been the key social unit of many denominations[1] and religious traditions; it provides a sense of community centered on shared convictions. Congregations are communities that nurture and support participants. Congregations are also *interpretive communities*, or collectivities that share strategies of interpretation of media (Fish, 1980; Lindlof, 2002). In other words, when media use is a defining element of a congregation, it becomes an interpretive community.

Lindlof (2002) identifies several types of religious interpretive communities.[2] Some groups are *genre* communities where worship revolves around particular categories of media. Reading novels with a religious theme, for example, is a common activity for some Southern Baptist congregations, and listening to classical music is part of worship for many

Lutherans. Some interpretive communities emphasize resistance to or rejection of unsavory or deleterious media. Such communities include the Nazarenes who, for many years, were discouraged from going to movie theaters, and the Mormons, who rally around strong admonitions to avoid R-rated movies. These and other types of interpretive communities are explored in this chapter.

Religious Organizations and the Media

Five major world religions: Christianity, Judaism, Islam, Hinduism, and Buddhism are examined. A number of denominations within these broad traditions are also explored. Specific beliefs are discussed as well as media use. I conclude by discussing opportunities and challenges for institutions in the current age of numinous media.

Media are enigmatic for many religious groups. On the one hand, denominations perform service and take action; media perform educational, humanitarian, and community functions. On the other hand, parishioners are exposed to competing messages that blur the line between the sacred and secular. Some religious leaders attribute weakening religious commitments to the popular media. A number of groups create their own television channels, Web sites, and publications to preserve fundamental beliefs. In urban areas, however, individuals live in complex environments with multiple information sources; so the media's boundary function of preserving some level of isolation is harder to achieve. All religions use the media to reinforce sacred beliefs; they also instruct members regarding which media outlets should be avoided or scrutinized.

Christian Audiences

Christianity is a multifaceted religion comprised of numerous denominations. According to Hitchcock (1979),[3] approaches to the media are best explained in terms of the *Christian paradox of the world*. While Christians believe the world should be embraced for its beauty, knowledge, and opportunities for experience, it must also be simultaneously rejected in terms of its evil and deleterious aspects. The same is true with the media. Educational and artistic media become catalysts for religious learning and meditative activities, while gratuitously violent and sexually explicit content are shunned.

This paradox is explored within four broad Christian audiences: Catholics, Mainline Protestants, Conservative Protestants, and Mormons. While there are considerable commonalities between these groups, there is also remarkable diversity in how the media are perceived and used.[4]

Roman Catholics

One of the oldest and enduring forms of Christianity, Roman Catholicism's relationship with the media is complex and not easily summarized.[5] The media, in various forms, are an integral part of worship. According to Vance-Trembath (2006) the denomination is basically friendly to communication and media: "Catholicism's approach to communication is guided by its foundational insight that all of creation is saturated with the presence of God" (p. 63). Some of the world's most highly treasured architecture, statuary, paintings, and other forms of art have emerged from Catholicism. By the same token, media that are considered unholy have been strongly denounced and at times prohibited.

The leadership hierarchy is central in Catholic theology and, generally speaking, members seek direction regarding the media from the Pope and other members of the clergy. In an official teaching on communications, Pope John Paul II declared that: "Only communication can, through true dialogue, bring about a desire and expectancy of a warm peace, seen as a necessity, in the hearts of peoples" (John Paul II, 1987a).

Numerous directives about proper media use have been issued. These include an encyclical (letter from a pope) on motion pictures in 1936 and another in 1957 discussing radio and television (Vance-Trembath, 2006). Additional statements address the ethics of advertising (Pontifical, 1997) and use of the Internet (Pontifical, 2002).

Catholic theology embraces media that evoke the holy and reinforce beliefs. However, there is a longstanding tradition of restricting media thought to undermine the sacred. As Jelen (1996) observes, Catholic leaders have not shrunk from censorship at times. Since the Second Vatican Council (1962–1965), however, matters concerning the media have shifted, somewhat, to the control of local bishops, resulting in greater autonomy among parishioners.

Catholics have a deep tradition in the sacred arts. Da Vinci's painting *The Last Supper* and *The Pietà* statue by Michelangelo are historical examples of sacred artistic media thought to inspire and uplift. Pope John Paul II (1987b) explains that:

> Authentic Christian art is that which, through sensible perception, gives the intuition that the Lord is present in His Church, that the events of salvation history give meaning and orientation to our life, that the glory that is promised us already transforms our existence. Sacred art must tend to offer us a visual synthesis of all dimensions of our faith. (Part IV)

While aesthetics is celebrated in Catholic theology, attempts to restrict media use are common throughout history. One example is the altering of Michelangelo's painting the *Last Judgement* by adding fig leaves to nude figures. Such activity may be rooted in the culture of ancient Rome where censors were appointed by the state as early as 443 BCE (McCormick & MacInnes, 1962). At first, these officials worked on the census, determining the size of the population. Eventually, however, they were authorized to condemn behaviors in conflict with the city's moral standards. According to Berger (1982), even elected senators were at the mercy of the censor, and many were publicly ridiculed and occasionally removed from office. Such practices were preserved with the emergence of the official Church.

Catholics cite the *little ones* concept in the book of Matthew in explaining their approach to media. It admonishes that little ones be protected and not permitted to go astray (Hagstrom, n.d., p. 149). To many Catholics, the little ones concept isn't merely confined to children, but covers any individual vulnerable to temptation.

Efforts to protect parishioners accelerated with the advent of the printing press in the 15th century. Early presses were taxed in fear that they would ultimately undermine the Church (Pool, 1984). Next, the *Index of Forbidden Books* was created to sanction certain texts and effectively kept many works out of circulation. The *Index* endured for centuries, and was not discontinued until 1966. By the mid-20th century, Catholic organizations such as the Legion of Decency were making recommendations about Hollywood films. Lists of films criticized by the Legion were published and used as a regular guide by parishioners.

While occasional directives are still issued, Vatican II emphasized the individual; the *Declaration of Religious Liberty* emphasizes personal conscience in these matters. The incorporation of rock music (i.e., "rock mass") into church services by some parishes in the 1970s and 1980s reflected this trend. According to Hagstrom (n.d.), this shift is an effort to participate in activities of the world community rather than fall into isolation through censorship strategies. The Pontifical Council for Social Communications states that "a merely censorious attitude on the part of the Church...is neither sufficient nor appropriate" (Pontifical, 1989, n. 30).

Catholics use both religious and secular media today. The Catholic newspaper *The National Catholic Reporter* is an example of the former, and *The Curious Case of Benjamin Button* and *Slumdog Millionaire* are secular films popular among Catholics. They also use the Internet: a Google search for "Catholic Web sites" in early 2007 yielded 1,320,000 results (Arasa, 2008, p. 16). Web sites differ widely throughout the denomination, however, reflecting regional cultures and varying purposes. The Vatican Web site, for example, centers on doctrinal information sources such as archives, digital libraries, and online museum collections, while the site for the Archdiocese of Los Angeles, given its proximity to the Hollywood film industry, contains specific admonitions about media use.

Protestants

Protestantism has its roots in the Reformation; it emerged out of rejection of Catholic hierarchy, resisting the line of authority between the Pope and common church members. In terms of the media, the Protestant audience is best seen as three broad interpretive communities: *Conservative Protestants, Mainline Protestants,* and the *Anabaptist* family of churches. Each reflects contrasting approaches to media use and interpretation.

Conservative Protestants   This category includes some churches within Evangelical, Fundamentalist, Southern Baptist, Pentecostal, and Lutheran traditions; it often reflects what Schultze (1996) calls an "uneasy alliance with the media" (p. 61). On the one hand, the media are used strategically for missionary work and other religious purposes, but on the other, campaigns are launched against "worldly" media that threaten God's purposes.[6] Some church members engage in public protests against the showing of movies and television programs as well as boycotting entertainment media that they consider deleterious to religious values.

Virtually any form of media or genre that accomplishes the greater good can be put to use. Newspapers, magazines, brochures, books, radio, television, recorded music, and the Internet are just some of the media that can be dedicated to religious purposes. James Dobson's *Focus on the Family,* a Christian-based radio program, attracts 2 million daily listeners (MacQuarrie, 2005). By the beginning of the 21st century, contemporary Christian music achieved "resounding success in the commercial market, primarily through sales in Christian bookstores" (Cusick, 2010, p. 388). Other popular media genres for Baptists and other Evangelical Christians include faith-based novels, cyberchurches, Jesus rock, and even televised Christian professional wrestling (Christian Wrestlesrs, n.d.).

Mainline Protestants   The mainline churches embrace a progressive theology that stresses independent thought over the admonitions of a single authority. According to Ferré (2010), mainline churches include the Disciples of Christ, Episcopal Church, some Lutheran Churches, Presbyterian Church (U.S.A.), United Church of Christ, United Methodist Church, and the American Baptist Convention (p. 359). Approaches to the media are more moderate than those taken by Conservative Protestants.[7] Mainline Protestants feel "that people need exposure to secular media

even if the messages are sometimes at odds with church teachings"
(Buddenbaum, 1996, p. 53). In other words, media selection is primarily
a matter of personal choice. It should be pointed out, however, that some
conservative branches also exist within these groups.

While Conservative Protestants complain about biased news coverage of religion, members of Mainline churches are also concerned about
the lack of depth or superficiality of such coverage. Media are expected
to raise awareness of social issues such as poverty and the need for better
education; they are important vehicles of political activism. Buddenbaum
(2001a) argues that Milton's concept of *the marketplace of ideas* underpins
Mainline Protestant thought when it comes to media; it's important to
grapple with media options and ultimately make good selections. For this
reason, Mainline churches engage in media literacy campaigns, urging
their members to develop critical skills in media selection and interpretation (Ferré, 2010). Mainline churches emphasize the community dimension of their Web sites, offering bulletin boards, online discussion, blog
access, Q&A posts, and devotional e-mail.

Anabaptists Anabaptists are descendents of the European radical
reformation; congregations formed in Switzerland and Germany. They
resist many forms of media but are less public than other groups in
expressing their viewpoints. Separation between church and state is
stressed, and adherents passively accept government rule. The Bible is
interpreted literally; teachings about the media are didactic, and abstention
from various technologies is expected.

Anabaptist branches include the Amish, Mennonites, and Hutterites;
each of which teach the doctrine of separation: believers should live apart
from unbelievers. Some Mennonite groups reside in the general population, however. Members can be excommunicated for breaking moral
codes. Entire classifications of media have been prohibited at various
times.[8] Television and radio are forbidden to Hutterites, and the Amish
use electricity cautiously out of fear it will lead to unnecessary connections
to the larger society. For this reason, Amish use generators to power computers and prefer telephone booths on the outskirts of the community to
personal home telephones (Strayer, 2010). Hutterites approach the Internet selectively and with considerable skepticism; they use it primarily for
educational purposes.

Some Anabaptists embrace the practice of *rumspringa,* a period when
teenagers confront the decision of either remaining in the religious collective or choosing life in the outside "English" world. During this time,
behaviors normally prohibited are overlooked (e.g., driving automobiles,
wearing secular fashions and hairstyles, viewing television and movies,

drinking alcohol, etc.). Rumspringa was the focus of the documentary film, *Devil's Playground* (Cantor, 2002) in which youth are depicted violating a number of Amish norms as they contemplate the future. Some Anabaptists claim that rumspringa is misunderstood, exaggerated, and overdramatized by outsiders. They argue that not all youth participate, and that the majority return to the community. For many Anabaptists, it is simply a time when the immaturity of youth is tolerated to a greater degree.

Mormons

Mormons claim that God restored the original Christian church to the Earth through Joseph Smith in the early 1800s. Subsequent prophets have directed the flock through what Mormons term "modern-day revelation." Such guidance includes proper media use as demonstrated by Brigham Young, who, in 1847 exhorted the early settlers in Salt Lake City to enjoy the theater, but to avoid tragedies, which produce fear in "our women and children" (Young, 1977, p. 243). Many of the modern-day revelations stress the sacred role of the family, and the concept of the eternal family is at the heart of Mormon theology. Consequently, teachings about the media focus on both strengthening the family as well as protecting it from negative influences.[9] In this way, media use is an enigma in Mormon culture. Unsavory aspects of the media such as violence and gratuitous sexuality are shunned, but Mormons also consume secular media. This stems from the simultaneous effort to keep religious commitments on the one hand, but also to be active participants in the larger society. Mormons produce official instructional films, books, and Web sites. Unofficial genres such as Mormon movies, popular fiction, and recorded music also exist.

Unlike Anabaptists, Mormons rarely prohibit entire classifications of media. Strong warnings are issued by leaders, however, to be highly selective in using secular media. When leaders speak to the entire church membership, proper media use is a frequent topic.

Avoidance of R-rated movies is a common practice. Church-sponsored Brigham Young University prohibits R-rated films on campus, for example. In the last decade, demand has risen for Mormon film. Unofficial feature-length films such as *God's Army, Real Life Singles Ward,* and *Midway to Heaven* depict the norms and daily life of Mormon culture through both serious drama and comedy. The Work and the Glory series of enormously popular novels contains Mormon history. Interest in contemporary Mormon music has also grown, but only hymns and classical music are permitted in official church meetings.

While directives about media are consistent, actual audience behavior varies. In terms of television, some Mormons feel the medium plays a positive role in family life, while others see its overall influence as det-rimental (Stout, Martin, & Scott, 1996; Valenti & Stout, 1996). Golan and Baker (2011) find that Mormon students at Brigham Young University do not rate the news media highly in terms of trustworthiness, credibility, or moral content. There are distinctively different interpretive communities within the larger one. Mormons living in the city of Las Vegas, for exam-ple, are more likely to view exposure to secular media as an important test, and necessary for personal growth, while Utah Mormons are more likely to reject such media outright (Stout, 2004; Stout, Martin, & Scott, 1996).

While LDS church leaders approach the Internet with caution, often warning about the dangers of pornography, exhortations to use the Web to defend the church have increased. Cautious about social media at first, Mormon leaders now urge members to actively spread the Gospel in cyberspace; church officials use Search Engine Optimization (SEO) and other strategies (Chen, 2011).

The Jewish Audience

Judaism represents an historical interpretive community that has endured over many centuries; it is a knowledge culture celebrating learning and the written word.[10] For centuries, Jews, along with Muslims and some Chris-tian denominations, have been known as the People of the Book. Media that educate, illuminate, and inspire are valued in Jewish communities. Learning is a sacred activity, and knowledge a sacred gift that is passed on from one generation to another. While there are several denomina-tions within Judaism (e.g., Orthodox, Conservative, and Reform), shared emphasis on education, ritual, and ethics give media the purpose of raising one's status by emulating God.

The Torah or first five books of the Hebrew Bible is helpful in under-standing media-related behavior. Jewish audience members favor media that raise moral standards, promote sexual morality, and respect God. Media use is restricted on the Sabbath, and Jews frown upon personal dis-closures or invasion of a person's privacy in the media (Cohen, 2010). That is, the value of privacy supersedes the right-to-know in Jewish culture. For this reason the subject of the private sexual lives of politicians, while fas-cinating to many TV viewers, does not surface as often in Jewish news outlets as elsewhere (Cohen, 2001).

Members of the *Haredi* or ultra-Orthodox community often reside in tightly knit neighborhoods, usually in urban areas. Motivated by mem-ories of anti-Semitic propaganda in newspapers and editorial cartoons depicting Jews as devils, Rabbis are often fearful about the power of the media to incite persecution (Wigoder, 2002). Televisions were banned in certain neighborhoods in Jerusalem in the 1960s, and considerable effort is made to shield children from secular media (Cohen, 2010). In Conservative and Reform Judaism, however, Jewish life is perpetuated without isolation from many secular influences and media (Aviv & Shneer, 2005).

For Conservative and Reform Judaism, the media question is paradoxical. Restricting media use to scripture, sacred music, and Jewish art is a means of building identity within the faith. These within-group rituals are stressed by Jews concerned about growing assimilation, especially in the United States (Dershowitz, 1997). Secular education, however, has also become part of life for many Jews. Based on the principle of *Haskalah*, or "enlightenment," broad education has become both a means of personal development as well as a way of contributing to and improving society (Wigoder, 2002). Writers dealing with Jewish assimilation and the contemporary struggle to preserve one's heritage while at the same time participating in the larger society have also been popular. These include Bernard Malamud, Chaim Potok, Philip Roth, and Saul Bellow. Examples of popular films or plays depicting these dilemmas are *The Jazz Singer* (Fleischer, 1980), *The Chosen* (Kagan, 1981), *Yentl* (Streisand, 1983), and more recently *Angels in America* (Nichols, 2003). Television programs dealt with the stresses of Jewish assimilation in the 1980s in *Frank's Place* and later in *Thirtysomething* in the early 1990s. In a less serious manner, *Seinfeld* deals with similar issues using a comedic self-mockery style.

A key concept underpinning Conservative and Reform Jewish interpretive communities, then, is an effort to integrate at an optimal level while resisting assimilation. For this reason, media literacy is stressed.

The Islamic Audience

Islam is a religion with over a billion adherents; it accounts for about a fifth of the world's population (Barrett, 2001). The majority (80–90%) of Muslims are Sunnis, and 10 to 20% are of the Shia denomination. Despite a popular misconception, most Muslims (about 75%) reside in countries outside the Middle East (Toronto & Finlayson, 2001). Islamic beliefs derive from the Quran, the core religious text, which was revealed to the Prophet Muhammad. During the Middle Ages, Islamic society flourished, making important contributions to science, mathematics, and literature. Various forms of Western architecture, music, and crafts are influenced by ancient Islamic styles and art (Peterson, 1995). Islamic approaches to media today are influenced by history as well as contemporary culture and politics.[11]

The *Five Pillars* of Islamic life are: (a) profession or witnessing of faith, (b) prayer, (c) almsgiving, (d) fasting, and (e) pilgrimage. Of these, witnessing faith is a key to understanding Muslims' approach to the media. Nothing should come before Allah, and Muhammad is the only way to Allah (Toronto & Finlayson, 2001). When a Danish newspaper published cartoons featuring the Prophet Muhammad, Muslims around the world considered the depictions blasphemous. Twelve countries initiated trade embargos against Denmark; embassies and consulates were attacked (Klausen, 2009, p. 1). The *fatwah* issued on Salman Rushdie for his novel *Satanic Verses* (1988) illustrates a similar effort to protect the sacredness of the Quran. Gratuitous sexuality and depictions of violence in Western media are often offensive to Muslims (Palmer & Gallab, 2001).

According to Abdollahyan (2008), younger generations of Iranian Muslims experience discord between formal religious media and secular media such as the Internet; this has created "challenges" to "their religious identity" (p. 4). Muslims often disagree about the need to shift between sacred and secular environments in order to achieve shared discourse and a public sphere. For this reason, religious or regionalized media outlets are favored over secular ones by some Muslims. *Hybrid genres* that combine religious teaching with secular formats are increasingly popular. The Islamic satellite TV channel *Al Risala* ("The Message"), for example, resembles Western television and features Egyptian actress Sabreen, a talk show host who some consider the Islamic equivalent to Oprah. According to *Al Risala* general manager Sheikh Tarek Swidan, "In our understanding, Islamic media is any clean media, so any program [is appropriate] that is clean and has a message to improve a human being—improve them religiously, ethically, socially; push them towards being productive and effective, having ambitions" (quoted in Lindsey, 2006).

Many secular genres from feature-length film to romance novels have been used for religious purposes. Radio Islam has a vast global listenership and offers teachings from the Quran; its call-in talk show is popular in Chicago. For children 10 to 12, *Salidin* is an animated action DVD series with Islamic themes, and hip-hop artist Abdul Aziz is popular among Muslims in many countries. In Indonesia, the country with the highest Muslim population, Islamic movies, books, and recorded music are in great demand. *Ayat Ayat Cinta*, a movie based on an Islamic novel, drew thousands to theaters across the country (Collins, 2008).

The Hindu Audience

Hinduism is the third largest religion next to Christianity and Islam; adherents are based primarily in India and number over a million in the United States. It is one of the oldest religions, perhaps dating back to 10,000 BCE. Hinduism is multifaceted with no single dogma or central authority; many theologies are accommodated, making it one of the most tolerant world religions. A common belief among Hindus is Karma or the idea that actions have consequences and moral behavior has positive results. Other traditions include Dharma (ethics and duties), Samsara (rebirth), and Moksha (liberation from the cycle of Samsara). Reincarnation plays a key role in Hinduism as does the Bhagavad Gita, an important Hindu text. The Bhagavad Gita stresses the eternal nature of the soul as well as devotional service, commitment, meditation, and the importance of gaining knowledge. Due to its diverse nature, in Hinduism there is no single approach to the media, nor is there a specific theological view of the nature of communication. Therefore, it is best to think of Hinduism in terms of several interpretive communities rather than a single audience.[12]

While few studies of Hindus and contemporary media exist, Luthra (2001) identifies two distinct interpretive communities. The first are small *textual communities* of *Satsanghis,* comprising a "society of pious people" (p. 126). These informal groupings can be found in Indonesia, Canada, the United States, and other countries; they are loosely connected by "informal networking mechanisms" (p. 126). Satsanghis gather to discuss and interpret a *vani* or text of the spoken words of a guru. According to Luthra's (2001) study, the guru rarely if ever instructs Satsanghis about how to use the media, which is consistent with the Bhagavad Gita, where knowledge is conveyed to Arjun, but he is never told specifically how to act; consequently, Satsanghis "vary tremendously in their use of media" (p. 128).

Another important finding in Luthra's study is that Satsanghis become so absorbed in the study of *vanis* that popular media become secondary, and are frequently ignored altogether. It is a phenomenon occurring in a number of religious communities where engagement in study, mediation, and other daily activities not only assigns contemporary media to secondary status, but renders them generally unimportant. This finding suggests that religious decisions about media aren't always a matter of whether to use or abstain, but can also be part of a process of prioritization.

Virtual communities are also playing a role in Hindu life. Unlike the smaller group of Satsanghis, Luthra (2001) found that the Internet is facilitating media activism. Through Web sites such as that of the American Hindus against Defamation (AHAD), Hindus participate in an interpretive community centered on opposition to media stereotypes; they are increasingly concerned about overemphasis on caste and idol worship as well as the portrayal of Hindus as lacking in social values. In Luthra's research, Hindus participated in a public protest against the television program *Xena, Warrior Princess,* and its use of Krishna for entertainment purposes. Of particular concern was the portrayal of Krishna as a fictional character. Media activism can benefit the religious community not only because it takes a stand against defamation, but can strengthen identity and institutional solidarity as well (Warren, 2001).

A third type of interpretive community revolves around Hindi film or feature-length films in the Hindi language. Hindi film is a complex and enormously popular genre combining elements of history, mythology, devotion, nationalism, and secularism. While contemporary Hindi film also has an expanding secular dimension, it continues to illustrate how movies play a vital role in religious culture, sustaining belief and observance (Dwyer, 2006b). In recent years, *masala* films have emerged, representing a strain of Hindi movies that combine several elements from suspense to romance to religion. Hindi film continues to be an important element in Indian culture; the growth rate of the movie industry is more than triple that of India's gross domestic product growth (Kripalani & Grover, 2002).

The Buddhist Audience

Little has been written about Buddhism and contemporary media.[13] Historically, sacred architecture, statuary, and printed texts have been salient; Internet use is expanding within some Buddhist sects.[14] The emphasis on personal responsibility, or the idea that each individual is his or her own master, is the key to understanding the role of the media in relation to Buddhist observance. Buddhists do not embrace a personified external God, but instead stress the internal searching that all must do to reach higher enlightenment. Media that assist one on this journey are highly valued, especially if they enhance study and contemplation.

According to Holmes (2010a), electronic and print media are having a "global impact on Buddhism" (p. 53). This includes periodicals (e.g., *Tricycle: The Buddhist Review, Bodhi Magazine, Shambhala Sun*), scholarly publications (e.g., *Journal of Buddhist Ethics, Journal of Global Buddhism*), and Web sites such as Access to Insight, which contains an archive of translated texts, and the Buddhist Channel which offers global news. The Dhamma Media channel, a Thai cable television station, provides guidelines and principles for daily living.

A Buddha is an awakened one; a person who has been enlightened. Media that foster enlightenment, therefore, are valued the most. All have the Buddhist nature within, and offer the chance to be enlightened. The first step is looking inward, examining one's thoughts and feelings. The

goal in Buddhist theology is to get beyond anxiety about past and fu~~
by achieving right mindfulness, or keener awareness of what is occurring
in the present. Therefore, meditation is central; it allows one to progress
through different states of consciousness toward Nirvana, the ultimate
state of enlightenment. While physical temples and in-home shrines are
key places for meditation, the Internet provides access to meditative environments through cybertemples, online chanting, and devotional music.
The Akron Buddhist Cyber Temple and the Cyber Temple of Shaolin Zen,
for example, facilitate immediate access to symbols, sacred texts, and Buddhist virtual communities.

Denominational Audiences and the Numinous

We have explored several religious audiences in this chapter. Reflecting on
this discussion, one point stands out: the media play a key role in numinous experience. We see a dramatic shift from congregation to audience—
the media touch all aspects of religiosity from community to belief, from
deep feeling to ritual. Within religious audiences, media help create environments in which numinous experiences can occur. Conservative Protestants illustrate how the numinous can be experienced through virtually
any medium, even those not usually associated with religion such as rock
music and video games.

Another point underscored by this discussion is that members of the
various religious groups do not blindly embrace media; they create standards of evaluation. Critique and resistance can also lead to religious
experiences and the numinous. Mormons' attention to the movie rating
system is one example. Such actions can strengthen belief, provide ritual,
and sustain community. The Internet is an outlet for the numinous as well.
Its flexibility, interactivity, and accessibility provide numerous possibilities for worship. It is still unclear, however, whether audience members use
the medium optimally in religious contexts. Church leaders and parishioners are just beginning to develop the critical skills necessary to use the
medium in a way that sustains religious values and preserves the sacred.
In the future, learning what it means to be an audience member is likely to
be as important as knowing doctrine.

Numinous experience outside denominations is a key issue facing religious leaders. Whether media of popular culture detract from or enhance
commitment is a question that has not yet been fully explored. Parishioners will likely participate in several audiences offering opportunities
for the numinous.

Key Terms

almsgiving: Giving materially to another as an act of religious virtue.

catechism: A summary of beliefs and principles of the Catholic Church, often in question-and-answer format.

censorship: The restriction or prohibition of information dissemination.

dogma: The established belief or doctrine of a religion.

fatwah: A religious opinion on Islamic law issued by an Islamic scholar.

Five Pillars (of Islam): The five duties required of every practicing member of the Islamic faith. *Shahadah* (profession of faith), *Salat* (ritual prayer), *Zakat* (almsgiving), *Sawm* (fasting during Ramadan), and *Hajj* (pilgrimage to Mecca).

interpretive community: The theoretical concept that groups share strategies of interpretation that are worked out in social interaction.

Krishna: A Hindu deity portrayed in different sects of Hinduism as either a god-child, a prankster, a model lover, a divine hero, or the Supreme Being.

marketplace of ideas: The condition where any idea is considered in public discourse. As a result, the best ideas surface.

pilgrimage: A long journey or search of great moral significance, sometimes to a sacred place or shrine important to one's beliefs.

the Reformation: A reform movement started by Martin Luther in Europe in 1517 as a response to practices of the Catholic Church.

Questions to Ponder

1. Do you think that denominations are relatively similar in their uses of media or do they differ significantly? Explain your answer.
2. Do you feel that *audience* is a better term than *congregation* in describing religious groups?
3. Is censorship ever justified in religious contexts? Explain your answer.
4. Why do some denominations restrict media use while others encourage it?
5. Do you feel that the Internet enhances religious experience or undermines it? Explain your answer.

CHAPTER 5

Cultural Religion

In this chapter we examine audiences of cultural religion.[1] As pointed out in chapter 1, the postmodern era requires a broader view of worship; denominations don't fully account for the expanding range of religious and numinous experiences. The media of popular culture are also important; they orient one's beliefs, elicit strong feelings, involve ritualized behaviors, and enable individuals to form communities. When this occurs through the Internet, film, television, and other media, users often describe their experiences in religious terms (Mazur & McCarthy, 2001; Sylvan, 2002, 2005). This book argues that religion is defined by individuals in everyday life; it should be studied wherever and whenever it occurs.

This chapter examines the following examples of cultural religion: the Oprah Winfrey phenomenon, Deadheads and Parrotheads, Elvis fandom, Trekkies, sports fans, and the Rothko Chapel community. Each illustrates the four elements of the numinous: community, belief, ritual, and deep feeling.

The suggestion that these audiences are religious is controversial.[2] Rock music fans and television viewers aren't typical parishioners in the traditional sense. Recent developments, however, indicate that belief systems and community do indeed form around popular media apart from organized religion. This is the expanding domain of cultural religion, and it deserves serious attention in media studies.

Considerable religious activity has occurred outside denominations in the United States over the last two centuries (Albanese, 2007); some of it

is traceable to Europe. Numerous immigrants with denominational affiliations arrived in the United States, while others sought truth outside these
boundaries. Institutions have never been the sole domains of ritual and
belief. Pluralism underpins this situation.[3] Distinct pursuers of truth exist
side-by-side, both denominationalists and independent believers. According to Berger (1981), pluralism offers choice, and "the lines between insid-
ers and outsiders have become blurred" (p. 41). This isn't attributed to the
media alone, but information access and greater sharing allow individuals
to question, search, and pursue truth in new ways.

Two groups illustrate cultural religion. Uncomfortable with institutional limits, baby boomers look for truth in new places (Roof, 1999).
Younger adults are also experimenting outside the concrete and mortar
of church buildings; their affinity for popular media developed in the
formative years, and is now woven into daily activities. Beaudoin (1998)
describes them this way:

> Here is a generation that stays away from most churches in droves
> but loves songs about God and Jesus, a generation that would score
> very low on any standard piety scale but at times seems almost
> obsessed with saints, visions, and icons in all shapes and sizes.
> These are the young people who, styroform cups of cappuccino in
> hand, crown around the shelves of New Age spirituality titles in
> the local book market and post thousands of religious and quasi-
> religious notes on the bulletin boards of cyberspace. (p. ix)

Beaudoin's reference to "cappuccino" and the "book market" reminds
us that cultural religion cannot be separated from the free market. As
noted by Einstein (2008), religion is a "commodity product" (p. 13); DVDs,
novels, and music downloads are made available by commercial industries. As we will see later in the chapter, however, this doesn't minimize
the role such goods play in the lives of many. I now discuss audiences of
cultural religion as well as the type of religion they practice.

Audiences of Cultural Religion

Christians, Jews, Muslims, Hindus, Buddhists, and members of other
faiths all use media to varying degrees. But, what about religious groups
grounded in the media of popular culture? Do Elvis fans constitute a religion? Do they share a community and system of beliefs in the same way
that members of denominations do? Do audiences of cultural religion participate in meaningful rituals and express deep religious feelings?

The Oprah Winfrey Phenomenon

The most popular talk show host in the history of television, Oprah Winfrey is a highly influential public figure. The range of her work expands far beyond entertainment; she offers educational programs, imparts advice on personal and family matters, engages in worldwide philanthropic activities, and participates in public affairs and politics. While the TV show's recent 25th anniversary season was the last, her magazine O, book club, Web site OPRAH.com, and other media promote self-improvement and community service. The recent book, *The Gospel According to Oprah* (Nelson, 2005) argues that the religious engagement of Oprah's audience is serious and meaningful.[4] The author gives 10 reasons why Oprah is a spiritual teacher: 1) She is very human in her approach, 2) She tries to relieve suffering, 3) A community is provided, 4) Self-examination is encouraged, 5) She teaches gratitude, 6) Her message is easy to understand, 7) As a leader she listens, 8) She teaches generosity through role models, 9) Forgiveness is emphasized, and 10) She provides a reminder service for accomplishing important things (pp. xv–xvii). The show was broadcast to 145 countries, and five U.S. presidents, one reigning queen, one former queen, seven princes, and six princesses appeared as guests (Adding it, 2011, p. 166).

Oprah held confession on the television program, imploring guests to be truthful and faithful to spouses. She chastised author James Frey for embellishing parts of his popular book. The Monday through Friday show has been a ritual for millions. The "Thought for Today" can be accessed on the Web site, and Oprah viewers are expected to read certain books. When she recommended Tolstoy's *Anna Karenina,* it became a bestseller a hundred years after its initial publication. Oprah's Angel Network provides an outlet for volunteerism, with the goal of improving elementary schools around the world.

Although she attended the Trinity United Church of Christ in Chicago growing up, the Oprah religion is more postmodern than denominational. Unlike traditional religion where one makes an appointment with a religious leader, Oprah offers immediate advice and assistance. It's a "let's get right to it experience" without the red tape of institutions (Nelson, 2005).

As one examines this phenomenon closely, it's evident that Oprah is more than a television personality and Web site; she offers a multidimensional spiritual experience not unlike traditional religion. Oprah builds community, suggests a clear set of values, expects audience members to behave in a particular way, and engages participants' deep feelings. In short, it embodies all elements necessary for a numinous experience.

Elvis Fandom

Elvis Presley is one of the most highly recognized names of the 20th century. More than 30 years since his death, he sustains a global audience through recorded music, movies, memorabilia, and fan clubs. Presley not only had an excellent singing voice, but also developed a rock-and-roll performance style known for its sex appeal. His provocative gyrations onstage were signature elements of his act, capturing both young imagination and the ire of community leaders. At concerts, devotees were provoked to a frenzy, erupting in ecstatic screams of adoration. While the precise number has not been officially validated, fan Web sites claim Presley sold more records than anyone in history (Keene, 2008). The Official Elvis Presley Fan Club of Great Britain has 20,000 members (Duffett, 2001). Presley also appeared in movies and was one of the most popular Las Vegas nightclub acts.

Since his death, Elvis fandom, also referred to as Elvis worship, has expanded exponentially. Graceland, the Presley home in Memphis, Tennessee, has become a pop culture mecca, where fans from around the world assemble annually on the date of his death to pay tribute to "The King." A group of fans known as Elvi, dress like the singer, usually with carefully coiffed black hair and the signature one-piece white sequined Elvis nightclub jumpsuit.

Whether Elvis fandom qualifies as a religion is the subject of current debate. While Doss (1999) notes that Elvis fans describe their experiences in religious terms, Duffett (2003) feels that the religion moniker goes too far; he doubts that the phenomenon has sufficient institutional structure to be called a religion.[5] Arguments that Elvis is a religion are gaining support, however (Chadwick, 1997; Denisoff & Plasketes, 1995; Rodman, 1996). A closer examination of Elvis fans reveals a number of religious behaviors.

They form a subculture with many rituals. Doss (1997, 1999) notes the prevalence of in-home Elvis shrines and altars. A similar phenomenon is the Elvis room, where an even larger space is devoted to regular contemplation of the entertainer. On these shrines, images of Elvis are displayed in a variety of ways including photos, statuary, and paintings. Observing Elayne Goodman's *Altar to Elvis*, Doss (1997) found tiny vials and boxes containing "simulated bits and pieces of Elvis's hair and fingernails" (p. 6).

Whether the Elvis audience embraces a clear set of beliefs has not been fully determined. Disagreements about this stem from the complexities of his life. On the one hand, he expressed respect for religion, but on the other he created controversies; he respected his conservative Protestant roots, yet abused drugs and engaged in womanizing at various times. Devoted Elvis fans, however, note the entertainer's many positive values. In a study by Fraser and Brown (2002), fans not only saw Elvis as a role model, but altered behaviors in order to emulate him. These values include pursuit of a simpler life, generosity, respect for parents, multiculturalism, and spirituality.

Although the religious dimensions of Elvis fandom are not yet fully understood, there appears to be evidence of the numinous. Community, an emerging set of beliefs, ritual, and expression of deep feeling are present among the most committed fans.

Trekkies

Although the original television series *Star Trek* was canceled in 1969, it has generated a vast community of devoted fans around the world. Known as *Trekkies,* these enthusiasts attend annual conventions, commit episodes of the TV series to memory, and often dress like characters from the program. Trekkies exist in many countries throughout the world; some have *Trekrooms* in their homes where parts of the spaceship *Enterprise* are recreated, and others acquire tattoos of *Star Trek* characters. While Trekkies represent a wide range of interests and goals (some prefer the name Trekkers), audience members embrace a positive view of science; they also engage in community service.

Life for Trekkies revolves around the convention. In 1972, convention attendance was in the thousands and by the end of the 1990s, there was a Star Trek convention somewhere in the world every week (Nygard, 1999). At these events, participants discuss episodes of the program, listen to lectures by actors, and display costumes and other Star Trek paraphernalia. A feeling of openness abounds at conventions; they are outlets for imagination and free expression. Individuality not tolerated in the larger society is welcomed and nurtured at Star Trek meetings. Attendees feel accepted, they often compare the convention to being in an extended family, and creativity is praised at all levels (Greenwald, 1998).

Despite some variations, a fairly consistent Star Trek belief system is emerging. It centers on a positive vision of the world and how it can be improved through innovation and technology. Trekkies believe that science and the imagination combine to do great things. Egalitarian values are also stressed, and Trekkies predict what certain program characters would do in various ethical situations.

Activity occurs outside the convention as well. Trekkies form clubs or "ships" that perform particular missions. They engage in charity work and community assistance. Each TV episode has a moral, and members of local units carry out its ethical code. Some ships engage in hunger relief, and others support science education programs. Devout Trekkies extend Star Trek into the workplace, with some donning uniforms, and requesting that coworkers refer to them by their Star Trek name.

Deadheads and Parrotheads

Cultural religion often revolves around performers of rock music. Such is the case with the Deadheads and Parrotheads, the former representing fans of the Grateful Dead band, and the latter the enthusiastic followers of singer Jimmy Buffett. Both communities are drawing the attention of sociologists of religion. By applying analytical concepts of religiosity, much is being learned about cultural religion by studying these groups.

The Grateful Dead performed most of its concerts between 1965 and 1995, the year lead guitarist Jerry Garcia died.[6] Since then, performances have been infrequent. While they were not the only musicians to sell DVDs, create music videos, and play sold-out concert halls, they spawned a unique subculture that was deeply devoted to the band. Between 500 and 1,000 devoted Deadheads followed the band from concert to concert, some of them sleeping in cars and living hand-to-mouth in order to stay on the concert tour (McCray-Pattacini, 2000). Outside the concerts, Deadheads created a carnival-like atmosphere, listening to beating drums, dancing, and selling crafts or Grateful Dead paraphernalia. Speaking of how Deadhead religion differs from traditional religion, band member and lead guitarist Jerry Garcia observes:

> Here's the thing: since there's a squabble over reality on earth—in other words, consciousness is fighting over reality insofar as there are Moslems and Hindus and Christians and so forth, and they're all striving to create the reality which creates their God and only their God, and that's the truth of the matter and everything else is wrong—their copping to nail down reality. What I wondered is why those people were so afraid of everybody coming up with their own reality on their own terms, because they would mesh anyway. They have to come together somewhere out here in this common reality which we'll agree to experience together. (Garcia quoted in Gans, 1991, p. 82)

Similarly, the Parrotheads create a reality-seeking experience at concerts. In keeping with the beach and ocean motifs of Jimmy Buffett's music, Parrotheads don tropical shirts, sunglasses, and grass skirts; some bring inflatable sharks to concerts and even haul in sand to simulate a beach in the parking lot.

During concerts, Parrotheads sing with Jimmy Buffett about tropical paradise and the need for escape. Deadheads participate in fairlike festivities followed by the actual performance and postshow gatherings. The band plays songs with intermittent improvisations called "The Space," where musicians depart from set musical structures. During these interludes, Deadheads sway and trance; many consider it a spiritual experience (McCray-Pattacini, 2000). At Jimmy Buffett concerts, Parrotheads also engage in standardized behaviors. During the song "Fins," they sway in unison and repeat various hand movements.

In terms of shared beliefs, Deadheads stress freedom, individuality, and a peaceful world. This is illustrated by a subgroup called the Spinners, who twirl or spin their bodies during performances. Then, they assemble after the show, sharing and writing down their inspirations (Sylvan, 2002). Parrotheads, on the other hand, advocate a simple life that respects nature; many support environmentalist causes. According to Mihelich and Papineau (2005), the "meanings of Parrothead subculture" include the search for a laidback lifestyle and the reclamation of spontaneity, which they find missing from a nine-to-five, overworked society. Many Parrotheads are critical of institutions; Buffett himself has a particular aversion for traditional religion (Ingersoll, 2001). Yet Parrotheads engage in "the use of religious discourse to make sense of their fandom" (p. 176).

Both audiences represent a type of ideological communitas during a liminal period (Turner, 1974).[7] In other words, Deadheads and Parrotheads create a fellowship of resistance against the status quo in a transitional period in their lives. Their rituals are rites of passage. In Sylvan's (2002) ethnographic study, he observes Deadheads moving out of "the structures of daily life" into a new social identity. Community ties and concert rituals reinforce this experience (p. 98). Likewise, the Parrotheads are in transition to "Margaritaville," a place described in the Buffett song by the same name. In a study by Bowen (1997), some Parrotheads believe Margaritaville is an actual place like Key West, Florida. To others, it's an imaginary beach town with aqua blue ocean and beaches of bright white sand; it's a place to be yourself and reconnect with nature. At the concerts, Parrotheads live vicariously through Buffett who takes them to Margaritaville through song, costume, and dance.

These communities are neither superficial nor ephemeral. Parrotheads exist outside the concerts through Parrothead clubs, informal gatherings, and Internet Web sites. These activities contribute to identity as a Parrothead and provide a continuing sense of community. According to Ingersoll (2001), Parrotheads form groups or flocks (phlocks), often with fellow Parrotheads they've known for many years. The club network Parrotheads in Paradise had 15,000 members in 1995 and 81 separate clubs; that year an annual convention drew 750 attendees (Ingersoll, 2001, p. 259).

Despite the fact that the Grateful Dead has performed much less frequently since Jerry Garcia's death, the community seems to endure in some form. According to McCray-Pattacini (2000) Deadheads continue to assemble by "following other tours and bands, communicating on the

Internet, and other creative pursuits" (p. 1). The recent *jam band* phenomenon suggests that this type of numinous experience is continuing. Groups such as Phish and Widespread Panic are a few examples. Lady Gaga and her fans, "little monsters" comprise a religion-like phenomenon as well. At her concerts, they pass notes to "Mother Monster." She has 34 million Facebook friends and one billion YouTube clicks (Hiatt, 2011, p. 42).

Sports Fans

The connection between sport and religion is a natural one given shared values of preparation, improvement, and fair play. To honor the gods, gladiators fought to the death; according to Roman belief, the outcome was determined by a higher power. In the ancient Mayan cultures of Central America, ball games were highly ritualized; some resulting in human sacrifice in order to assure the well-being of citizens as well as plentiful agricultural yields. Today, sporting events are often preceded by team prayer with some athletes bowing their heads or genuflecting after making a score. Considered role models in religious circles, athletes often speak at church gatherings. Such was the case at Evangelist Billy Graham's television crusades; professional football player Roger Staubach gave motivational talks as did other athletes. Athletic teams symbolize hard work and tradition, as exemplified by the University of Notre Dame's "Fighting Irish" football team, a source of pride for millions of Catholics.

Technology, economics, and available leisure time elevate the religious aspects of sport; it has become a source of the numinous in its own right. Fans form communities, engage in rituals, and in some cases codify behavioral expectations. Regarding the Boston Red Sox baseball team, fandom can be a way of life. In his cultural history of Fenway Park, Borer (2008) observes:

> Not only do people pack the ballpark on game days, but hordes of baseball fans also flock to the bars and restaurants that surround Fenway and flow into Kenmore Square, which is only a stone's throw away. Certainly they could catch the televised broadcast elsewhere, but they are drawn to or near the park even when the team is out of town. The closer you get to Fenway and, once inside, the closer you get to the lush green field, the closer you are to "history." Just by being there, you become part of a shared history of triumph and tragedy, heroes and villains, beer and hot dogs. (p. 14)

For those unable to attend, media enable vicarious experiences with deep meaning. Large-screen high definition televisions and digital stereo sound engage the senses. Broadcasts can be instantly rewound if a play is missed or needs to be reexamined. While the awe of the event cannot be fully captured through media, improved technology engages the senses, bringing the viewer closer to the action. Through Web sites such as espn. com, viewers access statistics, player profiles, and news while simultaneously watching the game (or several games). Enthusiasts create their own "Fantasy" teams, competing against other fans in organized leagues; winners are determined by the weekly performance of professional players. "Super Bowl Sunday," the championship game of the National Football League (NFL) is a ritual comparable to national holidays, associated with both large and small gatherings. The 2010 contest between the New Orleans Saints and Baltimore Colts drew an estimated 106.5 million television viewers making it the most watched program in history, surpassing the 1983 final episode of the show *MASH* (Huff, 2010). Cooking, entertaining, and attending Super Bowl parties take up the entire day; the game itself is only one part of an elaborate social ritual.

Super Bowl Sunday, NASCAR auto races, and the Master's Golf Tournament reveal much about contemporary society. According to R.L. Moore (2003), they demonstrate the merger of sacred and secular culture. In the view of Robinson (2007), they have traces of religion, including a sense of holism, community, transcendence, common purpose, ritual, and development (p. 8). Albanese (1999) suggests that sports reflect many societal codes, including competition: "Rigorously prepared for the fight by their previous exercises in self-denial, those who compete to the end are expected to win the day—or, at the very least, to lose with the grace and dignity demanded by the code" (pp. 476–477). Religiosity of sport inevitably turns out to be a reflection of cultural values such as personal sacrifice, teamwork, and the quest for higher achievement. While many disagree about whether sport is a religion, there is a view, now well documented, that these activities serve many functions of the numinous (Prebish, 1993).

The Rothko Chapel Community

Opened in 1971, the Rothko Chapel in Houston, Texas is the home of a community that reflects upon spiritual matters and supports humanitarian causes. While not "popular media" in the typical sense, the Rothko Chapel illustrates the impact of religious iconography outside denominations. The abstract expressionist forms in paintings by Mark Rothko are icons of religious contemplation for the local community and other visitors to the chapel. Because they bear no resemblance to traditional symbolism, however, they facilitate worship with no denominational ties. The chapel is discussed here because it illustrates how culturally religious iconography, not the denominational type, can inspire worship, community, and ritual.[8]

The building is an octagonal structure displaying 14 Rothko paintings; patrons meditate upon them from the center of the chapel. Aligned with the Abstract Expressionist School of art, Rothko's canvases contain horizontally positioned rectangular shapes presented in various shades of color. These images have been widely circulated through prints and the Internet. Chapel seats allow reflection on the paintings from any angle. In this way both the paintings and the chapel itself combine to form a religious medium. All are welcome; the building can be used by any religious or ethically based organization.

Beyond the meditative experience, the chapel is a center point in the local community and a support to the surrounding neighborhood; weddings and memorial services are held there. Monthly group meditations take place as well as art festivals. The chapel functions as a forum with speakers on topics such as human rights and hunger relief. The chapel is a gathering point for informal discussions, an example of how an artistic medium can become the focal point for community discourse and ritual.

Blurring the Lines between Institutions and Popular Culture: Emergent Churches and Charismatic Megachurches

The emergent church audience is a compelling example of cultural religion. These churches retain belief in a deity, but stress community over traditional structure; they resist rigid dogma and draw heavily from secular media such as films, music, and the Internet (Gibbs & Bolger, 2005). There's little difference between the insider and outsider in an emergent church; participants are free to synthesize any number of religious philosophies as long as she or he professes belief in God and engages in service. It is acceptable to affiliate with other denominations simultaneously. In a way, it is a church that represents all denominations and no denominations; community is primary and doctrine secondary.

Outside Huntsville, Texas, the Universal Ethician Church illustrates the emergent church phenomenon. Through a Web site, participants learn about the church and how to participate in the community. A roadside chapel and a small temple provide sites for worship and meditation for all visitors. At Saturday sunset meetings, nonsectarian messages are shared; poetry is recited, stories are told, religious songs are sung, and a sacrament is shared. Participants help maintain the church's family cemetery.

Information technology is central in the emergent church. Participants recognize the changing nature of media, observing that denominations have been slow to do so. Traditional churches overlook the "language of culture" they argue, and criticism of popular culture reflects a lack of understanding of their flocks:

> The Reformation contextualized the Gospel for the print era, but there has been no corresponding information to bring the gospel to our image-based era. The church continues to communicate a verbal, linear, and abstract message to a culture whose primary language consists of sound, visual images, and experience, in addition to words. (Gibbs & Bolger, 2005, p. 20)

Media are also central in charismatic megachurches, but unlike emergent churches, they revolve around the teachings of a single leader or pastor. Defining characteristics of these churches include size (congregation of 2,000 or more) and reliance on media to accommodate and retain large audiences. An example is the Crystal Cathedral in Garden Grove, California. Although affiliated with the Reformed Church in America, it is attended by members of other denominations. It began as a drive-in movie theater, with participants worshipping from the family car (Loveland & Wheeler, 2003). Today, about 3,000 attend each week, and a much larger audience is reached through *The Hour of Power*, a cable television program that's also streamed on the Internet.

Some megachurches merge religious venues with leisure activities; they reflect the postmodern tendency of mixing sacred and secular spaces. The 24,000-member Prestonwood Baptist Church in Plano, Texas has a gymnasium, sports fields, an arcade, a bookstore, and a food court with a Starbucks coffee shop (Mega-Churches, 2005). The International Church of Las Vegas, also combines entertainment elements with those of traditional worship. The church lists "entertainment" as one of the six kingdoms of God.

Pastor Joel Osteen's 16,000-seat Lakewood Church in Houston, occupies the former Compaq Center sports arena. The megachurch's Web site claims that the weekly television broadcast reaches over 200 million households in over 100 countries. Osteen's sermons stress general themes such as honesty, charity, and thrift, rather than the doctrine of a particular religious institution. At the conclusion of Osteen's sermon, audience members are exhorted to affiliate with a Bible-based church of choice.

Given the large audience, media are vital to the megachurch experience. The auditorium itself is a highly mediated environment designed to stimulate feelings of awe and wonder. Stereo sound, video recordings, live music, and dramatic lighting set the stage for the sermon. While megachurches appear to lack the social relationship dimension of smaller, more intimate congregations, network ties may be more substantial than previously thought. The Internet provides an outlet for networking beyond the weekly services, and many megachurches offer smaller classes and activities during the week.

Cultural Religion and the Numinous

The key elements of religiosity (i.e., community, belief, ritual, and deep feeling) are found throughout the culture, not only within formal institutions. Media of popular culture provide quasi-religious experiences in many forms. Audiences of Oprah Winfrey, Elvis, Star Trek, the Grateful Dead, and Jimmy Buffett demonstrate this. By expanding religion to include the numinous, much is learned about individuals' deep involvement with the media. Future research is needed to examine religion as an emergent phenomenon, not one that is exclusively tied to past traditions.

Audiences of cultural religion are *media-centric*; they focus on a mediated event, personality, or genre. Such experiences, while not religious in the traditional sense, are deep and meaningful; they are numinous nevertheless. By studying media processes through the lens of religion, knowledge is expanded about their role in society.

Beyond the examples discussed here, others should be examined in the future. Travel and tourism, for example, is emerging as an area of research.

Key Terms

communitas: Rituals that promote social cohesion and a feeling of unity.

cultural religion: A phenomenon where elements of religion (i.e., belief, ritual, community, and deep feeling) are exhibited outside denominations, often through media of popular culture.

emergent church: An audience that while retaining a belief in deity, stresses community over dogma.

liminality: The feelings of openness and liberation that are associated with transitional periods such as rites of passage.

megachurches: Congregations of 2,000 or more attendees that meet regularly in highly mediated venues.

media-centric community: A religious audience focused on a particular media event, personality, or genre.

religious pluralism: A condition where numerous religions coexist in a society, and citizens are free to choose from among them.

Questions to Ponder

1. What do you make of the claim that denominations do not account for the myriad ways that individuals engage the religious?
2. How does cultural religion differ from denominational religion?
3. Some argue that cultural religion audiences such as Oprah viewers, Elvis fans, and Trekkies aren't really religious. Do you agree? Why or why not?
4. How does the concept of liminality explain Deadheads and Parrotheads as audiences of cultural religion?
5. In what ways are emergent churches unique as audiences of cultural religion?
6. How do nondenominational megachurch audiences differ from those associated with denominations?

CHAPTER 6

Media Criticism

Religion is depicted variously across the media. How such portrayals are interpreted is the subject of this chapter. How is the religious value of media assessed? How does one get the most from media treatments of religion? Such critique requires frameworks of analysis. *Criticism* is the examination of media from different perspectives; it requires *media literacy*[1] or the ability to make optimal use of the media. Media literate individuals know the fundamentals of media criticism; they possess skills to analyze and enjoy media. In an era when the numinous is omnipresent, media criticism is a vital area of study.

First, we explore specific techniques. Because religion is a sensitive subject, media criticism is difficult in some settings. Barriers to media criticism, therefore, are discussed. The lack of critical tools results in misinterpretations, sometimes with dire consequences. Galileo's imprisonment in 1633 and Anthony Comstock's censorship of fine art in the 1880s are examples. Then, the numinous is discussed in the context of criticism; it is a key concept in examining both sacred and secular media. The chapter ends with a sample critique of a movie containing religious themes.

Religious Media Criticism

Religious media criticism is the assessment of works from a religious and moral perspective (Young, 1994). It is a means of understanding messages as products of religious surroundings and influence. Without systematic approaches, such assessment tends to be casual, superficial, and offhand. For this reason, several types of criticism are reviewed here; it is important to have analytical tools at one's fingertips.

Didactic Criticism

Common among denominations is didactic criticism. Critics simply ask, "What are media teaching about religion?" Clergy, for example, use films to discourage drug use and premarital sex. Whether a religious principle is effectively communicated is the concern of didactic criticism. In Sheldon's (1896) religious novel, *In His Steps*, morally sound decision making is stressed through the question, "What would Jesus do?" The didactic critic assesses how admonitions are put across, and whether values are communicated clearly and effectively. Listed as the 39th best-selling book of all time (Ash, 2002, p. 109), over 30 million copies of Sheldon's book have been sold. Similarly, the film *Cipher in the Snow* (Whitaker & Atkinson, 1973) about the death of a teenager without friends, so captured the imagination that it is frequently shown in churches to discourage teasing and bullying.

Didactic criticism is a form of dualism; a text is either positive or negative regarding religion.[2] The strength of didactic criticism is its identification of both deleterious and moral images. This gives clergy an idea of the types of behaviors youth are exposed to. The major weakness is superficiality and inability to explore media from deeper and more thorough perspectives. A movie about a dishonest priest could be interpreted as a moral message rather than a negative statement about a denomination, for example. Because of its limitations, few are satisfied with didactic criticism in all instances.

Audience Response Criticism

Audience response criticism is quite different from didactic analysis; messages are less important than their interpretation.[3] It is similar to reader response criticism in literature:

> [T]exts have no life apart from readers. Until someone opens a book, it does not exist; and then it only exists as part of a reader's consciousness ... readers create texts as they read them. The text exists in the reader, or perhaps somewhere between the reader and the page, and for all practical purposes it exists nowhere else. (Cowles, 1994a, p. 159)

Some religious leaders are sensitive to audience preferences, incorporating media that parishioners relate to. Perceptions about media change through time. Some Greek statues were originally made to honor athletes, but statues found in cathedrals today evoke the sacred, adding to the aura of places of worship. Rock music was shunned by many Evangelicals in the 1960s, but is now common in megachurches. Whether it is religious or not, is for audience members to say.

Formalism

One means of discerning a work's meaning is by analyzing its form. Plot, characterization, symbolism, tone, and imagery reveal a great deal. Formalism is the analysis of storytelling devices. While *Star Trek* is a space adventure at one level, it conveys moral messages at another. Just as Jim Casy is a Christ figure in Steinbeck's *Grapes of Wrath*, movies such as *Simon Birch* (Birnbach & Mark, 1998) and *Ulee's Gold* (Demme, 1997) also deify characters. In the latter, beekeeper Ulee Jackson serves and redeems others, only to be sacrificed in a manner similar to Christ's crucifixion. *The Natural* (Johnson, 1984), a film about an over-the-hill baseball player, suggests the existence of a higher power. Thunder and lightning can be understood as symbolizing God's intervention in people's everyday lives.

Formalism is content-based criticism. The plot, for example, does more than move the story along; it conveys religious messages indirectly. In Shyamalan's film *The Village* (Mercer, Rudin, & Shyamalan, 2004), townspeople try to obtain medicine for a dying loved one. The plot involves a moral journey toward higher values. The characters learn tolerance and compassion through dealing with mounting adversity.

When the author's intent is known it helps uncover religious messages below the surface. John Updike's novels, for example, confront the reconciliation of Protestant obligations with the artist's urge to create, unburdened by family demands (Updike, 1999). George Bernard Shaw's play *Man and Superman* presents a similar conflict. These writers faced such dilemmas in their own lives.[4] While a story may not be overtly classified as religious, authors comment on moral issues through characterization, dialogue, and other devices.

Ethical Criticism

It is difficult to study mediated religion without attention to ethics. From fund-raising to accuracy, the present age is characterized by both honorable and unscrupulous media activity. In the mid-1980s, activities of Jim and Tammy Faye Bakker's PTL Club (i.e., "Praise the Lord") TV show resulted in criminal charges. Viewers purchased lifetime memberships for $1,000 entitling them to an annual 3-day stay in a luxury hotel owned by the Bakkers. The number of memberships sold, however, exceeded the capacity of the 500-room resort, so most applicants weren't accommodated. Nevertheless, the Bakkers made considerable profits in the venture. An earlier scandal occurred when the Jehovah's Witness *Watchtower* magazine advertised "miracle wheat" in the early 1900s. It was purported to be five times more productive than any other brand, and cost $1 per pound, a high price in that day (Miracle, 1913, p. 1). The deception, uncovered by the *Brooklyn Daily Eagle* newspaper, tarnished the reputation of Pastor Charles Taze Russell.

At one time or another, members of all denominations behave in questionable ways that involve the media. Ethical criticism is the ability to assess the moral character of messages, and by so doing, make sound judgments regarding media selection and religious claims. Christians, Fackler, McKee, Kreschel, and Woods (2008) exhort individuals to weigh values and loyalties when analyzing news, entertainment, advertising, and other genres. They use a framework developed by Ralph Potter to encourage thoughtful reasoning based on the work of moral philosophers such as Aristotle, Kant, John Stewart Mill, and others. The controversial *Show Me!* book, designed to teach children about human sexuality, provides a case in point. The volume's explicit photographs offended religious leaders, while sex education advocates lauded its frankness. Should children be protected from such images as a matter of moral principle, or does their use accomplish a greater good by educating young audiences about human physiology? Whatever one concludes, according to Christians et al. (2008), the decision process should be thoughtful and thorough. Moral assessments shouldn't be taken lightly.

Artistic decisions have ethical dimensions; they influence how groups are perceived. Because of its humorous depiction of sacred symbols, over 5,000 Hindus signed a petition urging Paramount Pictures not to release the movie *Love Guru* (Hindus, 2008). Similar complaints have been registered by American Hindus Against Defamation (AHAD), and summarized by Luthra (2001):

> One incident revolved around the use of pictures of Shiva and Krishna adjacent to pictures of women in revealing clothes displayed on the walls of Club Karma, a Chicago nightclub. Another centered around the cover of the compact disc *Nine Lives* pub-

lished by Sony, which used an altered version of an ancient Hindu painting showing Krishna conquering the serpent Kalinag, replacing Krishna's face with the head of a cat and his male chest with a female's. (p. 134)

Artists face ethical issues, especially in a numinous age where morality is pondered and learned through media. Yet if freedom underpins creativity, what is the obligation concerning fairness and accuracy? As Patterson and Wilkins (2011) contend, "No question in the field of aesthetics is more thoroughly debated with less resolution than the role of truth in art" (p. 277). This dilemma emerged in the making of *Rudy* (Woods & Anspaugh, 1993), a movie about an actual lower-middle-class teen striving to attend the University of Notre Dame; he wants more than anything to play on the football team despite his small stature. The film conveys a straightforward message: faith and hard work precede the miracle. Yet the screenwriter Angelo Pizzo deviates from the actual events by depicting the coach, Dan Devine, as an arrogant taskmaster, aloof to Rudy's dreams. With the clock ticking off the final seconds of Rudy's last chance to play, Devine remains indignant refusing to put him in the game. Only when the chanting crowd becomes unbearable does he relent, allowing Rudy to run onto the field, fulfilling his lifelong goal.

According to Devine's (2000) autobiography, he actually liked Rudy, and it was his idea to play him. Pizzo, however, insisted the coach had to be the heavy in order to create necessary conflict; the movie wouldn't work without the negative depiction. Devine agreed, if it would help Rudy whom he considered to be a friend. Nevertheless, the coach's legacy suffered; he regrets that some will forever associate him with the insensitive villainous character in the film. In defense of the film is the utilitarian argument that so many were inspired to pursue their dreams because of the movie. These are difficult decisions for artists, and ethical analysis is vital in an age when popular media are also numinous vehicles for teaching morality.

Marxist and Critical Analysis

Marxist analysis is a broad area of criticism. One branch, *critical studies,* examines media messages in the larger context of economics and political power. Religious depictions advance ideology and uphold interests of the state, according to this view.[5] For example, some urge the use of Hindi films to promote Indian nationalism (Dwyer, 2006a). *The Wizard of Oz* (LeRoy, 1939) is examined by Marxist critics; they see the film as a capitalist apologia (Brummett, 2006). Although it contains religious themes (e.g., belief in oneself, enduring to the end, serving others, etc.), the phrase, "There's no place like home," admonishes one not only to remember Kansas, but to accept the status quo in hard financial times.

Marxists also criticize denominational support of materialism, or the idea that happiness is achieved through consumption. One example of this is televangelists who promise financial success (e.g., prosperity doctrine, health-and-wealth, etc.). Others market religious products through advertising[6] (strategic communication is discussed at length in chapter 9). Suffice it to say that mediated religion not only communicates doctrine, but can also advocate a particular way of life. According to Marxist critics, it is the ideology of consumerism that is conveyed most often.

Media Criticism and the Numinous

As religionists' involvement with media expands, the tools of media criticism become more valuable; it is vital that clergy and parishioners develop the critical skills to assess religious messages wherever they appear. If media are outlets for the numinous, what's the best way to take advantage of such opportunities? Some argue, for example, that televised sports serve the purpose of religion. While sports fans engage in ritual behavior, do they have a belief system strong enough to guide the moral life? Today, numinous media are ubiquitous. Therefore, several dilemmas must be resolved:

1. *Alignment vs. Separation* or the question of whether popular media should be incorporated into worship or kept separate. Hess (2001) argues that movies, television programs, and other media are familiar to parishioners and should be used to teach religious principles. Beaudoin (1998) makes a similar argument, especially with regard to young adult audiences. Postman (1985) on the other hand, favors separate spheres in order to preserve the sacred.
2. *Personal vs. Collective Media Use,* of which religious leaders must obtain a deeper understanding. It isn't sufficient to define media use in terms of the group; an understanding of how parishioners use media independently away from the congregation is also essential.
3. *Simplification vs. Complexity,* or how congregations will be taught to analyze texts. Simplification is a didactic approach where works are rejected based on the presence of certain images (e.g., violence, gratuitous sexuality, etc.). Media literacy programs emphasizing complexity address several dimensions in addition to overt representations; these usually include aesthetics and form.

4. *Open vs Closed Systems* begs the issue of whether communities should establish their own media (e.g., Internet sites, radios stations, periodicals, etc.) as primary, or encourage exposure to secular media and genres such as news programs and popular films.

As religious leaders address these issues in their media education programs, parishioners begin to deal with the substantive questions related to today's complex media environment. Simply knowing how various media operate is no longer sufficient; media literacy is about giving congregations the tools to resolve media-related problems.

Barriers to Media Criticism

Predictions about the impact of media on religious life have not always been accurate, and critical skill is the best way to assure against conjecture and misguided assumptions. Historically, the lack of media literacy has resulted in unfortunate circumstances (Stout, 2001). For example, the incarceration of the great scientist Galileo, for his writings on heliocentrism (theory that the earth revolves around the sun), was partly due to the fact that many of his accusers had not actually read his treatises.[7] This tendency persists today: there's an overreliance on others' opinions without actually experiencing the original work. Another example is *Schindler's List* (Spielberg, Molen, & Lusting, 1993), an Academy Award winning movie about the Holocaust. Although acclaimed by critics as one of the most moral works ever produced, some U.S. government leaders initially denounced nudity in the film without having seen it.

The tendency to simplify texts is also a barrier to media literacy. The late-19th century religious leader and antivice crusader Anthony Comstock is a salient example. Heading the New York Society for the Suppression of Vice, Comstock was authorized by the government to police the flow of obscene materials in the mail; he destroyed 50 tons of books and 3,984,063 pictures thought to be obscene (Trumbill, 1913, p. 239). Of the 3,646 people Comstock arrested, 2,682 were convicted or pleaded guilty (p. 239). Soon Comstock expanded his authority by confiscating works of art; he incarcerated artists, writers, and art dealers. Actions taken against Walt Whitman delayed the poet from publishing an edition of his book, *Leaves of Grass,* in New York (Beisel, 1997; Reynolds, 1996). Comstock's ruthless censorship got so out of hand, that citizens finally pulled the plug on his authority, and the term *comstockery* became synonymous with prudery in the late 1800s. Historians concur that Comstock had a simplified, one-dimensional view of media and could not recognize their artistic or aesthetic elements.

The Comstock example raises the question of whether *censorship*, or the act of preventing the flow of information, is compatible with the concept of media literacy. Literacy is an audience-centered activity where decisions about media rest with the audience member. Implicit is the assumption that even within a religious structure, the individual ultimately decides what is desirable or deleterious. For this reason, censorship has been controversial both inside and outside denominations. The practice of censorship varies across religious cultures and is a theological, legal, and ethical question. Historically, people have been imprisoned and on occasion even put to death for disseminating profane messages. While these practices are commonly associated with an organization such as the Inquisition, they continue today as illustrated by the *fatwah* issued on the life of Salman Rushdie for his depiction of Muslims in the novel *Satanic Verses*.

There is a type of censorship that is unofficial but still persists today. *Indirect censorship* is the condition where one feels pressure not to create or use media even though it isn't expressly forbidden to do so. Implied media restriction is sustained informally in order to maintain moral behavior and norms. In the Protestant denomination of the Nazarenes, for example, an earlier mandate to avoid movie theaters continues to be adhered to by some, even though it is no longer an official directive. By the same token, many Mormons consider R-rated movies to be inappropriate, although there is no official policy regarding this. One characteristic of religious cultures is a tendency, perhaps for reasons of protection, to create culturally based rules and restrictions. Media literacy, then, is also a process of identifying and better understanding the origins of media and rules.

The examples of Comstock and Galileo illustrate the dangers that can occur when media-related decisions are made without sufficient information or understanding. Media literacy programs can become safeguards against such situations.

Sample Critique: Religious Themes in Tony Kushner's *Angels in America*

In order to illustrate the critical frameworks just discussed, the TV movie *Angels in America* (Costas, 2003) is examined. The value of media criticism is best understood through actual critique. *Angels* is appropriate given its critical acclaim; it was awarded the Pulitzer Prize as well as the Tony Award for Best Play. The HBO version earned 11 Emmy awards, more than any other miniseries including *Roots*. Exploring the interface between religion, politics, and the 1980s AIDS crisis, *Angels* asks the question: How well have religious and political institutions served us in a time of crisis?

The protagonist is Prior Walter, a New Yorker with terminal
gay lover, Louis Ironson abandons him at the worst possible
is visited by an angel; she declares him a prophet with a special m...
for the new millennium. Bewildered, he goes to the Mormon Visitors
Center inquiring about angels, prophets, and whether his disease is God's
punishment. Angelic visitations continue, and Prior's mission is clarified:
he will guide a society inadequately prepared for the AIDS catastrophe.
In the final scene, Prior speaks directly to the audience: "The Great Work
Begins."

Through subplot, symbolism, archetype, and other devices, Kushner
comments on contemporary religion. Religion is a matter of the heart,
and shouldn't be corrupted by political power. This message is teased
out through the device of multiple conflicts. One is the struggle between
conformity and honesty to self. Other conflicts arise as well. A young
lawyer, for example, is confused when his boss asks him to do something
unethical in the name of loyalty. A mother is conflicted when her devout
Mormon son discloses he's gay. Later in the story, two friends argue
heatedly about whether Mormonism is a cult. A wife and husband disagree
about religious orthodoxy. *Angels* is fraught with quandaries that, taken
together, raise an ethical question: In times of crisis, should institutions
cling to tradition if it means sacrificing lives?

A didactic critique yields an even more direct message: churches
are ineffective. If read literally, the play claims the country has failed
AIDS victims, and this is especially true of religious institutions. The
protagonist, Prior Walter chastises those who look the other way; he
represents hundreds of thousands crying for help. Abandoned by his lover,
he can't afford medicine. Visiting church, he comes up empty handed.
We're taken backstage to a horrific world of lesions, needles, hemorrhages,
and sickbeds. A few try to help, but the problem requires the collective
resources of society, and unfortunately, no mobilization is occurring.
Religious institutions must carry the blame.

Through dialogue, Kushner stabs at religion throughout the play. When
Louis is worried about the morality of his actions, Rabbi Chemelwitz
responds: "Catholics believe in forgiveness. Jews believe in Guilt." Louis is
critical of Judaism: "Jews don't have any clear textual guide to the afterlife;
even that it exists." Beyond its inadequacy in solving the AIDS problem,
religion has many flaws. When Louis finds out that Joe, his lover, is a
Mormon, he says it's "creepy" and that he doesn't like "cults." He inquires,
"How can a fundamentalist theocratic religion function participatorily
in a pluralist secular democracy?" To this, Joe responds: "The Church
of Jesus Christ of Latter-day Saints is not a cult." Louis retorts, "But
you're a lawyer! A *serious* lawyer!" A Marxist critic could conclude that

Mormonism symbolizes Republican political power of the mid-1980s, and that Kushner's real aim is the perceived ineptness of Reagan era conservatism.

The author's use of humor raises an ethical issue. Could the main point be made without comic depictions? Sacred Mormon iconography is borrowed liberally in this fashion. Just as Mormons claim the prophet Joseph Smith was visited by an angel, Prior also receives a visitation. When this happens, he's awestruck and whispers, "Very Steven Spielberg." Joseph Smith was instructed to unearth a sacred book buried near his farm, but Prior is told to retrieve them from under his kitchen floor: "Get the shovel or an axe or some tool for dislodging tile and grout, and unearth the sacred implements," the angel commands. To this, he responds, "I'll lose my security deposit." Some Mormons were also offended by their depiction in the animated TV series, *South Park*, and the Broadway musical, "Book of Mormon."

Dialogue is dappled with snipes. Salt Lake City is a place of "abundant energy; not much intelligence." At the Mormon Visitors Center, Harper and her mother-in-law Hannah engage in the following exchange:

Harper: Something's always bothered me. Everyone thinks the angel's name was Mormon.

Hannah: No, the name of the angel …

Harper: I know, I went to Sunday School. Moroni. The angel Moroni. So why don't we call ourselves Morons?

These comments, taken at face value, could offend the didactic critic; inexperienced viewers may take dialogue literally. Booth (1988) argues that works are accountable to some extent for the readings they provoke, even if the reaction isn't intended. Audience response criticism, however, suggests that interpretations aren't so easy to predict. The fact that Mormon symbols are used indirectly suggests the denomination has come of age, and is worthy of analysis. And the Mormon characters do act nobly at times, as when Hannah tells Prior his disease isn't a curse of homosexuality, but "a cancer, nothing more." She assures him the angel's there to "carry you, it's not to be afraid of." Likewise, Harper expounds upon the meaning of our earthly trials: "In this world there's a kind of painful progress, longing for what we've left behind and dreaming ahead."

Stout, Straubhaar, and Newbold's (2001) study of critics as audience found reviews of the play to be highly varied. Despite the number of Mormon characters, only 18% mentioned Mormons at all, opting to deal more with the work's larger themes of injustice and the dilemmas of pluralism (p. 193). Of those mentioning the denomination, some saw it as the American home-grown religion and a key element of U.S. mythology. Others noted that Mormons were politically conservative. Some critics thought Mormons were depicted as moralistic, conflicted, and neurotic. In short, there was "a rough balance" between positive and negative mentions (p. 211), thus suggesting that uniform audience reaction isn't likely.

Making the Most of Numinous Media

This chapter discusses ways of analyzing media, particularly those with moral themes. It provides building blocks toward media literacy, and the ability to explore artistic works in greater depth. Virtually all media are numinous in the current technological age. Tools of media criticism help one enjoy and get the most from texts that treat morality directly or indirectly. As religion diffuses into the media landscape, such skills are increasingly valuable.

Key Terms

audience response criticism: Critique of media based on how audience members make sense of and interpret messages.

didactic criticism: Ability to assess the instructional and informative qualities of media.

didacticism: A teaching-oriented approach to art emphasizing instructional and informative qualities of literature and other forms of media.

hybrid genre: The combining of existing media genres into a new genre.

media literacy: Having sufficient critical skills to use media optimally in everyday life.

religion media literacy: Skills necessary to evaluate media in light of one's religious goals.

religious criticism: A set of approaches used to analyze the religious assumptions of a work as well as its moral impact on the audience.

religious news publications: News publications created by specific denominations in order to create, sustain, and expand their religious communities.

televangelism: The use of television to disseminate religious information.

Questions to Ponder

1. What are the pros and cons of having a religion page in major newspapers?
2. How is the news genre vital to religious groups both internally and externally?
3. How has the increased media literacy of younger audiences changed the relationship between religion and film?
4. Think about how watching television makes you feel. List five different feelings you have (though not necessarily all at the same time) while watching television.
5. How would you go about evaluating the religious dimensions of a secular movie?
6. What are the different types of religious media criticism? How might you apply them in analyzing a TV show or film?

CHAPTER 7

The Internet

Of those who are affiliated with a religious group, the vast majority (74%) use the Internet (Pew data reported by Sifry, 2010). Among regular weekly church attendees, 75% own cell phones and 52% use text messaging. Fifty percent of online adults who also attend church weekly, have a social networking site profile (Sifry, 2010). More than 3 million individuals in the United States access online religious material daily (Larsen, 2004) and 64% of "wired" Americans go online for reasons related to religion or spirituality (Hoover, Clark, & Rainie, 2004). By the early 1980s, the Internet was being used for religious purposes (Campbell, 2010b). About 44% of U.S. churches have their own Web sites (National Opinion Research Center, 2006–2007). While religion is highly visible on the Internet, researchers are only beginning to grasp how this technology is used in religious worship.[1] Campbell (2010a) notes: "It is likely that as new innovations, programs, and networks emerge so will religious applications and alternatives" (p. 25).

When religion's online presence expanded in the 1990s, considerable speculation and conjecture ensued. Some raised the possibility that online religion might replace traditional congregations. A *Newsweek* cover story in 1996 went so far as to say that the Internet was changing "ideas about God" (Ramo, 1996, p. 60). Another claimed "… computers reveal to us new understandings of our … spiritual complexity" (Cobb, 1998, p. 23). According to MIT sociologist Sherry Turkle, "People see the Net as a new metaphor for God" (cited in Ramo, 1996).

Since these early predictions, more has been learned about religion online. Heidi Campbell's work is especially important in this regard; she argues that decisions about how to use new media are based on cultural context and personal reflection:

> Decision-making about a technology is often not a simple yes-or-no vote for religious groups. While a new technology, such as television, may provide a platform for preaching and proselytizing, it may also be seen as allowing problematic moral or secular content to invade the home. Therefore while the technology provides certain benefits for the community it may also introduce new dangers to its members. This means that religious individuals or groups may need to undergo a detailed process of evaluation and reflection to consider the positive and negative aspects brought on by the new technology before a decision can be made. (Campbell, 2010a, p. 5)

This decision-making process occurs both inside and outside denominations; Internet usage has both individual and communitarian features.

The Internet and the Numinous

The Internet, as a synthesis of several media, has a great capacity for numinous experience.[2] In the same way that religion combines belief, behavior, community, and feeling, the Internet's convergence of text, video, graphics, sound, and interactivity facilitates all four dimensions of worship. Beliefs are described and discussed; there's an opportunity for community-building through social networking. Users engage in rituals and other sacred behaviors online. In sum, the Internet creates an environment for both structured worship and serendipitous searching for truth. Denominations have a strong presence online, but they don't dominate cyberspace; the electronic frontier is a vast terrain for limitless expansion of spiritual pursuits as well as a combination of traditional and nontraditional worship.

Media of popular culture can also be tapped for their numinous elements. Film reviews from a moral perspective, uplifting quotes by noted authors or celebrities, and blogs on life's meaning are constantly available. The Internet is inherently a quester's medium that provides access to an immense spiritual marketplace.

The Community Question

Whether the Internet undermines denominational communities is of great interest to scholars. In his book, *Habits of the High-Tech Heart*, Schultze (2002) asserts that cyberspace "foster(s) individualism and self-interest over community and responsibility" (p. 18). Others argue that the community issue is more complex. What we do know is that what goes on in an online community cannot be separated entirely from an individual's face-to-face offline community (Campbell, 2004; Wellman & Gulia, 1999).

Sociologists provide helpful definitions of community. C. S. Fischer (1982) argues that it is not necessarily neighborhoods that comprise community but a person's day-to-day social relationships; Wellman (1999) agrees that the personal network is the vital component. But, do online communities foster strong or weak affiliations? The verdict is still out. With regard to the Internet, are communities *real* or *imagined?* Some online networks are restricted to specialized topics, while others explore a wide-range of subjects in depth resulting in friendship and sometimes intimate relationships. Early studies reveal that service and volunteerism is occurring online (Wellman & Gulia, 1999). Gruzd, Wellman, and Takhteyev (2011) conclude that "real" communities exist on the social media site Twitter in terms of forming "new social connections" and maintaining "existing ones" (p. 1). The Internet, however, doesn't act in isolation; its role depends on the culture of the user. Dawson and Cowan (2004) elaborate:

> The Internet has suffered from an excessive and effusive press—it has been hyped and demonized in the popular media to a point where fewer and fewer people may care to pay attention. But the rapidly changing social-literature on the Internet is discovering truth behind the hyperbole. Cyberspace is not quite as unusual a place as sometimes predicted. Life in cyberspace is in continuity with so-called "real life," and this holds true for religion as well. People are doing online pretty much what they do offline, but they are doing it differently. (p. 1)

Campbell (2004) argues that religious Internet activity is a reflection of the cultural shift toward autonomous religious worship and growing ambivalence about structured church participation, but warns against uniform assumptions about a medium with diverse uses (p. 81). To understand how religious communities are constructed online, one must know something about individuals' motivations. In other words, the users' values tell us a great deal about the nature and purpose of online community (Campbell, 2005).

The Identity Question

Beyond community, the Internet contributes to personal identity (Lee, 2009; Linderman & Lövheim , 2003). The Internet is being studied, according to Lövheim (2004), to see if it can "provide individuals with a greater diversity of ways of interpreting their personal experiences and relations through access to sets of meanings and practices not readily available in their local time and place" (p. 60). This includes the Internet's role in defining and integrating one's sense of a religious self. In a study of young Swedish men and women, Lovheim concludes that online interaction provides "some experiences that enrich young people in their efforts to create their own religious identity" (Lövheim, 2004, p. 70).

The flexibility of the Internet makes it relevant to the needs of most users. They can study and discuss a particular subject such as forgiveness, adversity, or altruism. On the other hand, those estranged from denominations can explore the sacred away from institutional expectations or guidelines. Some blogs, for example, criticize formal religion and attract the support of likeminded Internet users. Online, institutional affiliation isn't a necessary condition for personal religious identity.

The Authority Question

Authority is a quandary in cyberspace. Unofficial Web sites raise questions about the credibility and trustworthiness of sources. How should such messages be interpreted and heeded? This subject emerges in the Islamic world of cyberspace (Bunt, 2003). Given the multiplicity of online voices, Muslims draw on a culturally embedded decision-making process that strives for consistency between "Islamic primary sources" and online discussion of such sources in light of contemporary conditions (p. 127). Familiarity with ancient writings and teachings makes this possible. The question of authority is also addressed by Stout and Scott (2003); they note that official Mormon Web sites are highly controlled in terms of social networking features in order to protect the hierarchical leadership structure within the denomination.

The User Perspective

The relationship between religiosity and Internet use isn't fully understood.[3] Nevertheless, the instant-access nature of the medium aids individualized quests. Yet citizens care about community as well, and such values also emerge online; users connect with those on similar journeys. Cyberspace is informational and interactive, accommodating both needs for individualism and communitarianism.

The Internet reflects a growing desire for convenience. While many attend neighborhood houses of worship, the home is a refuge from work and hectic lifestyles. Cocooning or "staying in" is occurring (Clow & Baack, 2007, p. 74). Meals are prepared simply and quickly, and shopping is conducted online. The cyberchurch is one example; it is an online environment where comprehensive worship opportunities are provided by a single Web site. Many of these sites offer e-commerce or the purchasing of religious music, movies, and books; they create a mediated sanctuary without the need to leave home.

In the not-too-distant past, taking sacraments and offering tithes meant traveling, sometimes considerable distances. Online rituals are rites and ordinances performed in cyberspace. Prayer, online pilgrimages, and baptism are a few examples. Online confession, although discouraged by some, is commonly practiced. Universal Life Church On-Line, allows sins and misdeeds to be electronically submitted to get beyond mistakes of the past.

Social media satisfy users' desire for immediate fellowship through Facebook, Twitter, YouTube, dig, hulu, and MySpace; they make networking instant through computers and hand-held devices. According to Martin and Coons (2010):

> Social media is [sic] a wireless conversation. It fosters communion and sharing between social human beings compared with traditional media that delivers content at the expense of conversation. (p. 1)

Whereas traditional media are essentially one way, social media build relationships through two-way or multiple-participant exchanges. It's now the most popular activity on the Internet, with about 96% of Generation Y (i.e., those born between the mid-1970s and early 2000s) joining online social networks (Qualman, 2009). Members of religious groups seek advice through talk, and get information through others' posts. Let's suppose that an individual is in a doctor's waiting room. She checks Twitter as well as her Facebook wall messages. A post about a fellow parishioner's back injury reminds her that she volunteered to take a meal to that person's home. On Twitter, her friends are discussing a new book about overcoming adversity. She decides to pick it up from the bookstore on the way home. Instead of having to search for information herself, social media brought ideas to her through conversation.

Institutional Strategies

Denominational Web sites are designed to meet particular objectives.[4] Those in search of converts emphasize accessibility and interactivity; their Web sites make it easy to participate, join up, or enter into fellowship. On the other hand, denominations stressing face-to-face community keep interactive features to a minimum on their Web sites. Major strategies include proselytizing, maintaining hierarchy, and establishing information boundaries.

Proselytizing

Traditional missionary work involved canvasing neighborhoods, distributing tracts, and preaching on street corners. Such techniques emphasize information dissemination, but online proselytizing is relationship-based; it attracts truth-seekers through interactivity. The Mormon Church, for example, now has online-only missionaries that blog, answer e-mail queries, and post "stereotype-bursting" profiles of church members. The online missionaries "routinely participate in about 10,000 chats a week, with 3,500 people asking for in-person visits and 1,200 going on to hear the missionary lessons" (Fletcher-Stack, 2010). According to Ron Wilson, manager of internet and marketing for the Mormon Church, the Internet is a new version of the "town square" (quoted in Fletcher-Stack, 2010). Online proselytizing is growing more sophisticated through branding, database marketing, and Web site design.

Online proselytizing stresses two-way communication, much like symmetrical public relations where both insider and outsider are served. This is akin to *permission marketing* where consumers specify what they'd like to know and when. The Internet offers targets of proselytization greater control in the relationship; they can set the boundaries of the discussion and specify the type of information they desire. Curious site visitors volunteer information to churches, which is stored in a database. The relationship with outsiders is tailored by database proselytizing based on individualized e-mail messages that address the visitor's needs.

Maintaining Hierarchy

For denominations with strong hierarchical structures and rigid lines of authority, Internet Web sites tend to be more informational than interactive. In other words, some church Web sites are designed to protect offline face-to-face communities. This is the case for the cathedral church of Saint John the Divine in New York (www.stjohndivine.org), where site visitors get information about services, outreach activities, and cultural events, but chat rooms and blogs are rare. Links to the Episcopal Diocese explain governance, organization, and beliefs. Similarly, diocesan Web sites of the Catholic Church emphasize information above all else. Interactive features exist, but are usually tied to doctrine and teachings of the Pope. In an analysis of these sites, Arasa (2008) observes that "diocesan Web sites are indispensable points of reference for the institutions they represent and, thus, need to be the essential, official information that anyone would require from the institution" (p. 21). The site for the Diocese of Los Angeles (www.archdiocese.la) illustrates this approach. Emphasis is on instruction through links to scripture, official statements, and newspapers. It is not the purpose of the site to displace highly valued local Catholic congregations.

Establishing Information Boundaries

Each denomination establishes a border between the sacred and the profane. Web sites reflect such boundaries; they communicate what's relevant in the world in order for individuals to live a fruitful life—subject matter presented online signals what is to be discussed offline. Much can be learned about a group's belief system by examining its Web site. Hutterites, for example, live in isolated Christian communities in the Western plains of the United States. The Web site of the Hutterian Brethren Schmiedeleut Conference (www.hutterites.org) simply explains the lifestyle, history, and customs of the sect. There are no discussion forums to speak of, and very little about the world beyond Hutterite villages. The Web site for the Unitarian Universalist Association of Congregations, however (http://www.uua.org), addresses many topics. Social issues, ethics, adult education, and sustainability are all treated. The online bookstore features works on world religions and contemporary issues. Not only do Web sites inform outsiders, but also establish an information agenda for members as well.

Occasionalization: How Questers Find the Numinous Online

People vary in their uses of the Internet. This is known as occasionalization or online usage patterns (Study of, 2001, p. 1). There are different types of users, from "Quickies" who make brief visits to the Web site to "Surfers" who spend an average of 70 minutes per session, visiting nearly 45 sites each time (Study of, 2001). While occasionalization refers to general Internet use, this activity includes religious information searching as well. Key patterns or occasions of use are now discussed.

Full-Experience Occasions

For some, the Internet is the center of worship; it is in cyberspace that most rituals and interactions with fellow believers take place. One example is the cyberchurch, an online site offering a full range of worship activities. According to the cyberchurch concept, there's little need to travel to a physical church; all elements of religion (e.g., community, ritual, and belief) are found online (The Cyberchurch, 1998). One example is the online Church of Fools, a 3-D church where priests conduct services using avatars, computer representations of actual individuals. Parishioner avatars enter the building, introduce themselves to fellow worshippers (using speech bubbles); they listen to a sermon, pray, chant "Hallelujah!" if they feel inclined, and socialize after the service. It is not an extension of an offline face-to-face congregation; the experience occurs entirely in cyberspace. Cyberchurches can be found in Second Life, one of the most extensive computer-created virtual worlds, complete with cities, schools, and businesses. Second Life is the home of the ALM cyberchurch, Temple Beth Israel synagogue, and the Islamic Society mosque.

Social Network Occasions

Internet users seek the numinous by developing relationships or network ties. For example, the importance of tolerance might be discussed through a religious blog; users know each other within the context of that particular topic. Because the discussion is specialized, secondary rather than primary ties are cultivated. The latter connotes deeper relationships that result from wide-ranging conversations over time; they usually involve friends or intimates. Nevertheless, specialized blogs play an important role in building religious community; they often attract people who are struggling with their faith as well as those offering support. Some blogs are niche media, which address one particular aspect of religious culture. Examples include Kosher Blog (www.kosherblog.net), which contains dietary certification for Jewish kosher requirements. Facing Inward (blogs.ashtangi.net/fiw) discusses the practice of yoga and how it can be used to cope with the challenges of everyday life.

General social media are adapted for religious purposes. On YouTube, Hulu, Delicious, and Flickr users discuss and share videos, photos, TV segments, movie segments, recorded audio, and content from other Web sites. On YouTube, visitors view segments of the movie *The Passion of Christ;* they discuss, critique, and share it through posts and e-mail. Religious leaders are reacting to the popularity of social media. Through the Vatican's "The Pope meets you on Facebook" application, users send virtual postcards from the Pope to other Facebook users. Some Islamic groups, however, reject the new medium. Indonesian imams for example, fear that social media encourage flirtation and extramarital affairs (Eaton, 2009).

Religion surfaces on Twitter, an exchange of brief messages about what's happening in a person's life; it consists of frequent posts in real time. Twitter users with common interests, or Twibes, discuss topics from politics to popular culture. Religious twibes include adherents to particular denominations as well as alternative groups such as freethinkers, pagans, lucumi practitioners, voodoo practitioners, wiccans, and others. Based on keywords in a user's tweets, relevant twibes are recommended. In this way, a social networking site assists a user in locating a like-minded community. Some religious leaders praise social media, and believe they strengthen commitment. Others fear they erode authority within the offline congregation.

Online Searching Occasions

The Internet is an immense source of religious information. Some navigate it with a specific topic in mind; others are more spontaneous in their searching. The dominant search engines, such as Google, Yahoo! Search, and Bing are improving; they are useful starting points in religious study. Second tier sources are also available for more specialized research. Archives on religious art, media, and history are now available.

While online sources abound, searching skills are often lacking. Therefore, the Association of Religion Data Archives (ARDA) (www.thearda.com) organizes material on a Web site that's easily navigated. Studies, statistics, and lists are accessed quickly through the "Research Hub" feature. Not only does ARDA reflect a demand for information, it assists the user in sifting through a cluttered and complex online environment.

A Word of Caution: The Myth of Internet Neutrality

The Internet is dialectical. That is, religionists use it while simultaneously assessing its value. While this chapter describes opportunities offered by the medium, there's an ongoing critique, the purpose of which is to assure that it reinforces rather than diminishes the quality of life. Christians (2002) argues that media aren't neutral; they're inevitably tied to superstructures emphasizing efficiency and the material goals of the market. Religion has the capacity to keep these forces in check, he argues. *Valuing* is the process by which media like the Internet uphold a worldview. Religious groups not only make use of the medium, but curb situations where "moral purpose is sacrificed to technical excellence" (p. 39). What is the depth and quality of online religious experience? Following Ellul's (1964) reasoning, it is important that moral values win out; we mustn't place our faith in technology when it displaces concerns about human well-being. Schultze's (2002) personal reflection captures this idea: "such machines seem to divert ... attention from the central concerns of life—such as love, gratitude, and responsibility—to relatively trivial pursuits with little enduring value" (p. 13). Religionists, therefore, evaluate the moral worth of the Internet. This requires examination not only of the ideas conveyed, but how well technology aids the pursuit of truth.

Key Terms

cocooning: The social trend of spending leisure time at home. Hobbies, entertainment, and religion are experienced primarily through in-home media.

cyberchurch: An online environment with comprehensive worship opportunities. Rituals and community normally found in physical churches are simulated online.

database proselytizing: Missionary strategies that draw from stored information about prospective converts.

media neutrality: The assumption that media have no philosophical or ideological significance in and of themselves.

occasionalization: Patterns or styles of Internet usage. In the religious context, they include full-experience, social networking, and information searching occasions.

online rituals: Rites and ordinances (i.e., prayer, baptism, confession, etc.) performed in cyberspace.

permission marketing: Strategy in which organizations obtain Internet users' authorization to send them information on a regular basis, usually through e-mail.

primary ties: Online networks between good friends or intimates.

religious blogs: A personal Web site in which religious commentaries are posted and site visitors respond.

secondary ties: Specialized or focused online networks; relationships form around a single religious topic or goal.

social media: Internet-based applications involving conversation as well as sharing of content such as video, music, and photography.

valuing: When technology comes to symbolize and support particular worldviews or ideologies such as efficiency or materialism.

Questions to Ponder

1. Do you think there's a tendency to exaggerate the potential effects of media when they are first introduced? Why was this the case with the Internet and religion?
2. Some argue that the Internet is a "quester" medium and particularly conducive to the numinous. Do you agree? Why or why not?
3. What role does the Internet play in creating and maintaining community?
4. How do individuals use the Internet for religious purposes compared to organizations?
5. What are the primary online "occasions?" How do they help us understand religious use of the Internet?
6. Do you think that media are inherently neutral? Explain your answer using the concept of "valuing."

CHAPTER 8

Entertainment Media

Entertainment is a dominant activity in contemporary society; citizens invest considerable time and money pursuing pleasure, diversion, and recreation.[1] From novels to video games, entertainment media are ubiquitous. According to Sayre and King (2010) entertainment engages audience members "in an agreeable way" and is "attractive, stimulating, sensory, emotional, social, and moral" (p. 4). Traditionally, a distinction was made between entertainment and the domains of work and education, but such lines are blurring. Religionists are experimenting with various media and genres. As Ferri (2010) puts it, "technology allows us to work and play almost simultaneously" (p. 403). Gabler (2000) notes that "Every day someone finds more inventive applications for its use"; and at some point, entertainment "became the primary value of American life" (p. 10). Pervasive entertainment facilitates the numinous in ways previously unheard-of. This chapter argues that the expanding range of religion into the broader phenomenon of the numinous reinforces the "Republic of entertainment" Gabler describes.

Entertainment and Religion in Context

Entertainment was present in early religious cultures. Dance was an ancient ritual in tribal, Western, African, and Eastern religions, as were plays in Greece and Rome. Music is an enduring element in worship worldwide. Entertainment-oriented print media such as illustrated chapbooks of the 17th century and didactic novels of the 18th century had religious uses. Today, religious novels are enjoyed by Muslims, Jews, Christians, Hindus, and other groups. Entertainment genres such as talk shows and call-in shows are adapted for religious audiences. Reality TV, a genre once confined to the secular domain, now features religious themes, dilemmas, and characters.

Accelerating the fusion of entertainment and religion is the commercial market; today religious media are commodities. Not only are they sites of religious experiences, but also sources of profit.[2] According to Einstein (2008), this development has to do with a number of cultural shifts, one being the rise of personal religion and the desire to worship in the home and other locations outside traditional houses of worship.

Religious leaders use entertainment in order to compete in a saturated information environment. As individuals become increasingly reliant on information technology, clergy use these vehicles to get the attention of believers and nonbelievers. The lure of entertainment is strong. Sayre and King (2010) elaborate:

> If something is boring, we don't pay attention to it. Entertainment captures attention. As a result, an attention economy is also an *entertainment economy*. Whether you are making a film or an advertisement, if you do not hold the interest of your audience—that is, if you do not entertain them,—they will stop paying attention. (p. 16)

Use of nontraditional media seems limitless. Professional wrestling, Jesus rock music, and video games are popular among some Evangelical Christians. Other groups are more cautious. Generally speaking, the Amish abstain from entertainment-oriented movies and films, as do conservative Muslims in their efforts to reject gratuitous content of a sexual nature. The meaning of entertainment, however, is evolving in new ways. Rejected media of yesterday has religious uses today. When the state-owned Indian television channel Doordarshan began airing a weekly sacred soap opera with Hindu religious themes, it was clear that religion and entertainment were culturally intertwined. In other venues, the trend is subtle, as in the case of Catholic masses where traditional rituals of communion are accompanied by contemporary up-tempo versions of hymns accompanied by performers playing electronic keyboards, guitars, and drums.

Religion, then, is connected to the phenomenon of leisure. Citizens value time away from their labors. In earlier times, festivals, fairs, and feasts provided regular escapes for farmers and laborers. Industrialization eventually created more time and made more money available for leisure activities such as the theater and sporting events. In the spirit of missionary work, revivals of the late 18th century combined elements of church and theater to strengthen convictions and attract converts. Such events were emotionally charged, featuring artful oratory, loud singing, clapping, and dancing. Few were more successful than Dwight L. Moody, whose late 19th-century revivals often drew crowds of over 10,000 (Evensen, 2000b, p. 119). Moody ushered in the era of mass evangelicalism, a time where religious events competed with other entertainment events.

The Incompatibility Argument

The mixture of religion and entertainment is controversial. Some parishioners equate entertainment with triviality or even blasphemy in some cases.[3] Entertainment media are sites of experimentation and artistic freedom; they can contain explicit and gratuitous material eschewed by religionists. Others complain about the frivolity of entertainment, claiming it distracts from religious activities such as study and prayer. On occasion, devotees have held boycotts and protests.

Postman (1985, 1992) critiques the entertainment–religion interface; he argues that particular media do not lend themselves to the sacred. Television, for example, underscores the trivial; it emphasizes breadth over depth. The sacred requires respectful contemplation, but television rarely gets beyond the superficial. Print media, according to Postman (1985, 1992), are more conducive to reflection, a necessary element of worship. Television, on the other hand, "has no ritual, no dogma, no tradition, no theology, and above all, no sense of spiritual transcendence" (Postman, 1985, p. 119).

Q. J. Schultze (2002) observes the same triviality dimensions of the Internet; it emphasizes information-seeking over truth-preserving. "We rarely think about what it means to be good and wise people; instead, we focus on whether we are technologically connected" (p. 29). We so overestimate the capacity of "more efficient and powerful messaging systems that we sacrifice patience and contemplation.... As a quasi-religion, informationism preaches the *is* over the *ought, observation* over *intimacy,* and *measurement* over *meaning*" (p. 26). Incompatibility arguments are ultimately traced to fears of secularization.

The Compatibility Argument

Some people take issue with Postman and Schultze and contend that entertainment is not only compatible with religion, but actually promotes faith. This is attributable to a generation of young adults who are comfortable with merging entertainment with the sacred (Beaudoin, 1998; Clark, 2003). As discussed in chapter 1, religious "questers" (Roof, 1993,

1999), find religion in many places. To some, entertainment need not be trivial; movies and novels can be engaging and intellectually challenging. Entertainment need not be crass; "family entertainment" is often uplifting. Entertainment need not be all-consuming; literate individuals use entertainment media selectively and optimally.

Entertainment Media

Next, we explore various entertainment media with two goals in mind. The first is to describe how genres contribute to religious experience, and the second is how this occurs in the numinous domain outside denominations in the popular culture.

Popular Fiction

Historically, novels have not usually been associated with religious institutions (Petersen, 2010). During the Victorian era, in fact, Protestant clergy compared them with the vice of tobacco use (Douglas, 1977). Novels have evolved considerably as a genre, however. Today, they depict religion in a number of ways, both didactically and analytically.[4]

Some novels deal with personal struggle, offering a religious critique. These include Voltaire's *Candide* (1759), Joyce's *A Portrait of the Artist as a Young Man* (1916), and O'Connor's *Wise Blood* (1952). Authors use religious symbolism to tell their stories; examples include Steinbeck's *The Grapes of Wrath* (1939) and Tolkien's *The Lord of the Rings* (1954). The length and detailed narrative of the novel creates the potential for deep reflection about religious questions and dilemmas.

Other twentieth century works of literature have also addressed difficult religious issues. One example is Updike's series of novels beginning with *Rabbit, Run* in 1960. Featuring hero Harry Angstrom, the reader is introduced to a number of dilemmas regarding Protestant views of happiness and life's purpose.[5] Set in New York City Hasidic culture, Potok's *My Name is Asher Lev* (1972) also deals substantively with issues of faith.

Today, the subgenre of religious fiction is popular both inside and outside denominations. But, Conservative Protestant novelists are particularly active. The Left Behind books by LaHaye are enjoyed by an immense readership, stimulating considerable discussion about the importance of religious commitment in evangelical communities. Similarly, The Work and the Glory is a series of Mormon historical novels that deal with issues of personal sacrifice and obedience; they are among the most popular books outside Mormon scripture. Religious fiction is one of the leading growth areas of the publishing industry.

Radio

Radio has been a part of religious worship for over a century. The medium has many advantages, making it an important source of religious news, music, and inspiration.[6] Predictions that television would spell the demise of radio have not come to fruition. Because radio is confined to sound and lacks a visual element, it is highly personal to the listener. Audience members use their imaginations to create an image of the message; this can aid reflection and learning. Hangen (2002) elaborates: "a radio sermon—unlike attendance at an enormous mass meeting—could be experienced by a single listener like a personal chat" (p. 5).

Radio's portability makes it instantly accessible at any time or place. Mitchell (2010) comments on the omnipresence of radio:

> Radios are to be found in kitchens, bedrooms, restrooms, offices, gyms, cars, and buildings used for worship. Radio plays a central role in some people's daily lives; it defines the day; awakening us in the morning, accompanying us to work and soothing us to sleep at night. Radio can act as a speaking book for nonreaders, a friend to the lonely, and a guide for those who cannot see. (Mitchell, 2010, p. 371)

For diasporic religions, radio is particularly important in retaining a sense of religious community. World Buddhist Radio and Hinduradio are two examples. Evangelical religions have also benefited from the medium's ability to attract new converts. In the early days of radio, however, there was considerable disagreement about its viability as a sacred medium. One objection was its association with entertainment, and some religious leaders wondered whether it was serious enough for theological purposes (Bendroth, 1996). Nevertheless, radio is used in some manner by most major denominations.

Today, religious radio is becoming more specialized, utilizing multiple genres. Religious talk shows and music programs are common. Music stations include a number of religious formats from traditional hymns, contemporary, rock, rap, and country music. While dramas have all but vanished from mainstream radio, they are popular within religious communities. Each episode of the program *Unshackled!,* for example, tells an inspirational story about someone who benefits from belief in God; it is the longest running radio drama in history.

Religious radio has pioneered the hybrid genre, or mixture of secular and religious elements. James Dobson's *Focus on the Family,* for example, combines the format of the traditional radio talk show (i.e., interviews, call-in segments, recorded features, movie reviews) with religious messages for spiritual development. Because hybrid genres are relatively new, few frameworks exist for their critique. For example, should *Focus on the Family* be evaluated as a news talk show or as a religious sermon? Secular-oriented listeners often want more from such programs in terms of journalistic content while religionists crave the inspirational elements.

Radio is a numinous medium in that it is experienced at multiple levels. It is a common ritual for millions; many programs reinforce belief and have community followings. Music and the spoken word elicit deep feelings. These elements combine to create a religious experience that goes beyond casual listening that isn't necessarily tied to denominations.

Feature-Length Films

Denominations made use of films not long after their inception. While epics of the 1950s like *The Ten Commandments, The Robe,* and *Ben Hur,* were religous apologetics, filmmakers' treatment of the subject is diverse. According to Duncan (2010), this is true in both style and viewpoint; "real and legitimate" issues have been raised in various cultures (p. 151). Internationally, Duncan points out the critique of state religion in Czech film in the 1960s as well as increasing emphasis on individual expression in Chinese cinema in the 1980s and 1990s. More recently, Iranian film has dealt with interfaith tensions, and Japanese religious animation has many "delights and substance" (p. 151).

In the last 20 years, U.S. cinema has evolved considerably in its handling of religion.[7] *The Last Temptation of Christ* (De Fina & Ulfland, 1988), while controversial, stimulated much discussion in the late 1980s, as have the more recent movies, such as *The Apostle* (Brown, 1997), *The Passion of Christ* (Davey, 2004), and *The Da Vinci Code* (Grazer, 2006). Religion-affirming films are still abundant, but less didactic than 1950s epics. *Tender Mercies* (Hobel, 1983) and *Places in the Heart* (Benton, 2004) are examples. Films critical of denominations, while denounced by Medved (1992), do not necessarily negate contemplation of moral issues. *Dogma* (Smith, 1999), *Simon Birch* (Birnbaum & Mark, 1998), and *Saved* (Stipe, 2004) appear critical of institutional religion, but deal with larger issues of inclusion, forgiveness, and the dangers of fanaticism. Film is expanding as a medium for analyzing religion, and thus opens new possibilities for the numinous engagement by viewers.

As Hess (2010) argues, film is familiar to young audiences and "communities of faith are slowly and often painfully coming to realize that mass-mediated popular culture has become the primary database from which younger generations are drawing to make sense of their religious experiences" (p. 248). This realization is leading to experimentation with popular film in teaching religious subjects (Hess, 2001, 2010).

Television

Considerable disagreement exists about the role of television in religious life.[8] Some appreciate its ability to bring religious experience and instruction into the home; others see it as a great opportunity to evangelize. Opponents, however, see the medium as being too passive for viewers to engage in substantive religious experience.

Given that television is largely defined as an entertainment medium, Postman (1985, 1992) doubts it can connect viewers to the sacred as a book could do.[9] Television, according to Csikszentmihalyi (1993), "seems to have the following effects on viewers: It makes them feel very relaxed, but also significantly less active, alert, mentally focused, satisfied, or creative compared with almost anything else they could be doing" (p. 135). Kubey & Csikszentmilhalyi (1990) argue that without some level of media literacy or critical viewing skills, television can be a medium of low challenges, rarely delivering high-level educational opportunities.

Early examples of religious television such as Bishop Fulton Sheen's program in the 1950s and *PTL* with Jim and Tammy Faye Bakker in the 1970s and 1980s were praised for making religion accessible to large audiences, but became controversial due to their entertainment-oriented formats. Since that time religious television has been the focus of considerable study (Abelman, 1994; Abelman & Hoover, 1990; Abelman & Neuendorf, 1985; Ferré, 1990). As discussed in chapter 1, the latchkey generation of the 1970s and 1980s has now moved into adulthood. These television viewers had working parents, so they fended for themselves after school; the media of popular culture became a comfort and solace. As adults, this generation has a greater affinity for television than their parents had; they use it as a serious vehicle for worship (Beaudoin, 1998). Today, religion emerges in all types of programs from sitcoms to soap operas. Entire books have been written about religion in *The Simpsons,* for example.

Assumptions that television conveys religion superficially are giving way to more thorough assessments; programs are increasingly complex in treating the sacred, consequently, opportunities for reflection and instruction are expanding. A turning point was the 1990s drama *Touched by an Angel* (Williamson, 2003) which offered a more serious treatment of religion than previous shows such as *Father Dowling Mysteries* (McInerny, 2001), which was less about religion than it was about solving crimes. With the show *Nothing Sacred* (Kramer, 1997), the realities of life within a religious organization were portrayed in a substantive manner. Later, the nondenominational drama *Joan of Arcadia* (2005) conveyed the idea that God is among us in the form of a common person. In *The Book of Daniel* (Kenny, 2006) the Christ figure is an everyday person with imperfections and an offhanded sense of humor. The more recent miniseries *Big Love* (Olsen & Scheffer,

2011) is not only about a contemporary polygamous family in Utah, but also deals with the tensions of patriarchy and evolving family norms.

Religion is often a secondary theme. This trend seemed to begin with *Thirtysomething* (Herskovitz & Zwick, 1991) in the 1980s; one subplot involved a Jewish husband and Christian wife struggling to raise children within a religiously diverse family. In the early 1990s, *Northern Exposure* (Chase, 1995) treated new age religion, and later, the *X-Files* (Carter, 2002) contained subplots dealing with institutional versus personal religion.

Televangelism continues to have a strong presence; it creates a religious environment where the medium itself is the center of religious worship. While initially associated with U.S. conservative Protestant movements, Armstrong (2010) defines televangelism broadly to include "virtually any religionist with a message for a television viewer, no matter his or her religious background or the format of the program..." (p. 424).

Online Entertainment

As an entertainment medium, the Internet isn't easily described. Because it is a convergence of multiple media (e.g., text, video, interactive features), virtually any type of entertainment can be accessed online, from novels to movies. Yet the Internet is an entertainment form all its own. The combination of interactivity and multimedia makes cyberspace a unique place for leisure and enjoyment. Online surfing, socializing, and video gaming occur in religious contexts.

The Internet's *experiential* dimension is key to its entertainment value; it involves the user in a satisfying search for truth. Religion itself is a phenomenon of progress, as is the user's online journey for new experiences: "Web sites invite the cybersurfer to be an active explorer, with the next nugget of knowledge or inspiration only a hyperlink and a mouse-click away" (Peterson, 2005, p. 126). Religionists move through cyberspace as they read scripture, view sermon videos, and post comments on discussion boards. The Internet is "an intrinsically quester medium" (p. 128). The Web site for Houston NW Church (www.hnw.org) illustrates this; users click through pages titled, "live," "love," "learn," and "lead." Podcasts and videos entertain and inform. The interdenominational site Beliefnet is a cornucopia of spiritual diversion. Visitors are treated to films and forums. One can take a "Belief-o-matic" quiz, skim the news, or read a horoscope. The entertainment page offers a "joke of the day" as well as movies and games, all with a religious theme.

Crossover entertainment is now common. The social media site Facebook, for example, has Jewish, Islamic, and Buddhist versions. GodTube is a Christian alternative to the popular video site YouTube.

Religionists are tailoring their messages to the Web, and this includes entertainment fare. Hybrid versions of games, e-cards, and music sites confirm this adaptation. Beyond information, Internet users want amusement and escape. Churches meet this demand through Web sites that take advantage of the medium's capacity for discovery and play.

Through blogs, entertainment and religion intersect in a different manner. While blogging isn't confined to diversion, it is recreation for many. This is especially true with religious critiques of popular media. The site Christian Jonas Brothers Fans is an online faith-based discussion of rock musicians. Numerous blogs review movies from denominational perspectives. Beyond being an entertainment medium, the Internet is also a place where believers gather to comment on popular culture.

New Forms of Religious Entertainment: Melding the Sacred and Secular

Religion and entertainment are overlapping in new ways. A number of factors account for this, including the market, individualism, technology, and the need for leisure and escape. Today's religious entertainment would have surprised believers and nonbelievers 20 years ago. In some groups, religious entertainment is so far-reaching that few pop culture phenomena are left untouched. Bates (2002) elaborates:

> [Y]ou can also find shaved heads, body piercings, tattoos, soul patches, spandex, and Goth makeup. Music styles include hyper pop-punk, holy hip-hop, and something called hybrid death tuneage. A reviewer in the Christian magazine *HM* salutes Green Olive Tree for "the best worship disc for butt-rockers I've ever heard." (p. 25)

Commercialism accelerates the fusion of religion and entertainment, but it also has to do with hectic lifestyles. In the same way that stores offer one-stop shopping with banking, medical, and postal services in the same location, churches conveniently combine worship and entertainment. More than a house of prayer, Prestonwood Baptist Church in Plano, Texas is a place to play and shop. A gym, sports fields, arcade, bookstore, and food court with a Starbucks are available. A number of megachurches present rock concerts in auditoriums with theater-style seating.

We live in a day of religious theme parks, museums, and film festivals.[10] In terms of humor, there are comic books and anime; stand-up comedy is popular among many Jews, Christians, and Muslims. Las Vegas, a city known for gambling and adult entertainment, illustrates the synthesis of sacred and secular. Its architecture, symbols, and shows incorporate religion in numerous ways (Stout, 2004). Casino resorts blend sacred symbols into their design, as exemplified by religious art in the Venetian hotel and stained glass in the Tropicana. Dao, a popular nightclub is designed like a temple with Buddhist statuary. The House of Blues in the Mandalay Bay resort has Sunday brunch with gospel singers. The Brahma Shrine outside Caesar's Palace is modeled after one of Thailand's prominent places of prayer.

Religion and Celebrity

The intertwining of religion and entertainment often has to do with celebrity. Public personalities are adoringly exalted, sometimes to the point of deification.[11] John Lennon's comment that the Beatles were "more popular than Jesus" (Cleave, 1966) illustrates how Godlike attributes are assigned to performers. Since then, a celebrity culture has emerged where individuals from all walks of life are idolized:

> The majority of celebrities are entertainers but the celebrity status is open to many different occupations or callings: models and super-models, fashion and interior designers. TV queens, famous hostesses and society ladies ("socialites"), members of the rich upper classes, occasionally a politician (or his wife), even some criminals may join their ranks. But many of these other categories also provide entertainment: athletes, beauty queens, hostesses, histrionic politicians. (Hollander, 2010, p. 388)

Personal identity is tied to celebrity worship. By drawing close to the famous, desirable attributes are sought through association. The Dalai Lama, Joel Osteen, and former Archbishop Desmond Tutu are emulated for their religious values, but their public personas make them celebrities as well. Osteen fans have a Twitter account. The Dalai Lama and Archbishop Tutu have Facebook fan pages. When actor Julia Roberts announced her conversion to Hinduism, blog posts curious about the religion followed.

Celebrity, according to Rojek (2007), is "an imaginary resource to turn to in the midst of life's hardships or triumphs, to gain solace from, to beseech for wisdom and joy" (p. 171). It provides "peculiarly powerful affirmations of belonging" (p. 172). Celebrity, Hollander (2010) argues, can reflect insecurity and efforts to borrow an identity.

Today, the most intimate details about public figures are available: "Without the speed and ease of choice for consumers through interactive media, there would be little ability for the viral growth of the celebrity in America and the world" (Ferri, 2010, p. 404). This creates a dilemma for religionists. On the one hand, it provides access to role models for those seeking inspiration and guidance. An interview with actor Matt Damon on Beliefnet, for example, deals with the afterlife, and his hope that mortal experience has meaning. Religious professional athletes can be found on the inspirational lecture circuit. On the other hand, some feel celebrity worship is idolatry, a behavior shunned in many denominations. Engle and Kasser (2005) argue that idolization may be associated with image, materialism, and the desire for certain possessions. Such images are easily available through new media as fans speak like and dress like those they adore.

Celebrity worship is an expanding and complex phenomenon, however. The emotional reaction by millions to the death of singer Michael Jackson is one example. In this numinous age, celebrity and religion have many similarities: ritual, community, and deep feeling. The 10,000 mourners gathering annually at Elvis Presley's gravesite in Memphis is another example; they carry candles throughout the night and often leave gifts (Gibson, 2010). While clergy find this perplexing in the face of declining attendance at some houses of worship, Laderman (2009) claims that cultural phenomena such as celebrity worship "ground ultimate concerns, establish moral communities, and make lives meaningful" (p. xv). What we are witnessing isn't necessarily a diminution of religion; it's a new manifestation of the sacred in forms not yet fully understood by scholars.

Entertainment and the Numinous

Uplifting entertainment has a place in denominationalism. Yet rejection of the blasphemous is also inevitable. Such distinctions, however, aren't always obvious. What was once sacrilegious may be sacred today, and vice versa. In the larger realm of the numinous, entertainment itself has a religious aspect; it has become a way of life. As a dominant activity, leisure is evolving; it encompasses phenomena previously reserved for traditional institutions. As individuals gravitate toward diversion and recreation, they bring ritual and community with them. More is derived from entertainment; options are expanding and easily accessed through multiple media. Through time, religious aspects of entertainment are explored, and previous categories are broken down. In an anthropological sense, who is to say that celebrity worship is less meaningful than established religion?

Entertainment media are conducive to the numinous for additional reasons. Given their convivial and enjoyable nature, the same positive feelings associated with religion can be experienced. Entertainment media draw large audiences, creating possibilities for community formation through time. Speaking of ritual, media use is patterned, much like sacred behaviors within denominations. Because entertainment media (e.g., film, television, popular fiction) engage in storytelling, they often teach moral lessons about beliefs espoused by churches.

Key Terms

celebrity culture: A condition where celebrity worship has ritual and community dimensions. Fame is highly valued in secular and sacred domains.

compatibility argument: The assumption that entertainment has a place in religious life and worship.

crossover entertainment: When a secular media vehicle or genre has a comparable religious alternative. An example would be YouTube and GodTube.

entertainment: Activities that engage participants in a pleasurable, stimulating, and desirable manner.

hybrid genre: An entertainment form combining religious and secular elements. Examples include faith-based talk shows and gospel rap music.

incompatibility argument: The belief that entertainment is trivial and profane; it runs counter to the sacred.

leisure: Diversionary escape from one's labors. Time devoted to diversion and recreational activities.

televangelism: The use of television to broadcast religious messages. It ranges from the simple airing of church services to studio-produced programs featuring taped messages and music.

Questions to Ponder

1. Are entertainment and religion compatible? Why or why not?
2. What are the historical roots of entertainment?
3. How do you think the commercial aspect of entertainment has affected religion?
4. What has been the role of "celebrity" in religious worship?
5. Are some entertainment media more conducive to numinous experience than others? Why or why not?
6. Why has entertainment become a dominant activity in contemporary society?

CHAPTER 9

The News

The study of media and religion would not be complete without attention to journalism.[1] Vehicles such as Beliefnet, Shalom TV, and Christianity Today report the news from a religious perspective. But, secular news media set an agenda, suggesting what the public should know about particular denominations or movements. Therefore, journalists have a responsibility to be fair, accurate, and thorough. How religionists are treated in society ultimately depends on available information. Misinformation results in tension between groups and, in some cases, persecution and bigotry.

News reporting of religion has evolved considerably in recent years. Perhaps the most significant trend is increased participation by audience members. This shift, a type of community journalism, allows citizens to either create news outlets or add content to existing ones; these options include blogs, interactive Web sites, and talk radio. Audience members no longer rely entirely on the newspaper religion page or nightly network newscasts. This multifaceted, user-centered method of acquiring the news facilitates numinous experiences through increased interactivity, instant information access, and exposure to multiple media simultaneously. Community journalism has a two-way conversational element, unlike the linear format of traditional news reporting.[2] This is not to say that traditional news reporting has gone away; it remains vital in all societies. Contemporary news outlets, however, enable conversations about religion, thus adding an experiential and participatory dimension.

This chapter explores journalism's relationship with religion, a complex interplay that has endured for centuries. First, I present a brief history, followed by a discussion of how various religions are depicted in the news. Then, principles of good religion reporting are addressed. Next, religion-sponsored journalism is explored as well as denominational efforts to influence news media. The final section discusses the role of news media in the numinous.

Journalism and Religion Past and Present

While "the news" is commonly associated with contemporary media, it is not a new phenomenon.[3] Ancient Egyptian hieroglyphics conveyed information about the sacred as did papyri in early Rome. In a sense, all scripture from the Quran to the Bible is religious news. In fact, the term *gospel* derived from the old English *godspell* means good news. Citizens today, however, get much of their information about religion from secular news sources. How did we get to the point where journalists shape public opinion about religion? This question is a historical one that begins with Gutenberg's printing press.

The Printing Press and the Roots of Religion Journalism

The printing press played a key role in religious history. It created a situation where churches, regardless of the distance between them, could possess uniform doctrinal texts. "Already in the 1530s, pamphlets, books, broadsides, and sermons poured forth without end to address issues like antinomianism, the Trinity, and the authority of the scriptures" (Morgan, 2010, p. 316). It isn't clear, according to Morgan, whether early printing contributed to broader public debate about religious matters; it may have served mainly "to solidify and maintain group loyalties among those who have already made up their minds" (Morgan, 2010, p. 316).

The first years of a new technology are spent mimicking previous ones. Consequently, the first printed pamphlets were often faithful reproductions of earlier manuscripts. Gradually, however, the printing press ushered in an era where the clergy was no longer the sole disseminator of religious and philosophical ideas; one of its most significant contributions was empowerment of competing voices (Eisenstein, 1983).

Religion and Journalism in New England

According to Sloan (2000), two developments are key to understanding early religion journalism in America. The first was the growth of the city of Boston, the establishment of Harvard College in 1638, and the rise of intellectual culture and free expression. The second was the Puritan emphasis on independent religious worship, provoking public expressions against Anglicanism. Sloan (2000) argues that this launched a divergent religious discourse:

> Because they emphasized the individual, rather than the established church, as having the authority to interpret God's word, they declared that the individual must be free to inquire and that diversity of views had to be tolerated. (p. 33)

Anglicans responded in turn, and the *New England Courant*, established in 1721, became a vehicle of criticism against the Puritans. Similarly, the first U.S. religious magazine, *The Christian History* (1743–1745), was a forum for preachers such as Anglican George Whitefield and Presbyterian Gilbert Tennent (Hatcher, 2010).

While newspapers of the 18th century were a blend of religious and nonreligious content, they advocated righteous living and devotion to deity. If for example, a crime was reported in print, the story might also warn readers of the perils of disobedience to God (Buddenbaum, 2010). As Holmes (2010b) points out, the sacred–secular distinction was not always made clear in newspapers prior to the early 1800s. Newspapers were religious in that writers assumed public interest in the religious view.

Nineteenth-Century Journalism and Gilded-Age Revivalism

The distinction between theologically based media content (*religious* journalism) and objective secular treatments of churches (*religion* journalism) was common by the mid-19th century.[4] A number of factors brought this about. First, sophisticated methods of distribution were being set in place:

> It was the will to print, that first led American evangelicals into the business of mass media. By the 1820's, the Bible and tract societies would emerge as leaders in both printing technology and the organization of national distribution networks. (Nord, 2000, p. 69)

According to Nord (2000), this system helped lay the foundation for the popularization of print media. Soon social activists such as those of the American Anti-Slavery Society were taking advantage of mass printing, as were groups using the brief, concise, and sometimes entertaining missionary tract.

By the 1830s, there was high demand for quick information. In an expanding economy, newspapers were becoming businesses, and the religion story had to be a good story; it had to be engaging enough to sell copies. Consequently, James Gordon Bennett the publisher of the *New*

York Herald, ran articles conveying the drama and spectacle of religion,[5] which was covered in a fashion similar to crime or entertainment; reporters emphasized the controversial aspects.

By the time newspapers entered the Gilded Age in the mid-1860s, writers were clamoring to cover flamboyant evangelists such as D. L. Moody. Journalistic coverage of religion had much to do with bringing revivals, in all their excitement, to the people. Evensen (2000b) describes this moment in newspaper history:

> Beginning in Brooklyn during the fall of 1875 and continuing in Philadelphia, New York, Chicago, and Boston in the year and a half that followed there is a remarkable similarity in the front pages of the big city Gilded Age Press. Each would attempt to outdo the other in column inch after column inch of coverage of the famous evangelist D. L. Moody, who had come to these cities to proclaim the good news of Jesus Christ. In the twenty-five years that followed, he preached to an estimated 100 million souls on both sides of the Atlantic and was able to reach many more than that when one considers the outreach of press reports. (p. 119)

Moody's revival meetings were spectacles on a grand scale, and the preacher's charisma and message resonated with thousands. Moody's popularity had grown to such a point by 1876, the country's centennial year that he competed with P. T. Barnum for the accolade of having the "greatest show on earth" (Evensen, 2003). D. L. Moody illustrates a major shift in the way religion was depicted by the press; it represented an early manifestation of sensational news designed to engross and captivate.

The Modern Era and the Sacred–Secular Divide

Throughout the 20th century, journalism was defined by two distinct strains: the secular and the sacred. Secular media covered religion much like other topics, with the objective of achieving in-depth analysis, balance, and objectivity. But, denominations also published their own newspapers, and by the second half of the 20th century, they were creating TV programs and running their own radio stations. Both types of journalism are highly developed industries, with each serving an important function.

Religious journalism, or church-sponsored news, is partly the result of concerns about the secular press's critical tone (see Holmes, 2010b). In 1908 the *Christian Science Monitor* contained local and international news while at the same time presenting the ideas of Mary Baker Eddy, founder of the Christian Science movement. Religious radio blossomed during the first half of the 20th century, giving a spiritual perspective on national and world events. Charles Fuller's program *Old Fashioned Revival Hour* had 20 million viewers worldwide by the end of World War II (Mitchell, 2010). Since then, the number of religious radio stations has grown exponentially, making the medium an accessible source for news. By the 1940s most major denominations had some type of news outlet. The magazine *Commentary* reported news and politics from a Jewish perspective, for example, while *Christianity Today* provided an Evangelical viewpoint.

Religious journalists also covered stories overlooked by secular media. The Black church press, for example, ran stories about civil rights and later the AIDS crisis. Mormon media have covered disaster relief throughout the world. In the 1930s, the Jewish press opposed fascism in Europe and was politically active in the United States as well.

The late 20th century also saw the establishment of religion newswriting, a professional field in its own right among secular news organizations. Newspapers assigned reporters to the "religion beat" and television networks hired "religion news specialists." The establishment of the Religion Newswriters Association in 1949 signaled a commitment to elevate the standards of religion news reporting. Nevertheless, it is one of the most challenging areas for journalists given the complexities of religious belief and culture.

The sacred–secular divide is not without a degree of overlap. News shows combine preaching, music, and even prayer with the secular TV talk show format (see chapter 8). Televangelists Jim and Tammy Faye Bakker were pioneers of this approach; they interviewed guests on camera, much like *Good Morning America* or *Today*. Within a talk show framework, Pat Robertson's *700 Club* features prayer, preaching, music, set interviews, news anchors, and short film pieces. The religious magazine *World* features graphics that resemble those of such news publications as *Newsweek* and *Time*.

Into the Information Age

In the age of information, citizens are not entirely dependent on journalists. What is considered news, and what qualifies as a news outlet, is not the same today as it once was. The Internet offers new opportunities for community involvement. Voicing opinions through blogs, social networking sites, and e-mail, citizens participate in public discussion. Some Web sites, both religious and secular, allow readers to post their own news stories as well as respond to regular articles. Journalists no longer have the only say in the public forum.

An example is the HBO TV miniseries *Big Love* about a polygamous family in Salt Lake City. When the program depicted a Mormon temple ceremony, church officials issued a statement that this was disrespectful and an invasion of privacy. News reports raised the question of why it was necessary for some religious groups to have private spaces in their facilities. Through the online discussion board, *One Million Mormons on Facebook*, numerous opinions were injected into the national debate.

Sources such as BeliefNet, BuddhaNet, and the Islamic e-periodical *Renaissance: A Monthly Islamic Journal* typify good reporting while at the same time engaging readers in the discourse. Online houses of worship such as cyberchurches and cybertemples are additional sources of religious news through bulletin boards, chat rooms, and e-mail discussion groups.

What Religionists Want from News Media

Since the 1990s, uses of news by parishioners have changed, and vary across groups; initial studies focused on primarily Christian media preferences. For example, Buddenbaum (1996) observed that Catholics and Mainline Protestants (who were active in their faith, and interested in political issues) were more likely to subscribe to a general circulation newspaper. Committed Conservative Protestants, on the other hand, were less likely to trust or subscribe to a daily newspaper for political information. Conversely, less committed Pentecostals and Fundamentalists were more likely to subscribe to and use newspapers for this purpose.

Buddenbaum and Hoover (1996) found that "interest in religion news" was "widespread," but that preferences for local versus cosmopolitan coverage differed (p. 145). Affluent citizens, Mainline Protestants, and those with no religious affiliation preferred news from cosmopolitan sources; less affluent Conservative Protestants had a greater affinity for local news.

A study of radio news preferences found that Catholics who regularly attended church and shared beliefs were more likely to listen to National Public Radio (NPR) and talk radio (Buddenbaum, 2001, p. 246). Mainline Protestant NPR listeners also tended to be actively engaged in their church organization. Evangelicals and Pentecostals who listened to NPR and talk radio tended to be less committed to their faith traditions. Ideologically conservative Christian radio and talk radio that is ideologically conservative, on the other hand, was more likely to attract Conservative Protestants who are behaviorally and ideologically committed to their particular denomination (p. 247). Much has yet to be learned about media preferences beyond Christianity. Golan and Kiousis's (2010) study of Arab youths in Egypt and Saudi Arabia extends this type of research cross-nationally; one of their findings is that higher levels of religiosity positively relates with perceived credibility of domestic media.

New media create new outlets for sharing, discussing, and contemplating the news. In cyberspace, there's a fine line between sources and users, especially in the case of religious news blogs where anyone can post articles or comment on other stories. According to Campbell (2010a), religionists negotiate the value of media to assure its "compatible with their faith and tradition" (p. 136). This is done through group discourses so that media use achieves "valued religious goals" (p. 137). Cheong, Halavais, and Kwon (2008) find that blogs are used not only to communicate religious information, but for self-contemplation as well. In their analysis of 200 blogs mentioning religion, 22.5% dealt with social issues, 15.5% with news, and 7% with the coordination of events or gatherings. A compelling 44.5% had to do with the bloggers' personal religiosity (p. 115). One possible interpretation is that news is used with other forms of content to meet personal needs. Lee's (2009) study of Buddhist priests confirms the role of blogs not only as a disseminator of information, but also as a means of developing the self. In other words, news in cyberspace is folded into both the user's desire for information and need for personal contemplation.

Religion in the News

The question of whether news media depict religion accurately and fairly is a controversial one that has not been adequately resolved. Some religious leaders frequently bemoan media bias and inaccuracies. According to Olasky (1988), secular journalists are unnecessarily critical of religion and don't cover it thoroughly. Moses (2005) describes a common perception among religious groups:

> Journalists assigned to the religion beat find out very quickly that many of the people they cover suspect the news media are biased against them. Evangelical Christians, Catholics, Jews, and Muslims all complain that they are victims of unfair coverage. Christian broadcasters and such groups as the Anti-Defamation League, the Catholic League for Religious and Civil Rights, and the Council on American-Islamic relations assail alleged media abuses, sometimes calling for followers to boycott advertisers or cancel subscriptions. News organizations, striving to increase ratings or gain circulation, take such threats seriously. (p. 67)

Journalists and editors, however, defend present practices; they argue that religion must be reported objectively, even if the coverage is critical from time to time.[6] People have a right to know about the misuse of church finances, for example, or improper conduct by clergy. The fact of the matter is that neither the claim of media bias nor the assumption of objective, balanced coverage has been sufficiently validated by research.

While a relatively small number of studies have been conducted, the findings are limited in scope, disparate, and vary in their findings. Data indicate that 0.8% of all news is devoted to religion, about the same coverage given to education and immigration issues. Vultee, Craft, and Velker (2010) found religion coverage in the *Atlanta-Journal Constitution* and *Houston Chronicle* to be mixed. The Atlanta paper had more religious coverage in 2000 than in 1992, but the opposite trend occurred in Houston. Vultee et al. report that in regard to whether depictions were negative: "Our findings say 'no'" (p. 159). In a content analysis of network television news, Kerr (2003) found that Fundamentalist Christians were portrayed in a "mildly negative manner," and the "main focus of newscasts involving Fundamentalists is politics," with the most prevalent news value being "conflict" (Kerr, 2003, p. 203). In Greece, it was noted that newspapers were "predominantly negative" in tone when depicting Protestants (Bantimaroudis, 2007, p. 234).

In a study of newspaper and magazine articles, Chen (2003) found journalists' descriptions of Mormons during the 2002 Winter Olympics in Salt Lake City to contain "stereotypical images" (p. 29). Baker and Campbell (2010) offer a five-factor model for better understanding "media representation of Mormon identity," which includes the nature of media outlets, how Mormons influence media content, influences of other religions, secular voices, and the relationship between Mormonism and government (pp. 110–114). The model is a means of placing news coverage of Mormonism, such as that of presidential candidate Mitt Romney, in a larger cultural and historical context.

Gormly's (2004) study of how the Christian TV news program *700 Club* portrayed Islam after the September 11 attacks, reveals an unsympathetic portrayal of Muslims, framing the denomination as a threat to Christianity. Meer, Dwyer, and Modood (2010), however, find that while Muslims continue to be racialized in the British press, there is "a positive contrast" in terms of the greater variety of Muslim voices today compared to the earlier period of the 1980s (p. 216).

In terms of religion coverage related to politics, the literature is relatively thin, yet some recent studies are worthy of note. Hollander (2010) finds that news media attempted to debunk the myth that Barack Obama is a Muslim, but this "did little to moderate" the perception (p. 55). The Pope was framed more as a political leader than a religious one by the Turkish press after his visit to that country (Valenzano & Menegatos, 2008). According to McCune (2003), the recent debate on teaching evolution in Tennessee did not emphasize a single viewpoint as some may have thought, but was framed by opinions of several involved parties.

Silk (1995), however, disagrees that news coverage of religion is mostly negative; he argues that journalists' values inevitably turn out to be similar to those advocated by churches. When journalists cover religion, he contends, they stress the basic themes of good works, tolerance, hypocrisy, identifying false prophesy, inclusion, supernatural belief, and declension (p. 55). Silk argues that journalists are not immune from cultural values and upon careful examination their writing can be seen to reflect ethical and moral themes. In a case study of how Buddhism and the Dalai Lama is reported in the *Idaho Statesman* newspaper, R. C. Moore (2008) finds that while Silk's hypothesis holds up in terms of positive coverage, depth and nuance about Buddhism is missing from the reporting. In an earlier study, Moore (2003) critiques Silk's thesis that religious themes are embedded in news coverage; his analysis reveals that while religion news "may have some of its roots in a religious tradition" it may, at the same time, call "into question traditional religious practice" (p. 63).

While few agree about whether news coverage of religion is fair and balanced, consensus exists on another point: citizens' familiarity with and knowledge of religious groups is lacking (Prothero, 2007). Because many journalists have no formal education in comparative religion they often have to educate themselves on the job, thus producing stories that frequently omit important facts and details.

Principles of Good Religion Reporting

How do we know when journalists are covering religion effectively? It's hard to address this question without examining the role of journalism in general. In democratic societies, people have a right to know how religions impact the world they live in. In the 2008 U.S. presidential election, for example, citizens were concerned that candidates' denominational affiliation might influence governmental decisions. Religionists have been outspoken on stem-cell research, abortion, euthanasia, sex education, and in vitro fertilization. Taking a watchdog role, journalists assess their level of participation in society as well as the impact they may have on other citizens. This is no easy task considering both the vast number of denominations as well as the complexity of religious beliefs. For this reason, a set of principles or standards is useful.

Education

The best protection against inaccuracy is an informed community of journalists. This isn't possible without a foundational grasp of the world's religions (Postman, 1985). Religion, Postman argues, is key to understanding philosophy, history, and many other subjects. Knowledge of it broadens the writer's perspective and ability to describe culture in general. For this reason, organizations such as the Religion News Writers Association sponsor programs that enable journalists to take courses in comparative religion.

Further justification of such activities is given by Prothero (2007); he observes a declining trend in *religious literacy*, or "the ability to understand and use in one's day-to-day life the basic building blocks of religious institutions—their key terms, symbols, doctrines, sayings, characters, metaphors, and narratives" (p. 15). According to Prothero, the level of religious literacy in the United States is startlingly deficient:

> Americans are both deeply religious and profoundly ignorant about religion. They are Protestants who can't name the four Gospels, Catholics who can't name the seven sacraments, and Jews who can't name the five books of Moses. (Prothero, 2007, p. 1)

Given that citizens receive considerable information about religious groups from the media, it is crucial that journalists have an acceptable level of religious literacy. Whether a course in comparative religion should be required of religion newswriters continues to be discussed in media boardrooms.

Accuracy

Making accurate assessments of religious groups is a daunting challenge, and it is on this point that journalists are regularly criticized. Some writers incorrectly assume that denominations are homogenous, failing to capture the complexity of religious life. For instance, after the horrific tragedy of 9/11 speculation abounded about connections between Islam and terrorism, which resulted in inaccurate conjectures. Another example is the frequent labeling of members of the Church of Jesus Christ of Latter-day Saints (Mormons) as polygamists even though the practice was officially discontinued over a hundred years ago.

According to Buddenbaum (1998), journalists often misuse religious terms such as *Evangelicals* (i.e., those who proselyte and are demonstrative in their worship); they exist in many religions, but journalists often confine the term to describing Conservative Protestants. Despite the fact that few religionists prefer the labels "cult" or "fundamentalist" such pejorative terms appear frequently in the press. Such labeling may place religionists at risk; they may suffer ill treatment depending on the degree of inaccuracy as well as the size of the audience that is misinformed.

Writers should also strive for *nuance* and sufficient detail. The RNA Web site offers the following advice to journalists writing about religion:

> Religions deal with good and evil, but in everyday life, there's little black and white and mostly a thousand shades of gray. Honor that. When writing a profile of a minister who runs an amazing program for underprivileged kids, don't ignore the fact that he owes child support. When reporting on a family whose faith saw them through a crisis, include the fact that they don't go to church. Religion often confounds expectations, which is one reason it is fascinating to write about. (Religion in the News, 2008)

Optimal news coverage of religion also deals with conflicts in a thorough, calm, and balanced manner. Good stories present multiple viewpoints and perspectives; they examine religion not only inside churches, but everywhere in public life from coffee houses to the mall. In terms of denominational religion, excellent reporting occurs when writers actually visit mosques, synagogues, and other houses of worship instead of relying on second-hand information about what a particular group is like.

Inclusiveness

In an era of religious pluralism, many voices are overlooked. Larger denominations have aggressive public affairs departments disseminating information on a daily basis, making it easier for journalists to cover them. Other churches grab the attention of reporters by taking public positions on controversial issues such as abortion and stem-cell research. Generally speaking, however, numerous faith groups are ignored by the press. Consequently, citizens are often unaware of the richness and complexity of the cultural fabric that defines society; they may have only a superficial sense of the country they call home. The inclusivity principle requires journalists to get beyond restrictive perceptions and make a serious effort to cover as wide a range of religions as possible.

Efforts to be thorough, accurate, and inclusive are essential for optimal religion journalism. Yet it is also important to consider how religionists themselves approach the news reporting process.

Theologically Based Journalism and Media Activism

We often think of journalists as having ultimate power in determining the news agenda; public opinion regarding denominations, it seems, is strongly influenced by them. In many instances this is the case, especially when a writer has high credibility and access to large audiences. Yet, religious groups aren't necessarily passive in this process; they don't always sit by when threatened by potentially injurious information. Strategies are employed to assure that their interests are represented in the public forum. In this section I address two ways this is accomplished. *Religious journalism* is dissemination of news through church-sponsored media. Next, I discuss *media activism* or efforts to influence secular news coverage. This ranges from public relations activity to the more aggressive action of censorship.

Theologically Based Journalism

Somewhat overlooked in society, religious-based news outlets comprise a significant sector of today's media industry. As noted in the historical section, there were times when the dominant media in society were religious. Such was the case in medieval Europe and later in Puritan America. Hedgepeth-Williams (2000) argues that Puritans valued the exchange of ideas, so long as such expressions "did not blatantly detract from God" (p. 18). As Buddenbaum (2010) explains, "Three hundred years ago, religious journalism was the norm. Printer/publishers usually saw their newspapers as performing both civic and religious functions" (p. 200). Colonial newspapers reported good news "as signs of God's favor" and portrayed bad news as "evidence of God's wrath" (p. 200). Such publications debated the issues of the day, but arguments were often grounded in religious doctrine. This was the case even in the 19th century. According to Buddenbaum (2010), many issues were hotly debated in the pages of newspapers, but "very few papers provided anything approaching balanced coverage" (p. 200).

Today, religious journalism exists side-by-side with secular news media. Citizens may demand a *fourth estate* or media that act as a watchdog, but they also want to hear the religious view. Religious journalists report information that rarely surfaces in the secular press. In the Christian magazine *Books and Culture,* for example, readers enjoy literary commentary from a spiritual perspective. *Tricycle: The Buddhist Review* helps build religious identity by sharing information about Buddhist life in the West. When the Pope speaks in Rome, Catholics around the world can immediately access the message online through the Vatican Web site. Radio shows such as *Focus on the Family* address everyday issues such as the role of marriage and how to raise children according to religious values. Such information is difficult to locate in secular media.

Religious news media can be vehicles of worship as well. When the magazine *Ensign* publishes the words of modern Mormon prophets, it is considered to be a form of sacred scripture, much like the Bible. For the Jehovah's Witnesses, the *Watchtower* magazine not only updates adherents about church activities, but provides content for study and reflection.

A longstanding complaint is that secular media do not, and perhaps cannot convey religious viewpoints in a thorough and comprehensive way. Religious journalism is the means through which the world's events are filtered through values that millions of people share in various subcultures. Mainstream journalists lacking firsthand familiarity with denominations, do not always report stories in sufficient detail. This is the case regarding coverage of Native Americans and sacred burial rites; news stories are often limited to short quotes and brief background material.

Religious journalism, however, is not without its drawbacks and controversies. One is whether exclusive reliance on religious media impedes participation in a democratic system. For a democracy to be vibrant and functional, citizens must be informed. If their sphere is comprised essentially of religious information, both an informed electorate and robust political discourse are difficult.

The *closed system* phenomenon isn't new; there are relatively isolated religious communities in all societies. With the proliferation of religious media, concerns are raised about increasing isolation of some groups. For example, it is now possible that an individual could frequent mostly religious retailers, attend a religious college, view only religious television programs, and listen to popular music exclusively on religious radio. As Schement and Stephenson (1996) suggest, the present information society "stresses the individual, emphasizes distinct spheres of life" and "exploits the idea of information to maintain the partitions" (p. 268).

This partitioning has led to media *synergy,* a situation where organizations "maximize their presence across as many media channels as possible" (Turow, 1992, p. 236). Often used in business, this approach is a response to the burgeoning number of media channels that religions must compete with. One method of competing is to be visible in each of these media. Alongside secular newspapers there are religious ones. The same is true of radio; churches now have a strong presence on cost-effective Internet radio. The question is, if religious news media provide most of the information which citizens use to learn about the society around them, will they be sufficiently informed on political matters and issues of the day?

Regarding these questions, writer and philosopher Neil Postman (1999) argues for balance. In his book, *Building a Bridge to the Eighteenth Century: How the Past can Improve our Future,* he argues that citizens should study comparative religion; religious texts and media have value if they encourage compassion and ethical conduct. On the other hand, he warns us about insularity, which can lead to intolerance and separation from the larger society where citizens must share common ideals and have mutual respect (Postman, 1992).

Media Activism

In addition to owning their own media outlets, religious groups interface with secular media in order to assure their voices are heard. Religionists desire representation in the political arena; they want fellow citizens to know their position on the issues. It is no surprise, then, that religion is intertwined with contemporary politics. According to Meyer and Moors (2006), religions are participating in "new arenas of public debate":

> The presence of mediated religion in the public sphere is both con-
> stitutive of and constituted by political activism, especially iden-
> tity politics or the politics of difference. Modern religion refuses to
> be bound to a distinct religious sphere—as is imagined in modern
> notions of society as differentiated into separate domains—and
> appears to be intermingled with politics and sometimes violent
> political action. (p. 11)

We now turn to some of the ways religious groups participate in the public forum. The first, and perhaps the most controversial, is *censorship* (see chapter 6 for a discussion of censorship in the context of media literacy). This represents the prevention, alteration, or restriction of information said to threaten religion or sacred values. Censorship is difficult to comprehend without attention to the concept of blasphemy or actions thought to undermine or disrespect the sacred. While censorship isn't embraced universally by churches, it appears throughout history. With the arrival of the printing press, censorship strategies became more organized and systematic (Claussen, 2010).

Islamic censorship serves as a relevant example: according to El-Nawawy (2005), it is considered a civic duty in the Arab Middle East. Muslims recognize the importance of the press, but "freedom of expression does not include offensive or negative statements about Islam or religious beliefs" (p. 63). For example, in 2001 an editor was incarcerated for 3 years for an article about the alleged sexual behaviors of a Coptic monk.

Another example comes from Mormonism. Fearing that its publication would lead to persecution and even violence against his followers, Mormon prophet Joseph Smith had the *Expositor,* an Illinois newspaper, destroyed in 1844 (Bushman, 2005). A more recent example of religious censorship involves the Falun Gong, which launched a libel suit against the New York newspaper *China Press,* alleging that mistruths in the publication created unusual hardships for group members (Moses, 2005). Such actions reflect the view that the media are immensely powerful and have the ability to impede the progress of denominations.

Journalism and the Numinous

A compelling development is the incorporation of news into actual religious experience. The news can enhance belief, play a part in ritual, and help build community. An important function of journalism is to inform, but it can also figure into one's milieu of worship. Monks in medieval monasteries regarded books as sacred, and some news media are used in a like manner today.

Ritual is key to understanding the interplay between religiosity and the news. Carey (1989) discusses this extensively, suggesting that reading or viewing the daily news is communal and moral. An illustration comes from Buescher (2005) who observed Tibetan monks incorporating the Voice of America's Tibetan Broadcast Service news show into their religious activities: "While they clustered in silence around the radio, they clasped their hands together as if praying, or fingered their prayer beads. If a sound clip of the voice of the Dalai Lama happened to come on during a news report, they prostrated themselves as if in his presence" (p. 38). The researcher described one of the monks this way: "he found listening to our show to be in harmony with praying and walking his ritual rounds, which seemed extraordinary to me—after all, it is just a news show" (p. 37).

The PBS series Religion and Ethics News Weekly exemplifies how a news program is more than meets the eye. While known for its informative and objective news reporting, religionists can link to the stories online as part of their personal study program. As mentioned earlier, hybrid programs such as the *The Jewish Voice, Eternal World Television Network (EWTN)*, and *700 Club* are particularly conducive to the numinous because they fold elements of the religious meeting (e.g., audience, instruction, prayer, etc.) into the TV news-talk format which includes news anchors and live interviews.

Online, a news story may be discussed, shared, and viewed alongside other sources; it may be recommended as a means of solving a problem or inspiring another. Blogs often focus on volunteerism or assisting the poor. With blogs, the story becomes part of a larger discussion of doctrine, belief, and how to solve community problems.

While news media function as informers and watchdogs, their role in contemporary religious experience is complex. Depending on the situation, news can enhance religious community, elicit deep feelings, and deepen commitments.

The numinous is a useful concept in thinking about journalism in the context of contemporary religion. This is not to say that the sole purpose of news is a religious one; journalism serves society in several ways. In the information age, however, religionists engage the numinous in places previously thought to be exclusively secular; they use news media in ways that are only beginning to be understood.

Key Terms

closed system phenomenon: When members of a religious group refrain from using secular media.

community journalism: Citizens have a voice in the news agenda and often create their own news outlets or add to existing ones.

Fourth Estate: Another name for the press and its responsibility to contribute to the broad debate of ideas.

marketplace of ideas: The belief that all ideas should be made part of public discourse and as a result, the best policies will become known.

media activism: Effort to influence secular news coverage.

religion journalism: The reporting of news about religion by secular sources, aiming to be objective.

religious defamation: The communication of a false claim that contributes to a negative perception of a religious or spiritual group.

religious journalism: The reporting of news from the religious viewpoint.

Questions to Ponder

1. What role did the advent of the printing press play in religious cultures?
2. Do you agree that news media are more "interactive" than they used to be? Why or why not?
3. What is the difference between religion journalism and religious journalism?
4. Some say that journalists tend to be overly critical of religious groups, while others see them as espousing similar values. What do you think?
5. What are the principles of good religious reporting?
6. What are the potential effects of the "closed system" phenomenon?

CHAPTER 10

Strategic Communication

A typical citizen is exposed to more than 600 commercial messages each day, from radio spots to spam (Clow & Baack, 2007, p. 132), among which are advertisements from religious groups. Religious advertising ranges from something as basic as pamphlets distributed on a city street to more costly television commercials. One example is a print advertisement from an Episcopalian church in Maryland that depicts Jesus Christ being cruci-fied with the caption: "Of course people with pierced body parts are wel-come in our church" (Armstrong, 2000). Advertising is also used within denominations as with a campaign encouraging Jewish parents to consider increasing the size of their families (Ott, 2002). Religious involvement in marketing has been strategic and controversial. On the one hand, adver-tising enables churches to reach large numbers of people, attract converts, and solicit donations. On the other hand, many are uncomfortable mixing business with the sacred. One thing is clear, however; religious groups are increasingly applying the tools of marketing; they use advertising more than at any other time in history. The same tactics used to sell commer-cial products are being used to promote denominations. Some churches employ advertising agencies and have public relations departments that are staffed by communications experts.

This chapter explores the subject of strategic communication, particu-larly religious advertising.[1] It discusses both opportunities and controver-sies. Specific strategies and tactics are also described. Advertising serves many functions for religious groups; it rapidly disseminates information to large audiences and facilitates the acquisition of religious products by consumers who either are or may become members of the congregation; these products are increasingly in demand. Religious organizations' use of advertising is also highly criticized, however, and we look at the reasons for these concerns. The chapter concludes with a discussion of how religion is depicted in secular advertising.

Advertising and religion have a number of things in common: they both are goal-oriented and persuasive in nature. When new media emerge, advertisers and religionists move quickly to exploit them for their purposes. The religious tract resembles the commercial brochure and the sermon is not entirely unlike a product testimonial. Advertising and religion have enjoyed a reciprocal relationship; they make use of each other's techniques and tactics.

Advertising's rise can be traced to the Industrial Revolution, a period when more products were produced than could be immediately consumed; it wasn't long before modern marketing and consumer culture were born. With it came a sophisticated form of advertising designed to create a product image, a technique now used by many churches. Today, a product is not just a product; it is a brand. Einstein (2008) elaborates:

> Brands are commodity products that have been given a name, an identifying icon or logo, and usually a tagline as a means to differentiate them from other products in their category. Branding also occurs through the creation of stories or myths surrounding a product or service. These stories are conveyed through the use of advertising and marketing and are meant to position a product in the mind of the consumer. (p. 12)

Individuals have experiences with, and emotional attachments to products. Some prefer Pepsi over Coke or Hallmark Cards over American Greetings. It isn't surprising that the term *religious branding* has surfaced in the marketing lexicon.[2] Through the Home Front campaign, the Mormon Church positioned itself as a religion that stresses family above all else. Recently, the "I am a Mormon" campaign running in nine markets may have been an effort to defend the brand in the face of recent negative publicity (Chen, 2011). These ads depict everyday Mormons in various roles and occupations in society. Some speculate that the Church's critical depiction in the Broadway musical, *The Book of Mormon,* as well as public reaction to its participation in California's Proposition 8 made such a campaign useful. Through TV commercials, the Shandon Baptist Church in Columbia, South Carolina emphasized its friendliness as a congregation in its branding strategy. Religious brands represent more than a simple set of beliefs; they are the sum total of an individual's feelings for, and experiences with a particular denomination.

The Religion–Marketing Paradox

The relationship between religion and marketing is paradoxical; some embrace it while others denounce it as an affront to sacred values. Yet because the goal of religion is behavioral change, persuasive communication has been employed by denominations for centuries. As Moore (1994) contends, religion's relationship with marketing is not a new one:

> The argument is not that religion has only recently found it necessary to embrace techniques of commercial expansion to get ahead. Commercial aspects of religion can be traceable in any century. Markets once flourished in cathedral towns, and the Church shared the profits. Martin Luther complained about the sale of indulgences. Protestants made their critical conquests in Europe among urban merchants. To say that religion is involved in market trade is not to pose a unique problem of modernity. (p. 7)

The basic elements of advertising (i.e., salience, persuasion, and call-to-action) are also found in the sermon. According to Bliese (2010), the sermon's "raison d'etre is to persuade people to lead a new life" (p. 395). Rhetorical devices such as irony, repetition, and metaphor combine to get attention, maintain interest, and implore parishioners to take action. By the 16th century, sermons were immensely popular, and the skills of classical rhetoric were exhibited at the pulpit. It is no surprise that today the same techniques are employed in radio and television commercials promoting religion.

The *pamphlet* demonstrates how religious groups honed persuasive techniques in print media. They were a "brief, quickly produced, and inexpensive" means of persuading interested parties (Morgan, 2010, p. 315). Today, religious pamphlets look much like direct-mail advertisements. One need only open the mailbox and find letters such as those from the "Covenant Partner's Ministry" that contain a brochure and "Partner Registration Card" requesting a monthly donation. The point is, religious institutions and commercial organizations have had a reciprocal relationship in that each has made use of the other's communication strategies.

These approaches have also stirred controversy; some parishioners argue that marketing comes perilously close to materialism and manipulation. Such activities seem antithetical to religious ideals. Although advertising effectively spreads the religious message to large numbers, some fear it is an endorsement of greed and worldliness. In a study of young adult Christian Evangelicals, Haley, White, and Cunningham (2001) found that nearly half of those interviewed struggled to reconcile religious ideology with the principles of marketing.

Reasons for Growth

While the appropriateness of religious advertising is hotly debated, it grows ever more common among major denominations. Reasons include: (a) emerging religious pluralism, (b) expansion of material culture and availability of religious products, (c) the rise of the spiritual marketplace, (d) the development of new marketing approaches such as integrated campaigns, and (e) the increasing need for public relations to defend religious organizations and facilitate their growth.

Religious Pluralism

Religious organizations' experimentation with advertising is driven by pluralism. In many nations, denominations must compete for converts and resources. Even in countries where one or two groups dominate, marketing tactics are used to lure back those who may be choosing leisure pursuits over religious activities. Advertising is a means of staying in the public eye and maintaining top-of-mind awareness. Advertising can be more effective than face-to-face communication in attracting large numbers back to the fold.

Evidence of pluralism is not hard to find in American cities. Evangelical Christians call passersby to repentance on the streets of Chicago; Hare Krishna adherents distribute tracts on the street corners of Los Angeles; automobile bumper stickers in Atlanta carry messages such as, "Praise the Lord" and "The 10 Commandments Are Not Multiple Choice!"

Material Culture and Religious Products

Religious advertising coincides with the burgeoning interest in sacred statuary, in-home ornaments, recorded music, popular novels, toys, jewelry, clothing, and even religious theme parks.[3] Demand for such products has created entire industries dedicated to their manufacture and sale. Material culture is present in some form in all denominational structures.

Religious products reflect individuals' spiritual convictions as well as "the religious, mental, and spiritual configurations found in the society as a whole" (Golden, 2010, p. 234). Early Christians of the third century

AD worshipped in their homes using holy tables that displayed holy relics (Armentrout, 2010). In-home statuary, paintings, altars, and other objects facilitated prayer and reinforced religious identity. Although the use of in-home religious objects isn't new, never has there been such a proliferation of these goods. This situation is made possible through the methods of modern marketing. It began with the Industrial Revolution when these products were mass produced; they're now mass-marketed much like commercial goods. The catalogue for the retailer Family Christian Stores, for example, illustrates the similarities between religious and secular product advertising; it combines Bible quotes and advertising-style copy. The headline, "Overwhelm them with appreciation and love" accompanies photos of the Passion Nail Necklace and the Passion Lapel Pin inspired by the film, *The Passion of Christ*.

Proponents of religious products argue that these artifacts are important elements of worship. For example, Perry and Wolfe (2001) found that Christian recorded music played a role in prayer, family cohesion, and sharing sacred messages with others. So, the increased availability of such products is accompanied by the need to promote them. Advertising, then, is not only a means of marketing such products, but also a way of describing the religious experiences resulting from their use.

The Spiritual Marketplace

The widening availability of religious products is only one reason for the rise of religious advertising. Demand for these goods reflects a grander phenomenon in which individuals not only shop for religious goods, but for ideas as well. Roof (1999) argues that Baby Boomers are engaged in a quest; they explore new ideas and often draw from more than one religious perspective. Religious leaders are aware of such quests and use advertising to inform seekers about their options.

This situation, termed a *spiritual marketplace*, "reflects a deep hunger for self-transformation that is both genuine and personally satisfying" (Roof, 1999, p. 9). According to Roof, those without a traditional religious upbringing are seeking new insight, and those with a grounding in denominational religion are looking to expand their horizons. With this new thirst for ideas comes a willingness to experience religion through new forms of communication, and this includes advertising. Throughout their lives, Baby Boomers were exposed to advertising and its promise of a better life. They may come to question materialism and the values of consumer culture, but they may also appreciate advertising as a means of identifying sources of knowledge as they pursue their quest.

The Rise of "Integrated Marketing"

The rise of religious advertising also coincides with a major trend in marketing communication. This shift calls into question the dichotomous view that advertising and religion are oppositional phenomena. The concept of integrated marketing communication (IMC) takes a much broader view of strategic communication than that of traditional advertising. It takes into account all of the possible contact points between an organization and its targeted constituencies, not just persuasive forms. The emphasis is on building relationships between sender and receiver rather than on one-dimensional campaigns whose goal is manipulation through the "hard sell."

As commercial companies adopt IMC, churches are also adapting elements of this approach. IMC is attractive to religious groups for a number of reasons. First, it encourages a holistic perspective where multiple contact points such as architecture, décor, signage, the Internet, word-of-mouth, and public events are coordinated so that all media are designed with a consistent goal in mind. IMC is a contingency approach, where the advertising strategy depends on the needs and challenges of the religious organization; it stresses the use of multiple channels of communication, formal and informal; persuasive and informational.

Public Relations

Few disagree that external communication by denominations is needed in order to survive and flourish. The opinions of lawmakers, politicians, and citizens make a difference in how religious groups are treated and accommodated by the larger society. For this reason, public relations is an activity of growing importance. Misperceptions exist about religious groups, and public relations is a way of assuring that important information is made available. People often form opinions about religious groups based on what they see in the media, and an organized public relations effort can dispel rumors and combat misinformation. For example, the Islamic Circle of North America used 1,000 subway car ads to familiarize New Yorkers with the basic beliefs of Islam (Adler, 2008).

Campaigns are also mounted against religious defamation. The Anti-Defamation League, for example, is dedicated to fighting anti-Semitism and securing equal rights for the Jewish population through various communication strategies. American Hindus Against Defamation (AHAD) is a watchdog group dedicated to the preservation and protection of Hindu symbols and culture. To keep the public informed, these organizations maintain Web sites and participate in community events.

Religion in Secular Advertising

Religion also appears in secular advertising for common products and services. While such depictions often appear innocuous, as in the case of a TV commercial featuring a Catholic monk using a Xerox copier in a monastery, or the magazine ad that reads, "You don't have to be Jewish to love Levy's" rye bread, a number of concerns have been raised. Given the ubiquitous nature of advertising, some wonder whether casual and widespread dissemination of religious symbols might lessen their impact over time. Postman (1992) laments the overuse of religious imagery, terming it "the great symbol drain" (p. 164). He elaborates:

> It is possible that some day soon, an advertising man who must create a television commercial for a new California Chardonnay will have the following inspiration: Jesus is standing alone in a desert oasis. A gentle breeze flutters the leaves of the stately palms behind him. Soft Mideastern music caresses the air. Jesus holds in his hand a bottle of wine at which he gazes adoringly. Turning toward the camera, he says, "When I transformed water into wine at Cana, *this* is what I had in mind. Try it today. You'll become a believer." (p. 164)

In Postman's view, the overproduction of religious symbolism undermines its sanctity and historical significance. Hoover (2001) uses the term *symbol flattening* to describe a condition where symbols such as the cross are no longer "held in a hierarchical relationship to other, more secular or cultural symbols" due to the frequency of their depiction in media (p. 56).

According to Mallia (2009), advertisers are also using religion to shock the audience into paying attention. Because sexual imagery in advertising is so prevalent, it seems to be losing its salience; religion may be replacing it as the bold new attention-getting device. Examples include a nun passionately kissing a priest in a Benetton ad, and an ad for the morning-after birth control pill Levonelle features the headline, "Immaculate Contraception." Similarly, DaVinci's painting *The Last Supper* has been adapted in controversial ways. The fashion house Girbaud's parody of the painting features partial nudity and was found to be in violation of French blasphemy laws (Mallia, 2007, p. 11). An ad for the Irish bookmaker Paddy Power depicts Jesus and the Apostles using playing cards, poker chips, and a roulette wheel (p. 12).

Such advertising has renewed the relevance of the ancient concept of *blasphemy* in media criticism. Webster (1990), for example, cautions that such depictions, while seemingly trivial, can deeply offend the sensibilities of religious devotees. When particular groups perceive that the sacred has been trivialized, communication between groups is hindered and hostility can ensue. While it has long been the goal of marketers to understand their target audience, the controversial depiction of religion suggests that insensitivity persists from time to time.

Advertising and the Numinous

With all the controversy surrounding advertising's relationship with the sacred, one hesitates to ask whether religious experiences can be derived from it. Advertising is both promising and problematic as a vehicle for the numinous. Indeed, its connection with business may restrict its acceptability in a number of religious communities. Advertising, however, is a broad and complex form of communication and its place in worship is not yet fully understood. In a highly mediated environment, however, advertising's convenience and easy access suggest that some religionists will continue to utilize it in meeting their goals.

A study by Tilson and Chao (2002) indicates that a promotional campaign can exhibit elements of the numinous. These researchers examined public relations for the U.S. tour of St. Thérèse's relics by the Catholic Church. Touring artifacts of the French Saint Thérèse Marie Françoise Martin attracted millions in Europe, Russia, South America, and North America. Campaign media included advertising, news releases, and church bulletins. The exhibit drew positive news coverage in print and electronic media throughout the tour. Unlike secular marketing, this was a promotional-devotional campaign in that the media created a covenantal relationship between the religious institution and the audience. Tilson (2000) elaborates:

> A devotional-promotional public relations campaign that is religious in nature, may seek to instill great love or loyalty, enthusiasm, or zeal for a particular religious individual, living or deceased, or for a specific religion or faith. In so doing, the campaign may weave cultural, ethnic, political, and other socio-political/economic elements into a complex communication tapestry. (p. 1)

In the case of the St. Thérèse campaign, promotional media became an actual part of the religious event. These messages attract participants and build enthusiasm for a sacred experience. News coverage deepens understanding of the event and enhances its enjoyment by adding an additional perspective. When advertising is used to promote a religious event, it becomes part of the event itself. In this way, promotional communication can play a role in numinous events.

Key Terms

blasphemy: Speech or writing that is disrespectful of or makes light of religion.

consumer culture: A culture in which materialism and consumption of goods are dominant values.

Industrial Revolution: A period in the late 18th and early 19th centuries when major changes in agriculture, manufacturing, and transportation had a profound effect on socioeconomic and cultural conditions in Britain and subsequently spread throughout the world.

integrated marketing communication (IMC): An approach to marketing where all possible contact points with the consumer are coordinated into a seamless strategic message.

reciprocal relationship: Two entities making use of each other's tactics and techniques.

religious branding: The marketing of religion using positioning, symbols, and messages in order to distinguish one denomination from another.

religious defamation: The communication of a false claim that may have a negative impact on a religious group.

religious ideology: A set of tenets and practices regarding moral and spiritual claims about reality and human nature making up a system of abstract thought applied to public matters.

religious pluralism: The condition where many religious organizations exist side by side in a society.

spiritual marketplace: A situation where individuals feel free to draw from any number of religious sources for personal worship.

symbol flattening: When symbols are so widely disseminated through media that their historical significance is lost.

Questions to Ponder

1. Stout writes that "In some ways, religious communication has always been entrepreneurial." What are some historical attempts to sell religion using the tools of marketing?
2. Why is religious advertising and branding being used more frequently by denominations?
3. Why do some individuals, such as Baby Boomers, make use of the spiritual marketplace?
4. How do denominations use integrated marketing communication?
5. Do you think using religious symbols in secular marketing is blasphemous? Why or why not?

CHAPTER 11

In the Classroom

A Learning Activity

In this the final chapter, a classroom learning activity is suggested. Religion can be a sensitive subject given that students represent disparate cultural and religious backgrounds. How might teachers cover it thoroughly, and do so in a way that presents the material in a balanced and sensitive manner? While the topic can be approached like any other (i.e., lectures, discussions, etc.), drama in the form of readers' theater is an ideal way to engage students. When students see an issue through the eyes of characters in a story, they may be more willing to express their views and ask questions. The chapter introduces a play that can be used to explore the media–religion interface in an enjoyable manner that puts students at ease.[1]

Case studies, role-playing, and dramatic readings are popular pedagogical approaches in problem-based learning (Albanese & Mitchell, 1993; Armstrong, 1991; Hmelo-Silver, 2004). These methods shift the learning framework from the traditional lecture to the analysis of situations, cases, and stories (Duveen & Soloman, 1994; Kitzerow, 1990). Case studies are used extensively in media ethics courses (Christians et al, 2008; Patterson & Wilkins, 2011). Case analysis can also be effective in broaching sensitive subjects like religion, given that students are able to project their ideas into case characters; they don't have to voice personal opinions directly. One limitation of the method, however, is that teachers move rapidly from case to case, making thorough discussion of controversial issues difficult. For this reason, the play may provide a means for deeper, more thorough examination of the subject. Plays are usually of longer duration than cases, and offer in-depth character description.

The play is a longstanding pedagogical device in many fields (Brockett, 1968; O'Hara, 1984). It has been used in classroom study of literature (McCalib, 1968; McMaster, 1998); history (Cassler, 1990; Duveen & Soloman, 1994); education (O'Hara, 1984); social work (Whitemen & Nielsen, 1986); and sociology (Kitzerow, 1990). Despite new interest in drama in the classroom, it is more prevalent in the humanities than in the social sciences. Drama is not as common in journalism and mass communication classrooms. This may be due to the field's emphasis on empirical approaches and the scientific method in analyzing media-related phenomena. As drama continues to expand within the broader field of social science, and as new teaching materials are made available, it is likely that this approach will be more common in media studies.

The purpose of the play *Redeeming Value* is to introduce the topic of media and religion in a way that will make students feel comfortable. Specifically, the story deals with religion and the dilemmas of censorship. Discussions of additional topics such as secularization, culture wars, and media ethics can also be engaged through the play.

Brief Synopsis of the Play

The story revolves around Russ McBride, a doctoral student in history at a religious university. He fails his dissertation defense and is denied a PhD. Two members of his committee (George Fackler and Barbara McPhee) are deeply offended by McBride's claim that a late 19th-century newspaper article implicates the founder of the university in a serious crime, perhaps murder. Feeling he has been censored, McBride returns to the campus 2 years later to appeal the decision. He is aided by a team of friends in preparing his case, including another professor, a local bookstore owner, and a campus custodian. Together they search for a lost document that they hope will solve the puzzle. The play culminates in the appeals hearing where the truth is revealed.

Using the Play in the Classroom

The instructor should begin by explaining the purpose of the play, which is to explore the issue of religion and censorship as well as other topics from the course. The activity takes about 3 weeks of class sessions. In the first week, students read the play aloud and are assigned parts. During the second week, various issues are discussed in the context of the story. The final week is spent preparing for a readers' theater where the play is read to an audience of friends and guests. Audience members are invited to discuss the play at the end.

In the discussion phase, students are asked about the dilemmas in the story. They should be encouraged to assess the characters' actions and suggest what they might have done differently. It is important for the instructor to incorporate concepts from the course into the discussion. Questions might include:

1. Do you feel that Russ McBride should have been failed at his dissertation defense? Why or why not?
2. Why do some members of religious groups feel justified in censoring information? Do you agree that censorship is ever justified? Why or why not?
3. How do various world religions such as Christianity, Judaism, Islam, Hinduism, and Buddhism approach the ideas of information and censorship?
4. Russ McBride denounces censorship from a religious perspective while his professor, George Fackler, justifies it in the name of the same religion. How is this possible?
5. Through his research, Russ McBride learns that historical figure Anthony Comstock had tried to prevent publication of Walt Whitman's *Leaves of Grass*. What is your opinion about this?

The readers' theater performance at the end of the course is an important event. Knowing that they will be performing for an audience, students become motivated to read their lines well. For the public reading, students sit on chairs at the edge of the stage facing the audience. Costumes are an option, and simple props can be used.

REDEEMING VALUE

A Play by Daniel A. Stout

Characters

Russell McBride, A doctoral student who fails his dissertation defense, 25 to 30 years old.

Peter Bradford, Custodian at Comstock College and self-proclaimed "nightshift anthropologist," 40 to 45 years old.

Kay Kendell, Owner of the Peoples' Bookstore with unconventional ideas about education, about 30 years old.

George Fackler, Chair of the History Department and a member of McBride's committee, 55 years old.

Barbara McPhee, History professor and member of McBride's committee, 40 to 50 years old.
Ivan Sellars, Chair of Russ McBride's dissertation committee, 35 to 45 years old.
Christina Martinez, Dean of Arts and Sciences, 40 to 45 years old.
Tour Guide, Student, 20 years old.
Server, 30 years old.
Appeals Panelists, Three Comstock professors, 40 to 50 years old.

Notes

This play is a work of dramatic fiction and the characters are imaginary. References are made, however, to Anthony Comstock, an actual figure of the late 19th century. His infamous acts of censorship are in the historical record. As a work of imaginative narration, however, the play takes liberties by filling in details of the Comstock story.

In terms of staging, most scenes are in faculty offices, the library, a bookstore, and a restaurant. Therefore, furniture (e.g., bookshelves, desks, tables, etc.) can be arranged to facilitate easy and quick transitions from scene to scene and during split scenes.

ACT 1

Scene 1

A chilly October afternoon on the main lawn of the campus of Comstock University, 1969. A student is conducting an official guided tour of Comstock University. She is center stage and speaks to the audience as if it were taking the walking tour.

Guide: Welcome to Comstock University. I'm Virginia, your tour guide today. Feel free to ask questions at any time. The school was founded in 1907 by Anthony Comstock, a religious leader and one of the country's most celebrated antivice crusaders. He cleaned up New York City, reducing prostitution, gambling, and pornography. After Congress passed the Comstock Law in 1873, prohibiting the mailing of materials considered obscene, Comstock made 4,000 arrests, resulting in 3,000 convictions. Today, Comstock University is a nondenominational Christian school with moral as well as academic standards. The university grants bachelors', masters', and doctoral degrees. Comstock graduates hold positions at the highest levels of industry and government. Now, please follow me to the first stop on the tour. (*Guide exits*)

Scene 2

The same afternoon on the campus of Comstock University. Split Scene: (1) Professor George Fackler's office. The walls are lined with bookshelves and stacks of paper clutter the room. George is seated behind his desk and Professors Barbara McPhee and Ivan Sellars sit across from him. The meeting to discuss the dissertation proposal of Russ McBride has just begun. (2) A study table in the Comstock University Library. Russ McBride and Peter Bradford are seated and conversing.

Ivan: What's the latest on the book?

Barbara: Should be off the press next week, but that's what they said a month ago.

George: It's about time. Seems like it's taken 5 years.

Ivan: Congratulations. In advance.

George: (*Changing the subject*) Thanks for saying something. Listen, Ivan. Russell McBride. His dissertation proposal. It's, well, unsettling. No, I'll go farther than that. It's reckless. Really.

Barbara: Does Russell believe Anthony Comstock was capable of a horrible crime? He's implying that the founder of this university killed someone. Do I have this right?

Ivan: (*Ponders the question, which shocks him*) No, I don't think he's saying that.

Barbara: I agree. He's just a gadfly.

Ivan: I wouldn't say a gadfly.

Barbara: He likes to see people squirm.

George: He's probably violated the Honor Code.

Ivan: If there's a problem, I'd be happy to work with him.

Barbara: You can't. You can't work with gadflies.

Ivan: (*Assertively*) Perhaps we're getting ahead of ourselves. All he says is that Comstock may have known something about this incident.

George: I know you like him, but I can tell you right now he's on thin ice. Very thin ice.

Barbara: Ivan, who is this Russell McBride?

Ivan: (*Assuringly*) He's a solid student. Very bright. Good values. Struggles with clarity in his writing, but that can be overcome. He found a police report; an important document, I think.

Apparently, Comstock was the last person to see the writer Iris Crandall alive. It's just a few paragraphs though, not central to the overall thesis.

Russ:	(*Assertively*) They better approve it.
Peter:	Maybe they will, maybe they won't.
Russ:	I thought you were the night janitor. What are you doing here now?
Peter:	(*Annoyed*) Reading. What, custodians can't come to the library to read?
Russ:	Listen, I want you to read my dissertation.
Peter:	Read it last night.
Russ:	How did you get a copy?
Peter:	I read the one on George's desk. So what?
Russ:	(*Beat*) Spying again, ehh? You're gonna get fired, I hope you know that.
Peter:	I ain't no spy.
Russ:	What do you call it then, snooping all over Fackler's office at night?
Peter:	Anthropology. (*Beat*) Just call me the nightshift anthropologist.
Russ:	(*Amused*) You're a strange man is what you are. (*Shakes his head*) So, do you think they'll approve my proposal?
Peter:	Yeah, right.
Russ:	Why not?
Peter:	Like I gotta tell you.
Russ:	The part about Iris Crandall right?
Peter:	You're dead if you leave that in. You're not that stupid, I hope.

Ivan:	His dissertation has to do with Anthony Comstock and Walt Whitman. It's the best analysis I've seen of the tensions between them.
George:	Is that the best we can do at this school? Focus on the tension between historical figures?
Barbara:	I don't care if he studies Comstock and Whitman. But, to suggest the founder might have been involved in a murder. I won't tolerate it. If he wants to do that kind of research he should be at a secular school.
Ivan:	He'll do the right thing. I trust him completely.
George:	Okay. Here's what we're going to do. Ivan, you'll be his chair. (*Takes out a form and signs it*) We'll approve the proposal on the condition that the questionable section will not be in the final draft.

Ivan:	He'll be fine.
George:	(*Shuffling papers on the desk*) Let's see what you can do.
Russ:	Besides that one part, how did you like it?
Peter:	Verbose. You need to get to the point faster. But, it's a good read. Opened my eyes about Comstock.
Russ:	(*Encouraged*) Really? But, you'd get rid of the part about Iris Crandall.
Peter:	Only if I wanted a P-H-D. If not, hell, I guess I'd say all kinds of stupid shit.
Russ:	Be serious.
Peter:	You think you're gonna get a P-H-D from this place by claiming Comstock may have murdered someone? (*Irritated*) Listen. You say that, and it's over. Your career. Over.
Russ:	Do you want to hear the whole story?
Peter:	I'm listening.
Russ:	The Postal Service hired Comstock to keep pornography out of the mail. But, for some reason he decides that books by Iris Crandall are obscene. But, they're just books on human sexuality, you know, information to help newly married couples. Health education. Medical books. Comstock doesn't see it like that, though. Explicit illustrations in a medical book really offended him. So Crandall hears about his criticism and fires back. Calls him a buffoon in the newspaper. Needless to say he's pissed off when the judge finds her not guilty. The next day, a bullet in her head.
Peter:	New York was a rough town back then. Bullets flying everywhere.
Russ:	But, listen to this. For some reason, Comstock goes to her office the night of her death.
Peter:	So, how come nobody's talking about this but you? I've been poking around this place for 20 years and nobody has said anything about this.
Russ:	Comstock was never a suspect; police ruled it a suicide.
Peter:	Then it sure as hell was! Drop it. I mean, you can't be that stupid. He started the school, I mean, are you crazy?
Russ:	Okay, okay, but let me tell you one thing. No suicide note and her diary implies she was very happy.
Peter:	All I can say is Russ, don't blow this. Maybe you haven't thought about it, but this P-H-D, it's your ticket. That's it. Everything. Toto. The whole nine yards. Your life's gonna be very different if you mess this up.

Scene 3

Later that afternoon in The Peoples' Bookstore. Kay Kendell is seated at her desk. She's on the phone with George Fackler.

Kay: Hello, George Fackler? (*Beat*) Kay Kendell at The Peoples' Bookstore. (*Beat*) Fine, and you? (*Beat*) I wanted to congratulate you on your new book about Anthony Comstock and invite you and your coauthor Barbara McPhee to speak at our Author Forum on Saturday the thirtieth of this month. (*Pause*) Oh, Okay. Sorry to hear that. What about the following Saturday? (*Pause*) You can't. We could do it on Wednesday afternoon, then. Would that... (*Pause*) Doesn't work either. (*Growing frustrated*) Is there some reason you don't want to speak at our bookstore? (*Pause*) That's not true at all. We're not affiliated with the Socialist Workers Party. Where did you hear that? (*Pause*) We carry politically conservative material I want you to know. The fact that I invited you to speak, I mean, what does that tell you? (*Pause*) What? It's not the right audience? Is that what you said? I'll have you know we just celebrated our 10th anniversary. My father opened this store in 1959. We have a 1632 Shakespeare Second Folio and 20 antique leather-bound volumes. Does that give you some idea about my clientele? (*Pause*) You prefer to speak on college campuses. Don't you think the town's people might be interested in your book? (*Pause*) I understand. You won't change your mind? (*Pause*) You're going to pass. Got it. Doctor Fackler, can I say something about your first book? The one on the history of the Salvation Army? (*Pause*) Yes, I read it. Regrettably I might add. And you know something? A real dud if you ask me. It's polemical, didactic, and pretentious for starters. Your writing lacks nuance and the conclusions are simplistic. The book is both unfulfilling and uninspiring. Good to talk to you, goodbye. (*Slams the phone down*)

Scene 4

Lunchtime in a coffee shop near the campus. Russ McBride and Ivan Sellars are seated at a small table. It's 3 weeks before Russ's dissertation defense.

Russ: Last night I went to the Beach Boys concert in the Student Center.

Ivan: Ah, yes. Surfing music. Love it.

Russ: You dig surfing music?

Ivan: The Beach Boys at Comstock. Makes more sense than Alice Cooper or Black Sabbath, I suppose.

Russ: It certainly does.

Ivan: Brian Wilson's a genius.

Russ;   You know the song, "God Only Knows," right?

Ivan: Beautiful melody in that song.

Russ: They asked them not to play it.

Ivan: Really. Why?

Russ: Has the word "God" in it. Irreverent, I don't know. Everybody's waiting for them to play it though, and the concert's almost over and the crowd is yelling for the song.

Ivan: I hope they played it.

Russ: And Brian Wilson says, "They told us not to play it, but how can we refuse an audience like this?" As soon as they recognize those first three or four notes, the students go berserk.

Ivan: Full-scale rebellion at Comstock.

Russ: About 30 seconds into the song they pull the plug.

Ivan: (*Pause*) What?

Russ: They cut the electricity in the middle of the song! All of a sudden, all you hear is Dennis Wilson playing the drums. No electric guitars or keyboards. All you can hear is the drums! Really weird, man. (*They look at each other and erupt in laughter*)

Ivan: (*Regaining his composure*) You know, Comstock has quite a history of that kind of stuff.

Russ: Like what?

Ivan: Like Rodin's sculpture *The Kiss*.

Russ: You're kidding. They wouldn't allow it?

Ivan: Sent it back the minute it arrived. Said it would offend children's groups in the museum.

Russ: (*Exasperated*) But, *The Kiss!* It's a classic!

Ivan: Changing the subject, I finished the monster known as your dissertation last night. Took me 'til 2 in the morning.

Russ: And?

Ivan: I'm scheduling your defense for March 3rd.

Russ: That's in 2 weeks.

Ivan: It's ready. Needs some editing, but I think it's ready. I mean, why wait? Send a copy to George and Barbara after you look at my notes in the margins.

Russ: Great. I'll send it tomorrow.

        (*An uncomfortable pause. They drink their soft drinks and gaze about the room for a moment before Russ breaks the silence.*)

Russ: So, the part about Iris Crandall's okay?

Ivan:	No, it's not okay. It shouldn't be in there.
Russ:	Maybe I'll take it out. Listen, Ivan. I feel like I'm on to something here.
Ivan:	And your point is?
Russ:	I mean, that's what they drill into us at this school. Stand up for the right. Take a stand. The categorical imperative.
Ivan:	Not now. Not in your dissertation.
Russ:	(*Beat*) Why not?
Ivan:	(*Assessing Russ's sincerity*) Save it for later—after you get your doctorate.
Russ:	Play it safe, right Ivan?
Ivan:	Seriously, don't let me down. I set up three interviews for you at some of the best schools in the country. The ball's in your court. (*He signals the server who brings him the check. At that very moment Peter Bradford wanders in and approaches their table.*)
Russ:	Peter, come over here.
Ivan:	(*Standing up, tossing a ten-dollar bill on the table*) Hello, Peter. I've got to split, but sit down with Russ. Ask him about the Beach Boys concert.
Peter:	Don't run off, Ivan.
Ivan:	See you boys later.
Peter:	(*Pause*) Beach Boys, right.
Russ:	(*Takes a bite of a sandwich*) So, tell me, what's new on campus? Done any good snooping lately?
Peter:	Let me see. What's new. Oh yeah, you'll like this. Women professors at Comstock are paid 32% less than men.
Russ:	Wow. How'd they get away with that?
Peter:	The attorneys are looking at it, man.
Russ:	What else?
Peter:	Well, the dress code thing keeps coming up.
Russ:	Where'd you hear that?
Peter:	In the minutes of the President's Council. And if it passes, you're in big trouble.
Russ:	Why?
Peter:	Your hair. Nothing below the collar. And no beards.
Russ:	It'll never happen. Anthony Comstock himself had a beard!
Peter:	It's all about today, man. No hippies at Comstock.
Russ:	I'll never shave my beard.
Peter:	You've got more important things to worry about. (*They pause as Russ takes a drink of his Coke*)
Russ:	I'll probably take it out.
Peter:	That's the winning ticket, believe me.

Russs: You know what, Peter? (*Pensively*) Nobody knows Anthony Comstock. I mean, he's just a myth. He wasn't the great man everyone thinks he was.

Peter: (*Beat*) Don't you understand? He has to be a myth. It's not who he was; it's what people want him to be. (*Emphatically*) This place is named after him; his name has to be clean. You don't send your kids to a religious college named after a murderer. Yeah, I got my degree at Al Capone College. Where'd you go, Jack the Ripper State?

Russ: You made your point. But, what if he did it?

Peter: (*Points at the window*) Look at that university across the street. It's a great thing this school. Wouldn't be there without Anthony Comstock.

Russ: What would be there instead?

Peter: (*Perplexed*) A stupid cornfield, I don't know. A bowling alley, I suppose. Burger Chef. (*Both laugh*) The point is, we gotta damn good university and Comstock made it happen.

Scene 5

George Fackler's office a week before Russ's dissertation defense. George is sitting at his desk. Barbara rushes in with a copy of their new book.

Barbara: (*Ecstatic*) Have you seen it?

George: Hold on, I'm taking it out of the box right now. (*Unwraps the volume and admires the front cover*)

Barbara: George, we did it. (*Sitting down*)

George (*Flipping through the pages*) Very nice.

Barbara: This is a magic moment, George. Don't you have anything profound to say?

George: (*Facetiously*) Yes, what's the next book going to be about?

Barbara: Oh, come on. (*Reading from the book's back cover*) Listen to what the book jacket says: Anthony Comstock ushered in the modern era of civility. He cleaned up New York City and kept it from lapsing into anarchy. Comstock propelled America toward a moral society. In moments of strife, he believed religion could restore values to New York and then to an entire nation. George Fackler and Barbara McPhee, two of the nation's leading historians tell the compelling story of a forgotten religious leader.

George: Well said, well said.

Barbara: Is that all you have to say? How should we celebrate? Should I make a dinner reservation?

George: No, no, not tonight. I'm too tired. (*Shuffles papers on his desk*)

Barbara: I knew you'd say that.

George: (*Preoccupied*) Some other time.

Barbara: (*Beat*) I guess what they say about you is true.

George: What do they say?

Barbara: That you have no life.

George: They say that?

Barbara: You've got to loosen up a little, George.

George: (*Defensively*) I can celebrate when I want to. (*Takes a bottle and two glasses out of his desk drawer*) I was saving this for New Years, but let's have a toast. (*Fills their glasses*)

Barbara: (*Looking at the bottle*) Lagavulin. That's excellent Scotch.

George: What do they mean I don't have a life?

Barbara: (*Touching her glass to George's*) A toast. To us. To the book.

George: (*Pause*) We've come a long way.

Barbara: We started an entire field: Comstock studies.

George: All those articles in the *Journal of History.*

Barbara: And our first book, *The Comstock Reader.*

George: And you can't forget the *Comstock Encyclopedia.*

Barbara: We started the National Association of Comstock Scholars.

George: But, it's a major publisher this time. It's the definitive biography. We're talking thousands of readers.

Barbara: It's hard to believe.

(*They pause as the excitement gives way to a more somber mood.*)

Barbara: What's the matter? Something wrong?

George: It's nothing.

Barbara: I can tell something's wrong. What is it?

George: The book looks magnificent.

Barbara: You're not thinking about....You are. You're worried about McBride aren't you.

George: (*Sitting back down in his chair*) I'm a little distracted by it, yes.

Barbara: We have to trust Ivan. He'll take care of it.

George: (*Cheering up*) Of course he will. (*Pours Barbara another drink*)

Scene 6

The next day. The dissertation committee is assembled for the official "defense" meeting. A surreal and minimalist scene with Russ McBride under a spotlight at center stage. He is flanked on the right by George Fackler and on the left by Barbara McPhee and Ivan Sellars. All stand in a line facing and speaking to the audience. Russ nervously fields rapid-fire questions. The scene conveys the same type of tension found in a police interrogation of a suspect sweating under the hot glare of a bright light. As the scene begins, the meeting is well underway.

George: Are you questioning the founder's judgment?

Russ: I'm just saying he had a narrow definition of obscenity. He couldn't place pictures of the human anatomy in context. That's why he arrested medical doctors for distributing books on sexuality. He suppressed valuable information and many people suffered for it. I'm just making an observation.

George: But, did he not save thousands of children from the evils of pornography? We have to examine Anthony Comstock's actions from a religious perspective. People needed a clear standard back then. Why focus on the exception when the intent was clearly moral?

Russ: It's not a matter of focusing on the exception, it's just historical analysis. It's what the data tell us. I'm not looking for anything in a biased way.

George: We value research, but not when it undermines the mission of this university.

Russ: (*Frustrated*) Yes, but you're not getting the main point. My dissertation is about the divergently correct perspectives of Anthony Comstock and Walt Whitman and how they created different approaches to art and literature.

Barbara: I don't like the term *divergently correct*. Religiously speaking, how can something be divergently correct?

Russ: Comstock and Whitman were members of two distinct interpretive communities. Both communities nurtured different worldviews, each with a moral foundation.

George: Interesting, but why do you imply that Anthony Comstock participated in a terrible crime? A murder, no less. Don't you realize what this could do to the university?

Russ: I'm just describing documents, not drawing conclusions.

Barbara: (*Suspiciously*) Really, Russ. Is that all you're doing?

Russ: (*Defensive and adversarial*) Isn't that why we do research? The pursuit of truth, right? You teach it, but we better not do it.

George: I believe I've heard enough.

Barbara: More than enough.

Ivan: Russ could I ask you to step outside while we deliberate. (*Russ exits the stage. Ivan, Barbara, and George continue to speak directly to the audience*) Let's not make this bigger than it is.

George:	He was warned. We have no choice but to fail him. There is no redeeming value in this study.
Barbara:	How can we grant a P-H-D when he suggests the founder was a criminal?
Ivan:	Barbara, Let's be careful about what we're doing here. What about his future? I'll convince him to alter the controversial section. Let's find a middle ground so he can get on with his life. He has great promise as a professor. We shouldn't stand in the way of that.
George:	(*Pause*) I vote to fail. He's had his chance.
Barbara:	That's my vote as well. He fails. Sorry.
Ivan:	(*Upset*) This is crap, both of you know it. We've never failed a doctoral candidate. We've passed dissertations not nearly as good as this one.
Barbara:	(*Aggressively*) Ivan, he had plenty of chances; it's too late. We don't have a choice.

Scene 7

Two years later on a winter afternoon in mid-November. Split Scene: (1) The People's Bookstore. Kay Kendell is absorbed in her work behind the cash register as Russ McBride enters unnoticed. (2) The office of George Fackler. George and Barbara are talking.

Russ:	(*Timidly*) Hi.
Kay:	(*Looking up, she recognizes him and shakes her head*) Hi? That's it? You come back here and just say Hi?
Russ:	I want my job back.
Kay:	(*Resuming her work*) You've got to be kidding. Forget it.
Russ:	I need a job. I'm out of money.
Kay:	(*Sarcastically*) Okay, you're hired. And any time you feel like taking a 2-year lunch break, go ahead.
Russ:	That's all it's been, 2 years?
Kay:	(*Calming down*) You walk in here like nothing happened.
Russ:	(*Interrupting*) Kay, I'm sorry.
Kay:	You never even said goodbye.
Russ:	I couldn't.
Kay:	So, why'd you come back?
Russ:	(*More assertively*) I need a job, I told you.
Kay:	(*More calmly*) Are you okay? You look tired.
Russ:	I'm fine.
Kay:	Why'd you really come back?

Russ:	I don't know.
Kay:	I know why. Revenge.
Russ:	(*Sarcastically*) Well, maybe you don't know everything.
Kay:	Fackler and McPhee. You want to even the score.
Russ:	So, what's wrong with a little revenge? It's an underrated emotion if you ask me.
Kay:	Don't you ever learn? Fackler and McPhee are just puppets. You got steamrolled by an institution.
Russ:	(*Amused*) I love it when you talk like a socialist. (*Beat*) Maybe I came back for other reasons.
Kay:	(*A short pause as their eyes meet*) Just friends, remember?
Russ:	Who decided that?
Kay:	Just friends.
Russ:	So, I'm back on the payroll?
Kay:	(*Picks up the cash register receipt off the counter and begins reading it*) All right, I'll give you one more shot. You can sleep in the back until you get a place.
Russ:	(*Also gazing at the register tape*) Looks like we sold a lot of books today.
Kay:	Two hundred and seventy books so far this month. Stuff on UFOs, Duke Ellington, Abstract Expressionism, and the Rolling Stones. Lots of romance novels. Four paperback Catcher in the Ryes. A ton of Cliff's Notes.
Russ:	(*Looking around*) The store looks different. (*Taking off his jacket*) Should I shelve that stack over there?
Kay:	Why not?
Russ:	(*Talks as he shelves books*) You added more bookcases.
Kay:	We built a small lecture hall upstairs. We have weekly author forums.
Russ:	Really. Who are some of the authors?
Kay:	Abbie Hoffmann.
Russ:	I should have guessed.
Kay:	Where'd you go for 2 years?
Russ:	(*Evading the question, he looks at a book title*) The Electric Kool Aid Acid Test by Tom Wolfe. What a great book.
Kay:	Amusing, but I wouldn't say, "great." You missed our 10th anniversary. (*She pauses to fondly gaze around the store*) Two weeks ago I bought 20 antique leather-bound volumes.
Russ:	I guess there's money in used books after all.
Kay:	Oh, definitely.
Russ:	Can I see the antique books?
Kay:	If you tell me where you went.

Russs:	(*Still shelving books, he pauses before responding*) That night after the defense, I called my dad. "Hello, dad. Things didn't work out. I failed my defense. No, I can't repeat the class. No, I can't rewrite the research paper. No, I probably won't be a professor." He tried to understand, but he was disappointed, you can't blame him.
Kay:	Did you go home?
Russs:	Nope. Hawaii. The North Shore of Oahu.
Kay:	I knew it. The island fantasy escape. Sit on a beach and all your cares disappear. Men love that myth.
Russs:	Got a job at Sunset Pizza, across the street from the bluest ocean I'd ever seen.
Kay:	I can just see you strumming the ukulele all day.
Russs:	Just trying to forget.
Kay:	Did it work?
Russs:	For a few weeks.
Kay:	Make any friends?
Russs:	Oh, yeah. My escapist buddies. Successful people, former accountant, a dentist from Detroit. Dropped out just like me. We sat on the beach, ate fresh pineapple, told stories.
Kay:	Then, you ran out of stories.
Russs:	Something like that.
Kay:	You can't forget, and you shouldn't try.
Russs:	The first night I slept on the beach gazing at this magnificent sky. In the middle of the Pacific the stars are so bright. I thought of Whitman's poem, *A Clear Midnight.* "Away from books, away from art, the day erased, the lesson done."
Kay:	You were homeless most of the time.
Russs:	How do you know?
Kay:	Your skin's been overexposed to the sun and you've lost weight. You drank too much over there.
Russs:	I suppose.
Kay:	When did the anger hit the fever point?
Russs:	(*Assertively*) What's with this anger thing? About a week ago.
Kay:	You feel guilty too.
Russs:	That would also be correct.
Kay:	Why?
Russs:	Maybe I did tarnish a man's good name, I don't know.
Kay:	(*Irritated*) You exposed a fraud is what you did.
Russs:	That's what I like about you. No doubts.
Kay:	What you need is some advice.

Russ:	From you, I suppose.
Kay:	(*Assertively*) You're going to appeal the decision.
Russ:	I don't think so.
Kay:	You've been planning it for 2 years.
Russ:	(*Smiling*) Sort of.
Kay:	Yes you have.
Russ:	I have a strong case.
Kay:	Yes you do.

George:	(*Concerned*) Is everything okay? When I didn't see you at the faculty meeting, I thought something must be up.
Barbara:	We had a faculty meeting today? (*Handing him a letter*) Here, read this.
George:	Okay. (*Takes the letter and reads it out loud*) Dear Professors Barbara McPhee and George Fackler, It is our great pleasure to inform you that your book, *Anthony Comstock, Forgotten Hero* has been awarded the Wordsmith Prize for distinguished biography. The judges, who consist of academics, critics, and authors were unanimous in praising your work as a great contribution, one that is certain to have lasting influence. With this award also comes a check for $5,000. Congratulations and best wishes as you pursue future projects. Sincerely, Wesley M. Peterson, President of the Wordsmith Awards Foundation.
Barbara:	What do you think of that?
George:	I think it's an excellent letter.

Kay:	(*Finishing typing*) Now, that's an excellent letter.
Russ:	(*Sarcastically*) We mail it today and I get my doctorate next week, right?
Kay:	You get a hearing before a panel of old fart professors who don't have the guts to rock the boat. But, we have to take our shot, right? And, if they turn you down, so what? Who said you have to have a P-H-D?
Russ:	Oh yeah, like I can just hang a shingle on the door that says, "Historian." People will make appointments and I'll charge them a fee for historical counseling.
Kay:	Ever heard of public intellectuals? Lewis Mumford, Susan Sontag, Tom Wolfe, Allen Ginsberg, Abbie Hoffman.
Russ:	Abbie Hoffman?
Kay:	Not a professor among them.
Russ:	Abbie Hoffman's a public intellectual huh. I'll have to think that over.

Kay:	They had ideas. Some of them spoke right here in this bookstore. (*Getting sidetracked*)
Russ:	Really? Susan Sontag? Tom Wolfe?
Kay:	No, Abbie Hoffman.
Russ:	(*Frowning*) I knew it.
Kay:	Know what he said? Read good books and stay out of college.
Russ:	Abbie Hoffman said that?
Kay:	And Aristotle.
Russ:	Aristotle. They didn't have colleges back then. At least not the kind you're thinking of.
Kay:	(*Interrupting*) Great scholars don't need institutions.
Russ:	You never went to college?
Kay:	I didn't say that.

George:	This comes at the right time. Perhaps we can leverage the Wordsmith Award into some kind of Comstock Center for Responsible Media or something.
Barbara:	I like what we're saying. Extend Comstock's legacy of family protection into the domain of contemporary media and popular culture.
George:	It's time to translate Comstock's philosophies into practical programs.
Barbara:	Through the Center, people will know the true Anthony Comstock.

Kay:	It's about time people knew the true Anthony Comstock.
Russ:	They will. That's why I came back.
Kay:	So, what are you going to say to them?
Russ:	Comstock kept meticulous records. He was always defending himself in his diaries.
Kay:	Why would he write down that he murdered someone?
Russ:	Intense guilt, for one thing.
Kay:	If it's on campus, Peter will find it; he knows every inch of that place.
Russ:	If he'll help me.
Kay:	You could have called him before you left. He was hurt by that. We stuck it out while you did your Hawaii thing. He came by the store several times asking about you.
Russ:	I'm gonna go see him. (*A pause as their eyes meet. Russ leans forward to kiss her, but Kay pulls back*)
Kay:	No, I can't.

Russ:	(*Embarrassed*) Yeah, you're right.
Kay:	Get back to work.
Russ:	No, let's talk about this. Why can't we be more than friends?
Kay:	Because we're different.
Russ:	Different how?
Kay:	I don't know, it's hard to explain. We're not loyal to the same things.
Barbara:	Do you think this could really happen? I mean it takes millions to build a center like that.
George:	The President said they're close to a very large gift that could involve new centers and even buildings. He wants our ideas.
Russ:	You say that, but I don't understand it.
Kay:	We're oceans apart.
Russ:	Why am I inferior because I want to teach at a university? We can't all drop out; some of us have to get degrees and go to work. I don't have a bundle of money from daddy to start up a little playhouse bookstore.
Kay:	Oh, and the playhouse bookstore is less valid than that anti-intellectual bureaucratic morass over there that calls itself a university?
Russ:	It's not the only university.
Kay:	They're all the same. And the people that come out of them are all the same. Like you. No guts.

Scene 8

A week later in the office of George Fackler. George, Barbara, Ivan, and Dean Christina Martinez are assembled for a meeting. They sit around a conference table.

Christina:	Thanks for getting everyone together, George.
George:	No problem. You have the floor.
Christina:	I received a letter from Russell McBride, a former student in this department. He's appealing your decision to fail his doctoral dissertation 2 years ago. School policy affords him a hearing before the College Appeals Committee. I've reviewed the documentation as well as the dissertation itself. This is your chance to fill me in on some of the details.
George:	(*Confidently*) Dean, this was difficult, and I know the disappointment Russ must feel. But, when a student says hey,

there's been a murder, let's see if the university founder did it, well, that's a clear honor code violation.

Christina: You're sure that's what he was trying to say?

George: Yes, and without one shred of supporting evidence.

Barbara: Dean, I like Russ. But, somewhere along the line he lost sight of our mission. And, now we've got a loose cannon situation.

George: I feel for Russ, but this is not just any university. It's one of the last remaining bastions of higher education where the sacred and the secular are integrated. We must not fail in our efforts to preserve the good reputation of this school.

Christina: Ivan, you chaired the committee. What's your take on this?

Ivan: (*Assertively*) He deserved to pass. It was a good piece of research. (*Getting increasingly upset*) Here's one of our best students, just trying to be thorough. And we ruin his career. Do you know where he's been for the past 2 years? Homeless. Lost.

George: Sorry to hear that.

Ivan: (*Aggressively*) I'm glad I don't have this on my conscience. You two sleeping okay?

Christina: While there are strong feelings, I expect that cool heads will prevail. (*Pause*) Okay, then. Feel free to come by the office if you want to discuss this further. Otherwise, I'll see you at the hearing.

George: Thanks, Dean.

(*Everyone stands up and the Dean shakes hands with George before exiting the room. Ivan also exits, leaving Barbara and George alone in his office.*)

Barbara: Well, he's going through with it.

George: (*Sitting down at his desk*) It'll be over before you know it.

Barbara: Do you think he has anything?

George: How could he have anything? They'll never find it. That's one thing we're good at here at Comstock, hiding things.

Barbara: He's quite determined.

George: He's hurt, but he'll get over it. Maybe this appeal hearing will convince him to get on with his life.

Barbara: I hope so. (*Pause*) Say, I'm having a few people over tonight. You're invited.

George: Thanks, but I can't.

Barbara: Why not, what are you doing?

George: I'm working on an article.

Barbara: Until how late?

George: (*Impatient*) Late. Barbara, I've got to get to these appointments.

Barbara: Too bad you don't have friends.

George: That's ridiculous.
Barbara: Who?
George: My students. You. Other colleagues.
Barbara: Okay, stay at home this weekend. Do whatever you do.
George: (*Impatiently*) Listen, Barbara. I really have to get going here.
Barbara: (*Moves toward the door*) The invitation's open should you change your mind.

Scene 9

Later that night in Peter Bradford's apartment. The room is tightly cluttered with stacks of documents and articles. Books, newspapers, and other artifacts are everywhere. Photos of past Comstock University athletic teams cover the walls as do posters of past campus events. It's about 10 p.m.

Russ: (*Knocking at the door*) Peter, it's me Russ.
Peter: (*Opening the door*) Russ? Hmmm, I used to know a Russ. (*Russ enters the room and sits in the chair Peter offers him*)
Russ: (*Gazing around the room*) You've got quite a place here. Very eclectic.
Peter: I call it home.
Russ: (*Nodding toward the corner shelf*) Who does that top hat belong to?
Peter: (*Handing the hat to Russ*) Your favorite antivice crusader.
Russ: (*Skeptical*) You mean to tell me this hat belonged to Anthony Comstock?
Peter: Bought it at an auction 20 years ago.
Russ: (*Taking something off one of the shelves*) What's this?
Peter: A deck of cards with girlie pictures. Comstock confiscated it in about 1880.
Russ: Obscene playing cards. Better not let George catch you with those.
Peter: Where the hell you been McBride?
Russ: You might say I took a little trip.
Peter: Kay's been in a funk since you left.
Russ: I just talked to her.
Peter: All forgiven?
Russ: I got my job back. Hey, you sure look good.
Peter: You sure as hell don't.
Russ: Thanks.
Peter: Where'd you get the sunburn?
Russ: Hawaii. It's a long story. Peter, how long have you known Kay?

Peter: Oh, I guess we met when she was teaching at Comstock. A few years ago.

Russ: She taught at Comstock?

Peter: Part-time while she worked on her P-H-D at Brown, I think.

Russ: Brown University?

Peter: Big problems in the classroom, though.

Russ: What kind of trouble?

Peter: (*Trying to remember*) Didn't like giving grades. Instead of A, B, or C, she drew peace signs on the tests. Wouldn't give grades, just peace signs.

Russ: Not surprising really.

Peter: And she told the smart kids not to come to class.

Russ: Why?

Peter: Hell if I know. (*Beat*) Russ, Listen. Sorry about your dissertation. Can't say I didn't warn you, you stupid ass. But, I've been thinking about it. Guess you gotta do what you gotta do.

Russ: I'm going to appeal.

Peter: You should.

Russ: Any ideas?

Peter: (*Taking something out of a plastic bag and handing it to Russ*) Be careful with this.

Russ: (*Delicately turning the pages*) I can't believe it. It's a diary of Anthony Comstock. Where did you get this?

Peter: Turn to the entry for May Seventh, 1909. Know what day that was?

Russ: The day before Anthony Comstock died.

Peter: That's right. Notice anything unusual?

Russ: There's only half a page, it's like the bottom half of the page has been cut out. Do you think…?

Peter: It might say something about that woman, what was her name?

Russ: Iris Crandall. Do you think…?

Peter: Got to be on the campus somewhere.
(*A knock at the door. Peter quickly puts the diary in a desk drawer and lets Kay in. She has a pizza and a six-pack of beer.*)

Kay: Best pizza in the world, right here.

Peter: Harry's Pizza. The best.

Kay: (*Places the pizza on the table*) C'mon, let's eat. (*They sit down and begin eating and drinking beer*)

Russ: That's what I missed about this town. Harry's Pizza. (*He grabs a slice and takes a huge bite*)

Kay: Russ, you know Peter made quite a few pizzas in his time.

Russ: Where?

Peter:	At Harry's. When I was a graduate student.
Russ:	Wait a minute. You were a graduate student? (*Beat*) Why didn't you tell me?
Peter:	You never asked. (*A slight pause as they continue eating*) First, I want to hear about the festival. Kay went to some festival where everyone was nude.
Russ:	Woodstock?
Kay:	Yeah, I went up there. It was wonderful. Everybody helping each other. The communal ideal. Half a million people sitting in a pasture listening to Jimi Hendrix.
Russ:	Half a million? How close were you to the stage?
Kay:	Very close. I could see the sweat on the performers' faces. Pete Townsend of the Who threw his guitar into the audience.
Russ:	So? He always does that.
Kay:	It bonked me on the head.
Russ:	You made that up. But, I want to know why you both have been holding back. Kay, you went to Brown and Peter was a graduate student?
Kay:	Well, I helped lead the tuition strike. We made a circle around the Administration Building and refused to let people in.
Russ:	Did you get arrested?
Kay:	Suspended from school for a year. But, they lowered the tuition the next semester. What happens is someone sticks their neck out, and change comes later.
Russ:	Nothing like that happens at Comstock.
Kay:	Your appeal. That's got an element of rebellion.
Russ:	Yeah, right.
Kay:	Others will benefit from what you're doing. It'll be a little easier for the next person.
Russ:	Now, Peter, you were a graduate student? At Comstock?
Kay:	You two have a lot in common. Wrote dissertations and never got degrees.
Peter:	Except that MY COMMITTEE loved me.
Russ:	I can't believe this.
Peter:	Should I tell him the story? Kay's heard it so many times.
Kay:	Embellish it a little. Make it more interesting.
Peter:	I was in the sociology P-H-D program at Comstock. Finished all my courses. I was on the short list for a job at Indiana University. (*He pauses to take a sip of beer*) My dissertation was about gambling in New York immigrant life before the turn of the century.
Russ:	They gambled a lot back then?

Peter:	More than in Vegas.
Russ:	Comstock tried to wipe it out.
Peter:	Had a chapter on why he failed. But, on to the juicy part. Two weeks before my defense, I'm eating in the cafeteria editing my dissertation. I get up to go to the men's room. It takes like 10 minutes. When I get back to the table it's gone. I went nuts.
Russ:	Someone stole your dissertation. You had copies right?
Peter:	Would I be here telling you this if I did? I only had a copy of the first chapter.
Russ:	How long…
Peter:	(*Interrupting*) Two hundred and eighty-seven pages.
Russ:	Ouch.
Peter:	So, I changed my career goals.
Kay:	He threw in the towel is what he did.
Peter:	Whatever you say.
Kay:	But, now he's the head janitor.
Peter:	Head of custodial services, I beg your pardon.
Russ:	What did you tell your committee?
Kay:	This is the good part.
Peter:	I didn't tell them anything. I never went back.
Kay:	(*Taking a bite of pizza*) Now you know why he's still at Comstock.
Russ:	To find his dissertation.
Peter:	You might say all three of us are looking for something.
Kay:	Peter and I, we're with you on this appeal thing. You need all the help you can get.
Russ:	(*Beat*) Thanks. (*Softly*) I really appreciate this. More than you realize.
Kay:	Just don't be late for work.
Russ:	You think I have a chance?
Peter:	Hell, no. But, it should be a good time.
Kay:	(*Passing out tablets of paper and pens*) So, tell us what to do.
Peter:	It's time to dust off my research tools.
Russ:	It's time for the nightshift anthropologist to go to work.

ACT 2

Scene 1

A chilly November afternoon on the main lawn of the campus of Comstock University. The student guide continues the official tour of Comstock University. She is center stage and speaks to the audience as if it were taking the walking tour.

Guide:	Some people ask, "What's the most important building on campus?" That's a tough question, but coming up on your left is the Comstock Library, which some say is the heart of the university. We're particularly proud of the Comstock Archive which houses the founder's papers and writings. They say it has 10,000 documents pertaining to Anthony Comstock. Don't ask me what they're about, I haven't had time to read them yet.

Scene 2

Late afternoon. Split Scene: (1) The Peoples' Bookstore. (2) George Fackler's office. It's 2 weeks before the appeal hearing. Russ, Kay, and Peter are seated at a table.

Russ:	Well, what did the nightshift anthropologist come up with?
Kay:	I've been waiting all day for this.
Peter:	Boy, have I got data! (He proceeds to dump the contents of two waste paper baskets on the table creating separate piles of objects) These are the discards of Barbara McPhee. The next pile is George Fackler's.
Kay:	This is a little creepy.
Peter:	It's a common method in field studies.
Kay:	Looking in someone's trash? Without permission? (*Leans forward, poking her finger into one of the piles as she examines the objects*) What do you think, Russ?
Peter:	It was picked up yesterday by the afternoon crew. It's public property now. That's the law.
Russ:	(*Eye-balling a fingernail file from McPhee's trash*) Most of this is innocuous. I guess it's okay to take a look.
Kay:	(*Takes a newspaper from McPhee's pile*) Hmmm. The *New York Review of Books*. Makes sense.
Russ:	(*Examining a ticket stub from Fackler's pile*) Looks like a ticket for horse racing. Fackler a betting man?
Kay:	George Fackler at the races. Hard to believe.
Russ:	Peter, why are we looking at this stuff?
Peter:	You have to understand the opposition! This stuff explains their motives.
Russ:	Are you sure it's worth the time? Looks pretty much like random junk.
Peter:	That's where you're wrong, my friend. These are clues. These artifacts represent a theme of a person's life.

Kay: My garbage has a theme? Like what? Peter, do you read trash cans like palm readers read palms?

Peter: It's like breaking a code. (*Examining some of the items in Fackler's trash*) Let's see. What do we have here? Look at this ad in the personals; he wants to meet women. And look at these travel brochures for Las Vegas.

Russ: So what? I like Las Vegas.

Peter: And these sales receipts. (*Examines the receipts*) Looks like he eats at Paul Revere's every Friday night.

Kay: The most expensive place in town.

Peter: Eats there by himself. Can't you see a dominant theme emerging?

Kay: He likes women, food, and travel?

Peter: A lot of ego here. His greatest loyalty is to self.

Kay: You get that out of this?

Peter: Now, McPhee is different; she's introspective. (*Reaches into McPhee's pile*) Four completed crossword puzzles. See what I mean? A crumpled up sheet of paper with very interesting doodles. (*Examining the paper*) She sketches desert scenes and half moons with planets around. Stuff like that. And look at these notices for late library books.

Barbara: Do you think Anthony Comstock was indifferent to art like McBride says?

George: Does it matter?

Barbara: (*Assertively*) Of course it matters. Art is divine. Did Comstock have the ability to appreciate beauty? In everything we've written about him, I don't think we ever addressed that question head on.

George: Of course he did.

Barbara: I was looking at McBride's dissertation last night. He claims Comstock couldn't see beauty. That he was aloof to the lovely things of the world.

George: McBride is wrong.

Barbara: But, you know, Comstock was quite reticent on the point of aesthetics wasn't he.

George: If your job is cleaning up New York City, maybe he just didn't have time.

Barbara: Look around this place. Few paintings and sculptures. And the buildings are so utilitarian. So sterile. So many straight lines; not many interesting architectural features. I have to say that the Administration Building may be the ugliest structure I've ever seen.

George: What's your point? Comstock had other priorities.
Barbara: That's what bothers me.
George: What.
Barbara: That you don't get it. You never talk about art's role in religion either. How God speaks to us through art. It's strange you never think about that. You walk by gardens without noticing. You rarely listen to music.
George: That's ridiculous. I can see you don't know me at all.

Russ: Peter, don't be offended, but I think this is a waste of time.
Peter: You've got to read the code. Her artifacts say she's authentic; really searching for something. For the love of it.
Russ: Okay, let's say you're right. How does that help us?
Peter: The key to George is his ego, and the key to Barbara is her sense of discovery. Appeal to those motives and these people will tell us a lot. They'll give us what we want.
Kay: I think Peter's right. I think I know how we might use this information.

Scene 3

Paul Revere's, an upscale restaurant. George Fackler sits alone at a table for two. Within a few seconds Kay Kendell, in disguise, approaches the table and introduces herself as Megan Thomas. Her hair is pulled back and she wears glasses. She is nicely dressed.

Kay: George Fackler? Are you George Fackler?
George: (*Startled*) Yes. Do I know you?
Kay: (*They shake hands*) No, no. I recognized your picture from the book jacket. I know you must get this all the time, but I loved your book on Anthony Comstock. (*Removes a copy from her bag*) Would you autograph my copy? I just bought it at the Peoples' Bookstore.
George: Yes, of course. (*Takes her pen and signs the book*)
Kay: I can't tell you how much this means to me.
George: And, you are?
Kay: Oh, I'm sorry. I forgot to introduce myself. Megan Thomas. From Cambridge, Mass.
George: It's a pleasure and I'm glad you liked the book.
Kay: Sorry, for interrupting you. (*Assertively, she sits down at the table*) Can I join you for dinner?
George: (*Cautious*) Yes, yes of course.

Kay: I love Italian food.
George: You look familiar. Have we met?
Kay: I don't think so. Are you ever in Cambridge, Mass?
George: No, but you seem familiar. Oh, well.
Kay: This is amazing. I can't believe it. Can I ask you questions about your book?
             (*The server hands them menus and takes their order for drinks*)
George: Uh, let me see. A white wine. Vidal Blanc, yes. Do you know that wine, Megan?
Kay: No, I don't believe I do.
George: Oh, you must try it, then. It has a delicate fruity bouquet; it's a well-balanced, dry wine. Superb with veal.
Kay: (*Studying the menu*) It sounds delicious.
George: It's a little sweet, but not flabby, with an interesting after taste.
Kay: (*Smiling at the waiter*) We're both having the Vidal Blanc.
Server: Excellent choice. (*He leaves to get their drinks*)
Kay: You really know your wine.
George: It's half the fun of dining out.
Kay: I went to a wine-tasting party once. People sitting around talking about the same glass of wine for 5 hours. I loved it.
George: So, what are you having for the main course?
Kay: (*Looking at the menu*) You mentioned veal.
George: It's excellent here.
Kay: (*Smiling*) Seems like all I eat is chicken these days.
George: The chicken is good here also.
Kay: Tell me about your work.
George: I'm chair of the History Department at Comstock University. We have seven professors on our faculty.
Kay: History professor. I'm envious.
George: What do you do?
Kay: Librarian. I archive and preserve 19th century American documents.
George: (*Intrigued*) Sounds like you're also an historian.
Kay: I guess, in a way. (*Flirting*) I can't believe I'm having dinner with a famous author.
George: (*Flattered*) It's an honor to have dinner with you as well.
Kay: What a fascinating man Comstock was. We need more people like that today.
George: One of a kind.
Kay: Do you think you'll win a Pulitzer?
George: (*Taken aback*) Well, actually we just found out that we won the Wordsmith for biography.

Kay: Congratulations! You deserve it. You tell a story that's never been told. Anthony Comstock's the true American icon. The embodiment of American values.

George: Unfortunately, his contributions have been overlooked.

Kay: That's too bad. It's refreshing to read about someone who says, "Hey, we've had enough" and then cleans things up.

George: Exactly. We have an annual convention on Comstock's life. Perhaps you'd like to attend?

Kay: Yes I would. Will you be there? I'd love to hear you speak.

George: Yes, yes, I'll be there.

Server: What would you like this evening?

Kay: I'll have the veal based on the recommendation of this gentleman. (*She glances at George and smiles*)

George: I'll have the same.

Server: Excellent. (*Exits to process their order*)

Kay: Comstock had quite a personality didn't he? Arresting hundreds of people all over town and confiscating lewd books and pornography. You must know some really interesting stories.

George: Lots of stories, yes.

Kay: Tell me one that isn't in the book.

George: (*Clearly enjoying the conversation*) Let me see. Oh, yes. When Comstock was a boy about 10, I think, his parents told him about the evils of alcohol and that bars were dens of iniquity. So, he breaks into this pub after closing time, opens all the taps of the huge barrels of ale and lets them drain all night onto the floor and out the door into the street. The whole neighborhood smelled like beer.

Kay: (*Absorbed by the story*) You're kidding me! What a little party pooper!

George: (*Confused by her comment*) Something like that.

Kay: Your book said that he rounded up all kinds of obscene books and photographs. From a librarian's perspective, I'm curious about how he stored this material so that it wasn't easily accessible to the public.

George: He used several censorship techniques, some dating back to the early days of the printing press.

Kay: (*Pretending to be absorbed by what he's saying*) I don't want to interrupt, but I want you to know how fascinating this is. Go on.

George: One such method is to bind the pages of a controversial book with a cover of a mundane work. Such as taking, for example, Kate Chopin's *The Awakening* and placing it inside the cover of, say, the *Dictionary of Accounting*. Important documents could also be hidden in the disguised volume.

Kay: I find this so fascinating.

George: Another thing they did was to actually hollow-out the inside of a book, actually cut out the center of the pages so that a smaller book or document could actually be stored inside a larger one.

Kay: Have you actually seen this kind of thing?

George: Oh, many times. Comstock did this kind of stuff all the time. We have much of it in our own library. He got the ideas from 15th century European monasteries.

Kay: So, what would keep people from accidentally stumbling upon these altered books?

George: Oh, they never go back on the regular shelves. They're kept in special storage rooms or even stored in locked cases. Mostly in library basements.

Kay: So, you must have some juicy things in your library.

George: Unique indeed.

Scene 4

The next day in the office of Barbara McPhee. Barbara reads at her desk listening to classical music. Peter Bradford knocks at the door.

Peter: Professor McPhee, got a minute?

Barbara: (*Looking up from her book*) Yes?

Peter: I'm Peter Bradford.

Barbara: Yes, of course. Come in.

Peter: I know you're busy, but first I want to say how much I enjoyed your new book.

Barbara: Thanks. How can I help you?

Peter: One thing I enjoy about working at the university is the library. I read a lot of history.

Barbara: Are you a student?

Peter: No, I'm the head custodian. Used to be a student. I read anything I can get my hands on by Anthony Comstock. It's part of my personal study.

Barbara: Good for you.

Peter: I was reading one of his diaries from the Comstock Archive. And it was really strange. One of the pages had been cut out of the bound volume.

Barbara: (*Startled by his interest in the missing page*) Have you discussed it with a librarian?

Peter:	I have. They don't know any more than I do about it.
Barbara:	Just because a page has been cut, doesn't mean it has significance. It may have been blank to begin with.
Peter:	No, if you examine the page closely, you can see that the top of a line of writing has been cut off.
Barbara:	Libraries have always edited their materials. Who knows, 80 years ago someone probably thought the section was superfluous and cut it out. In hindsight, of course, we know that was the wrong thing to do.
Peter:	So, let's say something like that did happen. Is there a chance the missing page is stored somewhere in the library?
Barbara:	(*A little nervous*) I don't know, I mean, I doubt it. I can check into it if you'd like.
Peter:	Would you? That would be great. Because the page I'm talking about was the last one he wrote before he died. The one he wrote on his deathbed. That page could have an important message on it, do you think?
Barbara:	Umm, yes, I suppose it could.
Peter:	If someone found that page I bet they could write a whole dissertation about it. Something we don't already know about Anthony Comstock.
Barbara:	I think we're getting ahead of ourselves; we simply don't know.
Peter:	I love a good mystery.

Scene 5

A week later in The Peoples' Bookstore. Kay is closing out the register and Russ is shelving books at the end of a busy Friday. The last customers are gone. They talk as they work.

Kay:	So, we're having dinner and I really buttered him up. Got him talking about his work and during the course of the evening he discloses where secret documents are kept.
Russ:	(*Smiling*) Fantastic!
Kay:	And, listen to this. (*Chuckles*) I tell him I'm a librarian and that I'm curious about censorship techniques.
Russ:	Perfect! (*Amused as he shelves books*)
Kay:	I felt terrible.
Russ:	It's for a good cause.
Kay:	I should've gone into acting.
Russ:	So, where's the missing diary page?

Kay:	In books with bogus covers or in books with hollowed-out spaces inside. Either in storage rooms or locked cases in the library basement. Apparently, there's a lot of stuff in that library nobody's supposed to see.
Russ:	We'll get Peter down there to take a look. A fine performance.
Kay:	Academy Award winning.
Russ:	(*Sweeping the floor*) Speaking of acting, come to the movies with us tomorrow. Peter and I are going to see *Citizen Kane* on the big screen.
Kay:	*Citizen Kane*, huh? I'll think about it. You, me, and Peter. All right, I guess.
Russ:	Seven o'clock tomorrow night. Be ready.
Kay:	We deserve a night out.
Russ:	(*Nervously*) I forgot to mention something.
Kay:	What?
Russ:	Peter can't go.
Kay:	What? So, it would just be you and me.

Russ moves toward her and they embrace passionately, kissing and caressing for several seconds. This is interrupted by a knock at the door. Kay gently pushes Russ away and walks to the door and unlocks it. Peter and Ivan enter.

Kay:	Saved by the bell.
Peter:	I brought somebody with me.
Russ:	Hello, Ivan. (*Pause*) Listen, it wasn't your fault.
Ivan:	I want to help.
Russ:	Okay. It's good to have you here. Let's get started. (*Everyone sits around the table*) Kay has learned that secret documents are kept in storage rooms or locked cases in the basement.
Peter:	I'll check it out.
Russ:	Good. Did you learn anything, Peter?
Peter:	I visited Barbara McPhee and asked her to help me find the missing diary page. Told her it was part of my personal study.
Russ:	So, now that they know someone wants this document, they'll probably try to move it.
Ivan:	I think they keep it where it is. George believes these hiding places are impossible to find.
Russ:	I agree. Peter, see if you can find one of these storage rooms or locked cases. And let's go through all the books in George's and Barbara's faculty offices just in case.

Scene 6

The next day in George Fackler's office. George and Barbara are discussing their upcoming lecture and publicity tour.

George: (*Handing her a copy of the itinerary*) Here's the schedule for the tour.

Barbara: (*Taking the paper from George*) What do they have us doing?

George: (*Reading*) "Meet the Press." That's marvelous.

Barbara: It's an important program. They have us on "Meet the Press?"

George: Just me. You're giving a lecture at the Riverside Church in Manhattan.

Barbara: (*Enthused*) Really. That's quite an honor, actually.

George: (*Reading*) Panel discussions at seven bookstores.

Barbara: (*Reading*) Lectures at Harvard, Stanford, and Rutgers.

Barbara: I'm overwhelmed by all this.

George: Very exciting. (*Becoming more serious*) Now, we have to talk.

Barbara: I know.

George: Russ McBride. He'll be looking for it.

Barbara: A custodian was in my office asking questions.

George: He's working with McBride.

Barbara: Really. Personal study, is what he said.

George: What?

Barbara: Nothing. So, do we move it?

George: I say we leave it where it is. They don't have a clue.

Scene 7

The next night. Split Scene: (1) Russ and Kay are shelving volumes in the Peoples' Bookstore. (2) Ivan and Peter (with flashlights) are opening and searching locked cases of books in the basement of the library.

Kay: (*As she shelves books*) I remember when you were writing your dissertation. Every afternoon you'd spread books and papers all over that table over there.

Russ: Notecards everywhere. I thought I'd never finish that thing.

Kay: (*Quoting Whitman from memory*) "O Captain! My Captain! Our fearful trip is done; The ship has weather'd every rack..." (*Looks pointedly at Russ*) What comes next?

Russ: "The prize we sought is won."

Kay: And, so it was.

Russ: The prize was won? No, I'd say the prize was lost.

Kay: You just don't understand the prize.

Russ: Right now I could be standing in a classroom teaching college students.

Kay: Upper-middle-class spoiled brats.

Russ: I could be grading papers this very minute.

Kay: Terrible writers. You wouldn't enjoy it.

Russ: I am enjoying the bookstore, though. (*Quoting Whitman*) "I celebrate myself. And what I assume you shall assume; For every atom belonging to me…" (*Gestures to Kay to complete the line*)

Kay: "As good belongs to you."

Russ: You know your Whitman.

Kay: So, if they change their minds and give you that P-H-D. What happens?

Russ: Who knows.

Kay: (*Interrupting*) What's wrong with working here?

Russ: For a career?

Kay: Why is it that I hate that word so much?

Russ: You've done great things with this place.

Kay: You can be part of it.

Russ: It's not what I want.

Kay: You don't know what you want.

Russ: (*Interrupting*) I know the world doesn't revolve around this store.

Kay: (*Sarcastically*) Oh, so it revolves around Cornell or Syracuse I suppose.

Russ: Bookstores and universities are different. Don't you think?

Kay: All I know is they come in here with fluff on their minds and leave with real books in their shopping bags.

Russ: So, what's your point, that you know how to browbeat people into reading books *you* like?

Kay: My point is that people don't have to go to universities to learn. Most people have no association with universities, don't you realize that? Being the big man off campus is better than being the big man on campus.

Russ: You're quite the academic bartender.

Kay: (*Removes a stack of books from a table*) This isn't just a store; people learn things here. I discover something new every day.

Russ: Really? You seem more like a knowledge preserver than a knowledge seeker.

Kay: Not true. One time this older gentleman walks in and says, "Where are your Bibles?" I told him this wasn't a religious bookstore.

Russ: Politely, I hope.

Kay: Then he asked whether the Bible could be read as a work of literature or history.

Russ: Smart guy.

Kay: Okay, so now we have 20 copies. And a huge religion section.

Russ: I can't see myself working here 10 years from now.

Kay: At some point you've got to let go of this Utopian dream you have about universities. Some day you'll learn there are no perfect situations.

Russ: You've got it figured out, sounds like.

Kay: (*Serious and more assertive*) There's one thing I know. You can't let people like Fackler and McPhee get in your way.

Russ: I haven't let them, I mean, that's why we're appealing the decision.

Kay: Aside from that. Where's your research? What have you written in the last 2 years?

Russ: That's my business.

Kay: A real scholar would have kept working. A real scholar wouldn't care what some chumps at the college had to say.

Russ: I don't know why I stopped writing.

Kay: Because you care too much about your *career.*

Ivan: Look at these books on sex. (*Pulling a book out from inside another book*) They've been placed inside larger books on cell biology and then sealed in this locked case.

Peter: (*Removes another stack of books*) Look, "World Book Encyclopedias," but they're really research papers and doctoral dissertations.

Ivan: What are they about?

Peter: Human anatomy, it looks like. (*Quickly leafing through the volumes*) And some of them are about Comstock. (*Hands a few of them to Ivan who skims their content*)

Ivan: Listen to this. (*Reading the title*) "The Depiction of Anthony Comstock in Popular Fiction." Interesting.

Peter: (*Opening another volume*) Wait a minute … (*Stunned by what he discovers*)

Ivan: (*Reading, he doesn't notice Peter's reaction at first*) What did you find? (*When Peter doesn't respond, he takes the volume from him*)

Peter: I found it.

Ivan: (*Reading the title*) The missing diary page? No, it's your…

Peter: (*Interrupting*) Yep, it sure as hell is.

Ivan:	Your dissertation.
Peter:	Every page. (*He picks up a stack of books and hurls them across the room in anger*) It was that bastard, George Fackler. He took my dissertation and locked it in this case. Now it's time to pay him a call. (*He starts for the door*) With this crowbar.
Ivan:	Peter, wait. (*Grabs his arm*) I know you're upset, don't do anything rash, put that down. (*Tries to take the crowbar from him*)
Peter:	(*Walking away*) Nothing rash my friend. Just gonna beat his brains out, that's all.

Russ:	It must be nice having all the answers.
Kay:	I speak my mind.
Russ:	So, I work here forever?
Kay:	As my assistant. If it works out, we could be partners some day.
Russ:	That's very generous, but I don't think so.
Kay:	You could run the educational programs. Author lectures and events. Things like that.
Russ:	Kay.
Kay:	But, maybe you don't have what it takes.
	(*The phone rings. Peter is on the line as Russ answers. The scene converges with both actors talking to each other by phone.*)
Russ:	(*Answering the phone*) The Peoples' Bookstore.
Ivan:	We found Peter's dissertation in Fackler's office.
Russ:	You're kidding. I'm coming over.
Ivan:	Peter left in a rage; he's going after George. You better do something fast. He's got a crowbar.
Russ:	Oh, Great. Okay, bye.
Kay:	What's happening?
Russ:	(*Puts on his coat and heads toward the door*) Get your coat, let's go.

Scene 8

A press conference. Dean Christina Martinez of Comstock University speaks to reporters from behind a podium bearing the university's logotype. She faces the audience.

Christina: Let me welcome members of the press to our campus. This morning I received a phone call from the Elizabeth Hart Foundation confirming that Comstock University will receive $15 million for the establishment of the Anthony Comstock Center for Responsible Media. A new building will be constructed at the heart of the campus just south of the Administration Building. (*Turns to George and Barbara*) We are deeply grateful for this generous gift and convey our appreciation to Elizabeth Hart. And I must also recognize the exhaustive efforts of Professors George Fackler and Barbara McPhee who were instrumental in bringing this about. Before I take your questions, let me also pay tribute to someone else. Without the courageous deeds of our founder, Anthony Comstock almost a hundred years ago, all this would not have been possible. We celebrate his unwavering defense of the family and disdain for profanity in the arts. Much of what we see in today's mass media is unsavory and offensive to Christian values. It is hoped that through the educational efforts of this center that thousands will acquire the critical skills necessary to use mass media optimally and in ways consistent with their religious standards. I will now take your questions.

Scene 9

A room on the Comstock campus 3 days later. The appeal hearing has just begun. The dean and members of the Appeals Panel sit behind a table. A podium is set up across the room. Russ, Kay, George, Barbara and other participants sit in chairs on both sides of the table. Dean Christina Martinez is explaining the procedures and is concluding her opening remarks.

Christina: Are there any questions before we begin? (*Pauses and glances around the room*) If not, let's start with Professor Fackler.
(*George walks to the podium and then addresses the panel*)

George: Good morning. Russell McBride was a promising student and researcher. But, to earn the doctorate at Comstock University, one must respect the mission of the School as well as demonstrate scholarship. The suggestion that Anthony Comstock may have been involved in the death of Iris Crandall has no basis in fact. There's not one shred of evidence. This dissertation is a violation of the Honor Code. All procedures were properly followed in its evaluation. While we understand Mr. McBride's deep disappointment, we see no reason to overturn the decision. If we give this a pass we would be supporting a rumor that could destroy the university's credibility. What allows us to do good in the world? Comstock's good name. Take that away, and we have no university. Our great moral cause has much to gain with an exemplary university, and much to lose if doubt is created about the founder of that university. Because our founder and our purpose are synonymous. Destroy one and you destroy the other. Therefore, I ask that the appeal be denied.

Panelist 1: (*Interrupting*) Has this claim been made by others that you know of? By other researchers?

George: Not one historian of record has stepped forward with a similar claim.

Panelist 2: If the student had deleted this passage before his defense, would you have passed it?

George: Yes.

Christina: Russell, would you like to question Professor Fackler?

Russ: Yes, Dean. Professor Fackler, you and Barbara McPhee are preeminent researchers of Anthony Comstock. In fact, you established the field of Comstock studies. And isn't it correct that you recently published a biography of Anthony Comstock?

George: That is all correct.

Russ: And, if it was found that Anthony Comstock was involved in a murder, the whole field of Comstock studies could be undermined, is that right?

George: Following your hypothetical, no I don't think it would be undermined. It would just evolve.

Russ: And, how about sales of your book, would they be affected?

George: I have no idea.

Russ: The fact is, you saw my dissertation as a threat to your academic career, is that right?

George: No, I do not feel threatened by your dissertation. The decision was all about principle.

Russ: (*Handing a book to George*) Professor Fackler please examine this volume and explain what it is to the panel.

George: (*Examining the inside pages*) It looks like a doctoral dissertation for Peter Bradford I believe is the name. From the title, it's about Comstock's efforts to wipe out gambling, it looks like. It doesn't appear to be signed by his committee, though.

Russ: And what does the cover say?

George: (*Reading the cover*) World Book Encyclopedia Volume Nine.

Russ: Can you tell us what you know about this dissertation and why the cover doesn't match the contents?

George: These are matters for librarians. We have a fine staff at the library to address these issues.

Panelist 3: Forgive me, but what does this have to do with the dissertation in question?

Russ:	I'm getting to that. Isn't it true Professor Fackler that you have engaged in censorship activities here at the university as have many professors over the years?
George:	No.
Russ:	Isn't it true that you place controversial books in the wrong covers to make access difficult?
George:	Again, ask the librarians.
Russ:	Isn't it also true that the Honor Code exhorts us to seek truth at all times?
George:	Yes, but what is the truth here? There's no truth in the suggestion that Anthony Comstock was involved in a murder.
Russ:	(*Feeling ill*) Dean Martinez, I'm feeling a little dizzy. Could we take a short break? I need some water.
Christina:	Of course. Are you Okay?
Russ:	I'll be fine. I just need a minute.
Christina:	Let's break for lunch, then. I'll see everyone at one-thirty.

Participants gather up papers and begin exiting the room. Russ and Kay take a walk together. After strolling a bit, they sit on a bench.

Kay:	Hang in there.
Russ:	It's not going very well, is it.
Kay:	You made some good points.
Russ:	Have you heard from Ivan or Peter?
Kay:	They're still looking. Nothing yet.
Russ:	I want this thing over with, now.
Kay:	(*Quoting a line from Whitman*) "The soothing sanity and blitheness of completion."
Russ:	(*Responds with the next line of the poem*) "The pomp and hurried contest-glare and rush are done." I can't believe you know that poem.
Kay:	That's what I like about you.
Russ:	My superb ability to quote Whitman?
Kay:	Yes. And that you believe in something.
Russ:	I better get back. I want to go over my notes.
Kay:	I'll see you this afternoon. (*Touching his cheek*) Don't let down. You know the real Anthony Comstock.

As Russ enters the building, he is stopped by Barbara McPhee. No one else is around.

Barbara:	I think this is what you're looking for. (*Hands him a document sealed in plastic*)

Russ: (*Inspecting the document*) Is this...I can't believe it.

Barbara: It's the missing passage from Comstock's diary.

Russ: (*Speechless*) What does it say?

Barbara: Read it yourself.

Russ: (*Studying the document*) You and George knew about this.

Barbara: Yes.

Russ: Why are you doing this now?

Barbara: You deserve to know the truth.

Russ: But, you and George. This could destroy your careers.

Barbara: Not if you do the right thing.

Russ: What do you mean?

Barbara: I expect you to destroy it.

Russ: (*Stunned*) What? Why would I do that? (*Gesturing to her with the document*) Do you know what this is?

Barbara: It's a new revelation. But, what's the greater good?

Russ: The greater good is that I'm gonna tell people about this.

Barbara: No, you can't. That would be immoral. And you are a moral person.

Russ: I'm a bit confused.

Barbara: Now, at this moment, you have your reward—knowing you did the right thing. But, much has happened since the deed was done. Four thousand students are counting on you to protect this university. The stakes are much higher now.

Russ: The truth is the truth. You're asking me to lie.

Barbara: You did the moral thing once. Now it's time to do it again. (*She exits, as Russ places the document in a file thick with documents*)

Scene 10

The student guide is concluding the tour of the campus. She speaks directly to the audience.

Guide: Follow me now to the south lawn. To your right is the site of the $15 million Comstock Center for Responsible Media; it symbolizes Comstock's future and its commitment to a better world. Perhaps the Center will be completed by your next visit. This concludes our tour of Comstock University today. Please visit us again soon.

Scene 11

The group has reconvened for the appeals hearing.

Russ: I have no further questions for Professor Flacker, Dean Martinez.

Christina: Would you like to call other witnesses?

Russ: (*Evokes disappointment*) No, Dean. Nothing else. I'm finished.

Christina: Are you sure Russell? I hardly think you've made your case sufficiently to overturn the decision.

Russ: (*Solemnly*) I don't have anything else to say about any of this.
            (*A short pause before Christina Martinez speaks*)

Christina: Well, then, we will adjourn to deliberate...

Peter: (*Interrupting, approaches Christina from the back of the room*) Dean, I am sorry to interrupt. I was sweeping the hall and found this document on the floor. Does it have anything to do with your meeting? It looks important.
            (*Realizing what has happened, Russ opens his file folder, looking for the document*)

Christina: (*Takes the document from Peter and reads it. Then, she pauses briefly before speaking.*) What I have here is the document that Russell has been searching for. I recognize the handwriting of Anthony Comstock and I'm going to read it to you now. (*Audible reaction by participants in the room. George and Barbara protest, but quiet down when Christina begins reading.*)

Christina: (*Reading the document out loud*) "September 20, 1915. As I find myself in the sunset of life I feel prompted to give account of an incident that is so horrible that I can barely speak of it. My life has been a rich one of service to God, but now I must give report regarding a terrible event that has been kept secret. On the evening of June 4, 1887, I went to the home of Iris Crandall upset about what she said about me. There she continued to mock our cause and said she would do whatever it took to end our crusade for morality. She said her friends in Washington would soon put a stop to our effort. I acted out of anger, silencing her forever. This is my confession. May God be my judge."

Scene 12

Two days later in the Peoples' Bookstore. Russ and Peter are seated at a table. Kay approaches with the morning newspaper.

Kay: OK, here it is. (*Reading an article in the newspaper*) "New Chapter in Comstock History. University Graduate Program Under Fire. Comstock University Dean Christina Martinez announced that two professors, George D. Fackler and Barbara M. McPhee of the History Department were being suspended for a year with-

out pay. Russell McBride and Peter Bradford will be awarded doctoral degrees as a result of the investigation."
(*Lights fade to black*)

End

Epilogue

As we conclude our introduction to media and religion, where precisely does this leave us? Some argue that religion remains a risky topic; it taints the larger discipline of media studies and threatens the empirical standards of science. But this is only a concern if the academic study of religion is confused with theology. If one avoids this assumption, then religion, as an analytical concept, broadens our understanding of media and society in general. Behaviorally, socially, and culturally, media and religion are much closer now. If we are willing to break down some old assumptions and replace them with new outlooks, great opportunities await us both intellectually and professionally.

Much hinges on the broadening of definitions, especially the use of the numinous concept in exploring a wider range of religionlike phenomena. Religion, in its most general sense, provides guidance for life. Today, an endless array of media-based activities extends the options for pursuing such guidance and meaning. It is a development that has been largely unexplored, and this book provides conceptual foundations as a springboard for future study. Why hasn't the concept of the numinous surfaced more often in media studies? Following Machlup (1979), a *stock* of information may exist within a discipline, but institutional barriers often impede the *flow* of knowledge.[1] Wiener (1948) noted this problem over half a century ago, and his assessment still applies:

> The result is like what occurred when the Oregon country was being invaded simultaneously by the United States settlers, the British, the Mexicans, and the Russians—an extricable tangle of exploration, nomenclature, and laws. There are fields ... in which important work has been triplicated or quadruplicated, while still

other important work is delayed by the unavailability in one field of results that may have already become classical in the next field. (p. 2)

This book takes an initial step in synthesizing knowledge about media and religion across disparate fields. Additional work is needed, however.

Is the new field likely to survive and flourish or become relegated to the less illustrious categories of "special subjects" or "occasional topics" in university curricula? Drawing from Machlup and Mansfield's (1983) typology of disciplines, I believe it important that media and religion become a strong *interdiscipline*. According to Littlejohn (1982), an *interdiscipline* is "a field of scholars who identify with various disciplines but share a common interest in a theme that crosses traditional boundaries"(p. 246). The theme that compels us is the ubiquity of religion and the numinous, and how media play an essential part in this phenomenon. Disciplinarity provides the apparatus necessary to expand knowledge of this important trend.

McCarty (2005) notes that full administrative facilities in the academy, such as autonomous departments, budgets, and faculties are lacking where interdisciplines are concerned. In the case of media and religion, despite more courses on the subject, new research centers, and faculty specialization in the area, the field remains in an early stage of development.

As Machlup and Mansfield (1983) point out, interdisciplines respond to needs not adequately addressed by existing fields; in short, they are vital in the pragmatic problem-solving sense. For example, the field of social psychology formed when the larger fields of psychology and sociology were not dealing adequately with the interplay of mind and interhuman activity; likewise, anthropological linguistics came about when neither anthropology nor linguistics fully dealt with the complex relationship between language and culture. In terms of the media–religion interface, no single discipline appears equipped to thoroughly investigate a shift where religion and media have become intertwined in so many strata of culture.

There is a great need for what Griffiths (2000) calls "boundary spanners" or those willing to go beyond what is typically treated in specific subject areas:

These individuals need to have a certain self-assuredness of their position and standing in their originating discipline; be open to new ideas and approaches; be patient enough to learn new modes of discourse (language, both formal and informal), foundational elements and methods; and be creative in applying their home discipline to new areas. (pp. 26–27)

University administrators can promote this self-assuredness by encouraging students to take a class in comparative religion, and by offering regular courses on media and religion. Students should not hesitate to ask questions or write about the subject despite the fact that few textbooks discuss it. As Moran (2010) argues, "the very idea of interdisciplinarity can only be understood in a disciplinary context" (p. ix). Therefore, increasing attention should be paid to theorists who have confronted the subject of religion head on, such as James Carey, John Durham Peters, and Neil Postman, among others.

In closing, let us all take up the challenge of exploring the interplay between media and the numinous more fully. Our awareness of the ritual, belief, and community dimensions of media will increase. As this happens, theorization about media will deepen and develop more fully.

Notes

Chapter 1

1. While it hasn't progressed as far as the sociology of religion, the psychology of religion, or the anthropology of religion, the subfield of the media and religion is making steady progress within the larger discipline of media studies. The International Conference on Media, Religion, and Culture is a leading forum for scholars of the subject. The founding of the Religion and Media Interest Group within the Association for Education in Journalism and Mass Communication (AEJMC) in 1998, and the creation of the *Journal of Media and Religion* in 2002 were also important milestones. University courses on the subject are common and research centers now exist at the University of Colorado, New York University, and the University of Edinburgh. The Knight Chair of Media and Religion has been established at the University of Southern California.

2. The problem of studying the media and religion as "autonomous foci" is eloquently addressed in Carey's (2002) preface to the inaugural issue of the *Journal of Media and Religion*. Hoover's (2001) article, "Religion, Media, and the Cultural Center of Gravity," also deals with this issue.

3. An extensive discussion of media and cultural conflict can be found in Hunter's (1992) book, *Culture Wars: The Struggle to Define America*. Browning et al. (1997) also explore the idea in considerable depth.

4. Several researchers point out the limitations of culture wars analysis in the study of media and religion. See, for example, Stout's (2001) essay, "Beyond Culture Wars: An Introduction to the Study of Religion and Popular Culture," as well as *Virtual Faith* (Beaudoin, 1998) and *Traces of the Spirit* (Sylvan, 2002).

5. A cogent argument for interdisciplinary studies in mass communication can be found in Budd and Ruben's (1979) book, *Beyond Media: New Approaches to Mass Communication*. In that volume, Hitchcock's (1979) essay on religion and mass communication is an early treatment of the subject.

6. An examination of 17 top journals in mass communication and sociology between the end of World War II and 1996 (50 years) revealed only 59 articles providing any data on the relationship between media and religion (Buddenbaum & Stout, 1996, p. 14).

7. Lohrey's (2010) *Speaking of the Numinous: The Meaning of Meaning* presents different scholarly perspectives on the numinous. For an example of ethnographic research using the concept see Sylvan's (2002, 2005) studies of popular music audiences. How psychologists

study and measure the numinous can be found in *The Psychology of Religion: An Empirical Approach* (Spilka, Hood, Hunsberger, & Gorsuch, 2003) as well as Hood (2005). Casement and Tacey's (2006) volume, *The Idea of the Numinous* argues that the numinous is being studied in psychoanalysis, anthropology, sociology, philosophy, and the humanities. A review of Otto's (1958) concept of the numinous can be found in Cipriani (2000). In the field of anthropology, Tuzin (1984) applies the numinous to the study of ritualistic sound and the Alahita Arapesh. Oubre (1997) discusses the evolution of numinous perception from the perspective of medical ethnobotany and consciousness. An empirical investigation of the numinous was conducted by Cameron and Gatewood (2003) in a study of museumgoers. Latham (2007) also explores numinous museum experiences. For a literary analysis of the numinous in modern British fiction see Arthur (1996).

8. "Rentheads" are loyal fans of the Broadway rock musical *Rent.*
9. "Deadheads" is another name for the deeply committed audience of the rock band *The Grateful Dead.*
10. The "Parrotheads" are ardent followers of the rock musician Jimmy Buffett.

Chapter 2

1. For a discussion of challenges facing congregations, see Wuthnow (1988, 1994). The rise of personalized religious worship is explored in depth by Roof (1999); his book, *Spiritual Marketplace: Baby Boomers and the Remaking of American Religion,* chronicles the religious quests of the baby boom generation.
2. Lyotard's (1992) *The Postmodern Explained* and Jameson's (1991) *Postmodernism or the Cultural Logic of Late Capitalism* broaden knowledge of the cultural shifts influencing contemporary approaches to religion.
3. The role of the human brain in trance and ecstatic states is discussed in Becker's (2004) *Deep Listening* and Rouget's (1985) *Music and Trance.*
4. For critiques of the secularization hypothesis see Dobbelaere (1989) and Hadden (1987).
5. The idea that each medium encourages a particular worldview is discussed extensively by Innis (1950, 1951), McLuhan (1964), Meyrowitz (1985), Mumford (1934/1963), and Postman (1985); Mumford (1986) uses the example of the mechanical clock, arguing that it accomplished much more than just providing the time of day; it became a symbol of production, efficiency, and regimen.
6. For a more detailed discussion of prehistorical communication practices, see Marshack (1995). Also see Schmandt-Besserat's (1995) article on the ancient symbol systems that led to primitive writing. Psychological and sociological roots of worship are treated in Evans-Pritchard (1965), *The Theories of Primitive Religion.*
7. The key works by Harold Innis on this subject are *The Bias of Communication* (1951) and *Empire and Communication* (1950). They explore the idea that various media are biased toward particular worldviews. Stone carvings of ancient Egypt, for example, encouraged an emphasis on the preservation of traditions.
8. Scholars exploring religious aspects of the orality-literacy transition were known as the Toronto School of Communication, which included Walter Ong, Harold Innis, Marshall McLuhan, Eric Havelock, and Northrup Frye (see discussion in Gibson, 2010b).
9. According to Ehrenreich (2006), festivals have many functions including the expression of collective joy, diffusing tensions of the working class, and rebellion against the status quo.
10. For a detailed and substantive religious history of the sixties, see Ellwood (1994), *The Sixties Spiritual Awakening: American Religion Moving from Modern to Postmodern.* Also see Lattin (2003), *Following Our Bliss: How the Spiritual Ideals of the Sixties Shape Our Lives Today.*
11. A general discussion of the information society is found in Schement and Curtis (1995), *Tendencies and Tensions of the Information Age.* For a focused examination of religion and

the information society, see Schement and Stephenson's (1996) essay, "Religion and the Information Society."

Chapter 3

1. The subject of mental states is given little attention in the media and religion literature. See Stout and Buddenbaum's (2002a) essay, "Genealogy of an Emerging Field: Foundations for the Study of Media and Religion," which urges researchers to draw more substantively from the field of the psychology of religion.
2. For a general discussion of brain anatomy and emotionality see Gerow (1992). A more focused treatment of the biological aspects of religion can be found in Tanner and Reynolds (1983).
3. Ehrenreich's (2006) book, *Dancing in the Streets: A History of Collective Joy,* discusses the roots of Western cultures' suppression of public displays of ecstatic states.
4. Various media were associated with trance in the 1960s. Sitar music, strobe lights, black-lights, psychedelic rock, and psychedelic art are some examples. For a discussion of the spiritual culture of the 1960s, see Lattin (2003), *Following Our Bliss: How the Spiritual Ideals of the Sixties Shape Our Lives Today.*
5. The psychologist Mihaly Csikszentmihalyi has written extensively about the phenomenon of flow. His books *Flow, the Psychology of Optimal Experience* (1990) and *The Evolving Self: A Psychology for the Third Millennium* (1993) provide general discussions of the concept. To see how flow is used in an analysis of television viewing, see Kubey and Csikszentmihalyi (1990), *Television and the Quality of Life: How Viewing Shapes Everyday Experience.*
6. Various kinds of possession and trance states are discussed in Rafferty's (2003) chapter, "Possession States across the World: An Anthropological Approach." For a discussion of the trance film genre, see Sitney (2002). Trance is also an active research area within ethnomusicology (see Becker, 2004; Rouget, 1985). Trance and contemporary music is discussed by Sylvan (2002); he also explores the topic with regard to dance raves (Sylvan, 2005).
7. For discussions of the spiritual aspects of the Burning Man Festival, see Lattin (2003) and Sylvan (2005).

Chapter 4

1. Here the term *denomination* refers to organized groups within larger faith traditions. Within Judaism, for example, denominations include Orthodox, Conservative, and Reform.
2. Thomas Lindlof has written extensively about interpretive community. His application of the concept to religion can be found in his essay, "Interpretive Community: An Approach to Media and Religion" (2002), as well as his article, "Interpretive Community" in the *Encyclopedia of Religion, Communication, and Media* (2010).
3. Hitchcock's (1979) essay, "We Speak that We Do Know: Religion as Mass Communication," is one of the earliest discussions of the media that draws from concepts in the sociology of religion. The issues it raises are still being studied today, such as media and secularization, formal and informal religion, and the duplication of religious symbols.
4. A general discussion of media and Christianity can be found in Buddenbaum's (2001b) essay, "Christian Perspectives on Mass Media." The essay describes Roman Catholic, Mainline Protestant, and Conservative Protestant audiences.
5. For an overview of Catholic perspectives on the media, see Jelen (1996), "Catholicism, Conscience, and Censorship." Vance-Trambeth's (2006) entry on Catholicism in *The Encyclopedia of Religion, Communication, and Media* is fairly detailed in its discussion of media in the context of Catholic theology; see Arasa (2008) for a discussion of Catholic Diocesan Web sites.

6. Quentin Schultze has written extensively about Conservative Protestants and the media. See Schultze and Woods (2008), *Understanding Evangelical Media: The Changing Face of Christian Face of Communication*. Also see Schultze (1996), "Evangelicals' Uneasy Alliance With the Media," as well as Buddenbaum's (2001a) discussion of the subject.

7. See "Mainline Protestants and the Media" (Buddenbaum, 1996) for a discussion of the historical, theological, and cultural dimensions of these denominations. Ferré's (2010) article in the *Encyclopedia of Religion, Communication, and Media* is also a helpful resource.

8. For a general discussion of Anabaptists and media, see Strayer (2006). Media and Mennonites is the subject of an essay by Iorio (1996).

9. For a summary of Mormon teachings about the media, see Stout's (1996) article, "Protecting the Family: Mormon Teachings about Mass Media"; also see Baker (2006). Several audience studies of Mormons have also been conducted (e.g., Stout, 2004; Stout, Scott, & Martin, 2006; Valenti & Stout, 2006). A review of the literature on Mormonism and media can be found in Baker and Stout (2004). See Stout and Scott (2003) for a discussion of Mormons and media literacy. In the special issue of *BYU Studies* on film, see Samuelson (2007), "Finding the Audience, Paying the Bills: Competing Business Models in Mormon Cinema."

10. Articles by Cohen (2001, 2006) discuss Judaism and the media. See also "The Jewish Contribution to American Journalism" (Whitfield, 2000). For more general discussions of Judaism and contemporary culture, see *New Jews: The End of the Jewish Diaspora* (Aviv & Schneer, 2005) and *The Modern Jewish Experience: A Reader's Guide* (Wertheimer, 1993).

11. The special issue of the *Journal of Media and Religion*, "Media and Religion in Iran," offers many insights about the Islamic audience (Hoover, Abdollahyan, & Yeganeh, 2008). Also see Palmer and Gallab (2001, 2006) for a general discussion of Islam and media. Also see Mowlana's (2003) essay, "Foundation of Communication in Islamic Societies." The book *Cartoons that Shook the World* (Klausen, 2009) provides an extensive case study of Islamic reaction to depictions of Muhammad thought to be blasphemous. For an examination of Islamic approaches to the Internet, especially in terms of its role in religious authority, see Bunt (2003); also see Lawrence (2002). For a broader discussion of Islamic art and architecture, see Finlayson (2001).

12. Luthra's (2001) article "The Formation of Interpretive Communities in the Hindu Diaspora" illustrates the diversity of media use and interpretation within this religious audience. For a general treatment of Hinduism and the media, see Rajagopal (2006).

13. An exception would be the Holmes (2010a) article on Buddhism in the *Encyclopedia of Religion, Communication, and Media*.

14. Lee (2009) found that Buddhist monks and nuns use personal blogs to cultivate believers as well as for spiritual self-development.

Chapter 5

1. For a detailed explanation of cultural religion as well as an historical perspective of the concept, see *A Republic of Mind and Spirit: A Cultural History of American Metaphysical Religion* (Albanese, 2007) and *America Religions and Religion* (Albanese, 1999). Also see Albanese's (1996) article "Religion and American Popular Culture: An Introductory Reader." A discussion of the related concept of popular religion can be found in *Modern American Popular Religion: A Critical Assessment and Annotated Bibliography* (Lippy, 1996).

2. Scholars vary in their assessments of the importance and veracity of the concept of cultural religion. Johnstone's (2001) text on the sociology of religion, for example, does not discuss the concept. For an argument for the study of religion in popular culture, see the essay by Mazur and McCarthy (2001).

3. Berger's (1981) essay "The Dilemmas of Pluralism" has relevance for the study of cultural religion. He explores both the opportunities and challenges of religious pluralism.

4. In addition to Nelson's (2005) analysis of the religious aspects of the Oprah phenomenon, see Primiano's (2001) article, "Oprah, Phil, Geraldo, Barbara, and Things that Go Bump in the Night."

5. Duffett (2003) argues that the Elvis-as-religion approach is reductionist and does not account for the complexities of fandom. His argument is partly based on the idea that Elvis fandom "is not an institutionally organized paradigm" (p. 515).

6. For comments about religious aspects of the Grateful Dead by band members themselves, see Gans (1991), *Conversations with the Dead: The Grateful Dead Interview Book.*

7. Applications of the concepts of communitas and liminality have been applied to television viewing and the televising of ceremonial events in particular (Katz, 1996; Katz & Dayan, 1985).

8. Rothko himself spoke of creating forms that would evoke contemplation and religious experience (Breslin, 1993). For a discussion of the religious dimension of Rothko's art see Valiunas (2006).

Chapter 6

1. Hess (2001, 2010) discusses media literacy from a religious perspective. For an overview of the general concept, see *Media Literacy* by Potter (1998) and *Media Literacy: Keys to Interpreting Media Messages* (Silverblatt, 2001). Arguments for media education are found in Kubey (1991); Kubey & Csikszentmihalyi 1990).

2. Medved's (1992) *Hollywood vs. America* is an example of didactic criticism; it argues that, generally speaking, movies "attack" religion. Wright's (1993) *Why Do Good People see Bad Movies? The Impact of R-rated Movies* also relies on dualism as a form of media criticism.

3. Clark's (2003) *From Angels to Aliens* is a study of teen audiences; it illustrates audience-response criticism, especially in terms of genres dealing with the supernatural. Another example of this approach is Loomis's (2004) study of college students; he found that the movies *Saving Private Ryan, Family Man,* and *Dracula 2000* prompted contemplation and feelings of personal growth. Mormon students' reading of John Stuart Mill's "On Liberty" is discussed in an article by Baker, Randle, Carter, and Lunt (2007). For an example of reader response criticism in literary analysis, see Radway's *Reading the Romance* (1984).

4. Playwright George Bernard Shaw was ambivalent about family life and perceived it as a distraction from artistic work (Miller, 1989). According to Heer (2009), John Updike's "life followed exactly the same arc" as most of his fiction.

5. A comprehensive discussion of religion, film, and ideology is found in Lyden's (2003) book, *Film as Religion.*

6. Steinberg and Kincheloe's (2009) *Christotainment: Selling Jesus through Popular Culture* discusses religious marketing from a critical studies perspective. A more comprehensive history of religion and commercial media is contained in Einstein (2008), *Brands of Faith: Marketing Religion in a Commercial Age.*

7. This unfortunate fact is discussed in Sobel (2000), *Galileo's Daughter: A Historical Memoir of Science, Faith, and Love.*

Chapter 7

1. Campbell's (2010a) book, *When Religion Meets New Media,* is a thorough examination of religion and the Internet; it describes how religious groups engage in decision making about new technologies. Her earlier book, *Exploring Religious Community Online* (2005), provides a good introduction to the subject. Also see Campbell's (2004) essay, "Challenges

Created by Online Religious Networks," in the *Journal of Media and Religion,* as well as her article in the *Encyclopedia of Religion, Communication, and Media* (Campbell, 2010b). Dawson and Cowan's (2004) edited collection, *Religion Online: Finding Faith on the Internet* discusses both mainstream and new religions. Zaleski's (1997) *The Soul of Cyberspace,* is also relevant to this discussion. For a detailed discussion of worship practices in cyberspace, see Brasher (2004), *Give Me that Online Religion.*

2. Lee's (2009) examination of blogging by Buddhist priests expands knowledge about the multidimensional nature of the Internet in a religious context. Shouse and Fraley (2010) argue that numinous experiences occur through humorous and satirical Web sites.

3. Armfield and Holbert (2003) found a significant negative correlation between religiosity and Internet use. According to Cheong, Halavais, and Kwon (2008), religious blogging has both personal and communal dimensions.

4. Smith (2007) finds that nonprofit religious organizations underutilize their Web sites. In terms of Catholic congregations, Cantoni and Zyga (2007) observe that "contemplative" units use the Internet less than those more involved in the "outside world." Furthermore, institutes dedicated to assisting the poor invest less in their Web sites than do other congregations. Sturgill's (2004) content analysis of Evangelical Christian Web sites reveals that "promotion of the church as an organization" and "evangelistic function" were key purposes.

Chapter 8

1. For a comprehensive discussion of entertainment in contemporary society, see Sayre and King (2010). Gabler's (2000) *Life the Movie* is an argument that entertainment dominates American culture. Postman's (1985) *Amusing Ourselves to Death* and Boorstin (1972) also have much to say about the reasons for entertainment's rise in modern society. A general overview of the entertainment–religion interface can be found in Lewis's (2010) article in *The Routledge Encyclopedia of Religion, Communication, and Media.* A treatment of the origins of religious theater by Samuelson (2010) provides helpful historical context.

2. Several books address commercial aspects of religious entertainment. Einstein's (2008) *Brands of Faith: Marketing Religion in a Commercial Age* is comprehensive in nature. Steinberg and Kinchloe's (2009) *Christotainment: Selling Jesus through Popular Culture* describes the historical and political context of Christian marketing; also see Hendershot (2004) and Moreton (2009). Ewen's (1976) *Captains of Consciousness: Advertising and the Social Roots of Consumer Culture* provides historical context for the general interface between media and commercialism.

3. Webster's (1990) *A Brief History of Blasphemy: Liberalism, Censorship, and "The Satanic Verses"* discusses the impact of blasphemy on society. For studies of religion and tolerance of secular ideas, see Coward (2000) and Hammann and Buck (1988).

4. Detweiler (1989) discusses literary analysis from a religious perspective. See Skinner and Millett's (1999) *C. S. Lewis: The Man and His Message, A Latter-Day Saint Perspective* for a denominationally based critique of literature.

5. A number of works explore religion in John Updike's novels. See, for example, *John Updike and Religion: The Sense of the Sacred and the Motions of Grace* (Yerkes, 1999). Also see Detweiler's (1989) chapter on Updike.

6. For an examination of radio from the view of religious history, see Hangen (2002), *Redeeming the Dial: Radio, Religion, and Popular Culture in America.* Also see Bendroth's (1996) history of fundamentalism and radio. Mitchell (2010) reviews global religious radio.

7. The literature on religion and film is vast. Duncan's (2010) summary is thorough and includes international genres. A volume of *Northern Lights: Film and Media Studies Year-*

book is dedicated to "mediatization of religion" (Hjarvard, 2008). In his book, *Sanctuary Cinema*, Lindvall (2007) analyzes the origins of Christian film. Hart and Holba's (2009) edited volume discusses apocalyptic movies.

8. See Warren's (2010) overview of television and religion as well as Armstrong's (2010) discussion of televangelism. A special issue of the *Journal of Media and Religion* is devoted to television (Stout & Buddenbaum, 2002a, 2002b). Davis et al. (2001) discuss television and religion from the perspective of media criticism. See Bluem (1969) for an early history of religious television programs.

9. A review of Neil Postman's cultural commentary on religion and television can be found in Strate (2006b).

10. Sayre and King (2010) list new forms of religious entertainment within their larger volume on entertainment and society.

11. Laderman's (2009) cultural critique of celebrity worship argues that such phenomena have religious elements. The special issue on celebrity in *Society* contains several relevant articles (Imber, 2010). Rojeck's (2007) article "Celebrity and Religion" deals with social and anthropological dimensions of this interface.

Chapter 9

1. On the subject of journalism and religion, a number of sources are available. Buddenbaum's (1998) *Reporting News about Religion: An Introduction for Journalists* explores the craft of writing about religion in a way that identifies common problems and presents guidelines for journalists. For an overview of journalism and religion that discusses history as well as print and broadcast media, see Buddenbaum (2006). Hoover's (1998) *Religion in the News: Faith and Journalism in American Public Discourse* is a cultural–historical treatment of the subject. The Web site for the Religion Newswriters Association (www.rna.org) is a comprehensive resource for journalists.

2. In addition to community journalism, the terms *public journalism, civic journalism,* and *citizen journalism* have also been used to describe situations where community members have a voice in what becomes news; see Lauterer (2006), *Community Journalism: Relentlessly Local* for an overview of the topic.

3. A number of works examine the history of the journalism–religion interface: see Underwood (2002), *From Yahweh to Yahoo! The Religious Roots of the Secular Press,* for a discussion of how the history of religion sheds light on the dilemmas facing the journalism profession today. Silk (1995) also provides an historical examination of news coverage of religion in his book, *Unsecular Media: Making News of Religion in America.* Buddenbaum's (2010) article, "Journalism" in the *Encyclopedia of Religion, Communication, and Media* also provides historical background. Sloan's (2000) edited volume, *Media and Religion in American History,* addresses subjects ranging from religion and colonial newspapers to revivalism.

4. For a discussion of the distinction between religion journalism and religious journalism as well as a thorough discussion of each, see Buddenbaum (2010).

5. A content analysis of religion news coverage by James Gordon Bennett's *New York Herald* was conducted by Buddenbaum (1986b).

6. A discussion of contrasting opinions by clergy and journalists regarding the nature of religion news coverage is found in Dart and Allen (2000), *Bridging the Gap: Religion and the News Media.*

Chapter 10

1. The seminal work on religious advertising is Moore (1994), *Selling God: American Religion in the Marketplace of Culture.* Also see Moore's more recent book (2003), *Touchdown Jesus: The Mixing of Sacred and Secular in American History.*
2. For a comprehensive treatment of religious branding, see Einstein's (2008) *Brands of Faith: Marketing Religion in a Commercial Age.* Also see Clark's (2007b) essay, "Identity, Belonging, and Religious Lifestyle Branding (Fashion Bibles, Bhangra Parties, and Muslim Pop)." A discussion of marketing of evangelical culture can be found in *Shaking the World for Jesus: Media and Conservative Evangelical Culture* (Hendershot, 2004).
3. For a discussion of religious products and marketing, see Haley, White, and Cunningham (2001). Also see Clark's (2007a) edited volume, *Religion, Media, and the Marketplace* for a discussion of religious material culture studies. See Golden's (2006) article on material culture as well.

Chapter 11

1. The play *Redeeming Value* has been used in classes at BYU, the University of South Carolina and the University of Nevada Las Vegas.

Epilogue

1. The problem of isolated disciplines that study information (e.g., artificial intelligence, linguistics, semiotics, communication sciences, telecommunication, etc.) is discussed extensively in Machlup and Mansfield (1983), *The Study of Information: Interdisciplinary Messages.* According to Griffiths (2000), Nobel Laureate Herbert Simon likened the book "to an anthropological exploration into islands whose inhabitants speak foreign tongues: attempts are made by the explorers to help learn the meanings of the strange sounds and try to make sense of what is seen and heard" (p. 25).

References

Abdollahyan, H. (2008). Gender and generations' modes of religiosity: Locality versus globality of Iranian media. *Journal of Media and Religion, 7*(1–2), 4–33.

Abelman, R. (1994). News on "The 700 Club": The cycle of religious activism. *Journalism Quarterly, 71,* 887–892.

Abelman, R., & Hoover, S. M. (Eds.). (1990). *Religious television: Controversies and conclusions.* Norwood, NJ: Ablex.

Abelman, R., & Neuendorf, K. (1985). How religious is religious television programming? *Journal of Communication, 35,* 98–110.

Adams, R. G. (2000). "What goes around, comes around": Collaborative research and learning. In R. G. Adams & R. Sardiello (Eds.), *Deadhead social science: You ain't gonna learn what you don't want to know* (pp. 15–50). Lanham, MD: AltaMira Press.

Adding it all up: The Oprah Winfrey show by the numbers. (2011, June). *O The Oprah Magazine,* 166–169.

Adler, M. (2008, Sept. 18). Spiritual subway: Islamic ads seek to educate NYC. *NPR.* Retrieved September 5, 2011, from http://www.npr.org/templates/story/story.php?storyId=94764831

Albanese, C. L. (1996). Religion and American popular culture: An introductory reader. *Journal of the American Academy of Religion, 59*(4), 733–742.

Albanese, C. L. (1999). *American religions and religion.* Belmont, CA: Wadsworth.

Albanese, C. L. (2007). *A republic of mind and spirit: A cultural history of American metaphysical religion.* New Haven, CT: Yale University Press.

Albanese, M. A., & Mitchell, S. (1993, January). Problem-based learning: a review of literature on its outcomes and implementation issues. *Academic Medicine, 68*(1), 52–81.

Arasa, D. (2008). *Church communications through diocesan websites: A model for analysis.* Rome: EDUSC.

Arens, W. (2003). Professional football: An American symbol and ritual. In K. Rafferty & D. C. Ukaegbu (Eds.), *Faces of anthropology: A reader for the 21st century* (pp. 79–83). Boston: Pearson.

Armentrout, D. (2010). In D. A. Stout (Ed.), *The Routledge encyclopedia of religion, communication, and media* (pp. 5–8). New York: Routledge.

Armfield, G. G., & Holbert, L. L. (2003). The relation between religiosity and Internet use. *Journal of Media and Religion, 2*(3), 129–144.

Armstrong, E. (1991). A hybrid model of problem-based learning. In D. Boud & G. Feletti (Eds.), *The challenge of problem-based learning* (pp. 137–149). London: Kogan Page.

Armstrong, K. (2000). *The battle for God*. New York: Random House.

Armstrong, R. N. (2010). Televangelism. In D. A. Stout (Ed.), *The Routledge encyclopedia of religion, communication, and media* (pp. 423–427). New York: Routledge.

Arthur, C. (1996, July 1). The English novel in the twentieth century: The numinous in modern British fiction. *Contemporary Review*.

Arthur, C. (1997). Media, meaning, and method in religious studies. In S. M. Hoover & K. Lundby (Eds.), *Rethinking media, religion, and culture* (pp. 184–193). Thousand Oaks, CA: Sage.

Ash, R. (2002). *The top ten of everything 2002*. Los Angeles: Sagebrush.

Aviv, C., & Shneer, D. (2005). *New Jews: The end of the Jewish Diaspora*. New York: New York University Press.

Bainbridge, W. S. (2002). A prophet's reward: Dynamics of religious exchange. In T. G. Jelen (Ed.), *Sacred markets, sacred canopies: Essays on religious markets and religious pluralism* (pp. 63–90). Lanham, MD: Rowman & Littlefield.

Baker, S., & Campbell, J. (2010). Mitt Romney's religion: A five factor model for analysis of media representation of Mormon identity. *Journal of Media and Religion, 9*, 99–121.

Baker, S., Randle, Q., Carter, E. L., & Lunt, S. (2007). Democratic learning and the sober second thought: The effect of reading John Stuart Mill's essay "On Liberty" on tolerance for free speech among highly religious, politically conservative students. *Journal of Media and Religion, 6*(1), 41–61.

Bantimiroudis, P. (2007). Media framing of religious minorities in Greece: The case of the Protestants. *Journal of Media and Religion, 6*(3), 219–235.

Barber, G., & Myers, M. (Producers). Schnabel, M. (Director). (2008). *The Love Guru* [Motion picture]. USA: Spyglass Entertainment.

Bar-Haim, G. (1997). The dispersed sacred: Anomie and the crisis of ritual. In S. M. Hoover & K. Lundby (Eds.), *Rethinking media, religion, and culture* (pp. 113–145). Thousand Oaks, CA: Sage.

Barrett, D. B. (2001). *World Christian encyclopedia*. Oxford, England: Oxford University Press.

Bates, S. (2002, December 16). The Jesus market: Christianity still may be struggling in the public square, but it's prospering in the public bazaar. *The Weekly Standard*, 24–29.

Beaudoin, T. (1998). *Virtual faith: The irreverent spiritual quest of generation x*. San Francisco: Jossey-Bass.

Becker, J. (2004). *Deep listening: Music, emotion and trancing*. Bloomington: Indiana University Press.

Beisel, N. (1997). *Imperiled innocents: Anthony Comstock and family reproduction in Victorian America*. Princeton, NJ: Princeton University Press.

Bendroth, M. (1996). Fundamentalism and the media, 1930–1990. In D. A. Stout & J. M. Buddenbaum (Eds.), *Religion and mass media: Audiences and adaptations* (pp. 74–84). Thousand Oaks, CA: Sage.

Benton, R. (Director). *Places in the heart*. (1984). [Motion Picture]. USA: TriStar Pictures.

Berger, M. (1982). *Censorship*. New York: Franklin Watts.

Berger, P. L. (1967). *The sacred canopy: Elements of a sociological theory of religion*. Garden City, NY: Anchor.

Berger, P. L. (1981, November–December). The dilemmas of pluralism. *Sunstone*, 38–43.

Birnbaum, R., & Mark, L. (Producers). Johnson, M. S. (Director). (1998). *Simon Birch* [Motion picture]. USA: Caravan Pictures.

Bleum, A. W. (1969). *Religious television programs: A Study of relevance*. New York: Hastings House Publishers.

Bliese, R. (2010). Sermons. In D. A. Stout (Ed.), *Routledge encyclopedia of religion, communication, and media* (pp. 395–398). New York: Routledge.

Boorstin, D. J. (1972). *The image: A guide to pseudo-events in America*. New York: Athenaeum.

Booth, W. C. (1988). *The company we keep: An ethics of fiction.* Berkeley: University of California Press.

Borer, M. (2008). *Faithful to Fenway: Believing in Boston, baseball, and America's most beloved ballpark.* New York: New York University Press.

Bowen, D. L. (2001). Respect for life: Abortion in Islam and the Church of Jesus Christ of Latter-day Saints. In J. W. Welch (Ed.), *BYU studies: LDS scholars engage Islamic thought* (pp. 183–198). Salt Lake City, UT: Brigham Young University.

Bowen, D. S. (1997). Lookin' for Margaritaville: Place and Imagination in Jimmy Buffett's Songs. *Journal of Cultural Geography, 16*(2), 99–108.

Bowra, C. M. (1965). *Classical Greece.* New York: Time-Life Books.

Brasher, B. (2004). *Give me that online religion.* New Brunswick, NJ: Rutgers University Press.

Breslin, J. (1993). *Mark Rothko: A biography.* Chicago: University of Chicago Press.

Bro, H. (1989). *A seer out of season: The life of Edgar Cayce.* New York: St. Martin's Press.

Brockett, O. G. (1968). Theatre in the education process. *Educational Theatre Journal, 20*(2) 299–302.

Brown, S. (Producer). Duvall, R. (Director). (1997). *The Apostle* [Motion picture]. USA: October Films.

Browning, D. S., Miller-McLemore, B. J., Couture, P. D., Brynoff-Lyon, K., & Franklin, R. M. (1997). *From culture wars to common ground: Religion and the American family debate.* Louisville, KY: Westminster John Knox Press.

Brummett, B. (2006). *Rhetoric in popular culture* (2nd ed.). Thousand Oaks, CA: Sage.

Bunyan, J. (1966). *The pilgrim's progress.* New York: Oxford University Press.

Budd, R. W., & Ruben, B. D. (Eds.). (1979). *Beyond media: New approaches to mass communication.* Rochelle Park, NJ: Hayden.

Buddenbaum, J. M. (1986a). Analysis of religion news coverage in three newspapers. *Journalism Quarterly, 63*(3), 600–606.

Buddenbaum, J. M. (1986b, August 3–6). *The religion journalism of James Gordon Bennett.* Paper presented at the annual meeting of the Association for Education in Journalism and Mass Communication. Norman, OK.

Buddenbaum, J. M. (1996). Mainline Protestants and the media. In D. A Stout & J. M. Buddenbaum (Eds.), *Religion and mass media: Audiences and adaptations* (pp. 51–60). Thousand Oaks, CA: Sage.

Buddenbaum, J. M. (1998). *Reporting news about religion: An introduction for journalists.* Ames: Iowa State University Press.

Buddenbaum, J. M. (2000). The religious roots of Sigma Delta Chi. In W. D. Sloan (Ed.), *Media and religion in American history* (pp. 206–216). Northport, AL: Vision Press.

Buddenbaum, J. M. (2001a). The media, religion, and public opinion: Toward a unified theory of cultural influence. In D. A. Stout & J. M. Buddenbaum (Eds.), *Religion and popular culture: Studies on the interaction of* worldviews (pp. 19–38). Ames: Iowa State University Press.

Buddenbaum, J. M. (2001b). Christian perspectives on mass media. In D. Stout & J. Buddenbaum (Eds.), *Religion and popular culture: Studies on the interaction of worldviews* (pp. 81–94). Ames: Iowa State University Press.

Buddenbaum, J. M. (2002). Social science and the study of media and religion: Going forward by looking backward. *Journal of Media and Religion, 1*(1), 5–12.

Buddenbaum, J. M. (2010). Journalism. In D. A. Stout (Ed.), *The Routledge encyclopedia of religion, communication, and media* (pp. 200–206). New York: Routledge.

Buddenbaum, J. M., & Hoover, S. M. (1996). The role of religion in public attitudes toward religion news. In D. A Stout & J. M. Buddenbaum (Eds.), *Religion and mass media: Audiences and adaptations* (pp. 137–147). Thousand Oaks, CA: Sage.

Buddenbaum, J. M., & Stout, D. A. (1996). Religion and mass media use: A review of the mass communication and sociology literature. In D. A. Stout & J. M. Buddenbaum (Eds.), *Religion and mass media: Audiences and adaptations* (pp. 12–34). Thousand Oaks, CA: Sage.

Buescher, J. B. (2005). Radio in Tibet: A portable window on the sacred. In C.H. Badaracco (Ed.), *Quoting God: How media shape ideas about religion and culture* (pp. 37–42). Waco, TX: Baylor University Press.

Bunt, G. R. (2003). *Islam in the digital age: E-Jihad, online fatwas and cyber Islamic environments.* London: Pluto Press.

Bunyan, J. (1984). *Pilgrim's progress.* New York: Oxford University Press. Originally pub. England: Nathaniel Ponder, 1678.

Bushman, R. L. (2005). *Joseph Smith rough stone rolling: A cultural biography of Mormonism's founder.* New York: Random House.

Cameron, C. M., & Gatewood, J. B. (2003). Seeking numinous experiences in the unremembered past. *Ethnology, 42*(1), 55–71.

Campbell, H. (2004). Challenges created by online religious networks. *Journal of Media and Religion, 3*(2), 81–99.

Campbell, H. (2005). *Exploring religious community online.* New York: Lang.

Campbell, H. (2010a). *When religion meets new media.* New York: Routledge.

Campbell, H. (2010b). Internet and cyber environments. In D. A. Stout (Ed.), *Routledge encyclopedia of religion, communication, and media* (pp. 177–181). New York: Routledge.

Cantoni, L., & Zyga, S. (2007). The use of Internet communication by Catholic congregations: A quantitative study. *Journal of Media and Religion, 6*(4), 291–309.

Cantor, S. (Producer). Walker, L. (Director). (2002). *Devil's playground* [Motion picture]. USA: Columbia Pictures.

Carey, J. W. (1989). *Communication as culture: Essays on media and society.* New York: Routledge.

Carey, J. W. (2002). Preface to the inaugural issue. *The Journal of Media and Religion, 1*(1), 1–3.

Carroll, B. D. (1997). *Spiritualism in antebellum America.* Bloomington: Indiana University Press.

Carroll, D. (1972). *The Taj Mahal.* New York: Newsweek Book Division.

Carter, C. (Producer). (2002). *X-Files* [TV series]. USA: 20th Century Fox Television Productions.

Casement, A., & Tacey, D. (Eds.). (2006). *The idea of the numinous: Contemporary Jungian and psychoanalytic perspectives.* London: Routledge.

Cassler, R. (1990). Creating historical drama. *The History Teacher, 23*(3), 255–262.

Castells, M. (2000). *The rise of the network society, 2nd ed.* New York: Blackwell.

Chadwick, V. (1997). (Ed.). *In search of Elvis: Music, race, art, religion.* Boulder, CO: Westview.

Chase, D. (Producer). (1995). *Northern Exposure* [TV series]. USA: CBS.

Chen, C. W. (2011, August 11). *Marketing religion online: The LDS Church's SEO efforts.* Paper presented at the annual meeting of the Association for Education for Journalism and Mass Communication (AEJMC). St. Louis, Missouri.

Chen, C. W. (2003). "Molympics"? Journalistic discourse of Mormons in relation to the 2002 Winter Olympic Games. *Journal of Media and Religion, 2*(1), 29–47.

Cheong, P. H., Halavais, A., & Kwon, K. (2008). The chronicles of me: Understanding blogging as a religious practice. *Journal of Media and Religion, 7*(3), 107–131.

Christian Wrestlers Body Slam for God. (n.d.). Retrieved from http://www.wftv.com/sports/8141328/detail.html

Christians, C. G. (2002). Religious perspectives on communication technology. *The Journal of Media and Religion, 1*(1), 37–48.

Christians, C. G. (2006). Jacques Ellul's conversions and Protestant theology. *The Journal of Media and Religion, 5*(3), 147–160.

Christians, C. G., Fackler, M., McKee, K., Kreschel, P. J., & Woods, R. H. (2008). *Media ethics: Cases and moral reasoning 8th ed.* New York: Allyn & Bacon.

Cipriani, R. (2000). *Sociology of religion: An historical introduction.* New York: Aldine de Gruyter.

Clark, L. (2003). *From angels to aliens: Teenagers, the media, and the supernatural.* New York: Oxford University Press.

Clark, L. (Ed.). (2007a). *Religion, media, and the marketplace*. New Brunswick, NJ: Rutgers University Press.

Clark, L. (2007b). Identity, belonging, and religious lifestyle branding (Fashion Bibles, Bhangra Parties, and Muslim Pop). In L. Clark (Ed.), *Religion, media, and the marketplace* (pp. 1–36). New Brunswick, NJ: Rutgers University Press.

Claussen, D. (2010). Sex and religion. In D. A. Stout (Ed.), *Encyclopedia of religion, communication, and media* (pp. 66–69). New York: Routledge.

Cleave, M. (1966, March 4). How does a Beatle live? John Lennon lives like this. *London Evening Standard*. Retrieved from http://beatlesnumber9.com/biggerjesus.html

Clow, K. E., & Baack, D. (2007). *Integrated advertising, promotion and marketing communications*. Upper Saddle River, NJ: Pearson Prentice Hall.

Cobb, J. C. (1998). *Cybergrace: The search for God in the digital world*. New York: Crown Publishers.

Cohen, Y. (2001). Mass media in the Jewish tradition. In D. A. Stout & J. M. Buddenbaum (Eds.), *Religion and popular culture: Studies on the interaction of worldviews* (pp. 95–108). Ames: Iowa State University Press.

Cohen, Y. (2010). Judaism (communication and mass media). In D. A. Stout (Ed.), *Routledge encyclopedia of religion, communication, and media* (pp. 206–212). New York, Routledge.

Collins, A. N. (2008). Islamic movie "Ayat Ayat Cinta" wows Indonesian audiences. Voice of America. Retrieved from http://www.voanews.com/english/archive/2008-03/2008-03-13-voa10.cfm?CFID=7535378&CFTOKEN=16198982

Cooper, T. (2006). The medium is the mass: Marshall McLuhan's Catholicism and Catholicism. *The Journal of Media and Religion. 5*(3). 161–173.

Cornwall, M., Albrecht, S., Cunningham, P. H., & Pitcher, B. L. (1986). The dimensions of religiosity: A conceptual model with an empirical test. *Review of Religious Research, 27*(3), 226–244.

Costas, C. (Producer). Nichols, M. (Director). (2003). *Angels in America* [Miniseries]. USA: HBO.

Coward, H. (2000). *Pluralism in the world religions*. London: Oneworld.

Cowles, D. L. (1994a). Reader response criticism. In D. L. Cowles (Ed.), *The critical experience: Literary reading, writing, and criticism* (pp. 159–179). Dubuque, Iowa: Kendall/Hunt.

Cowles, D. L. (1994b). Summaries of critical approaches. In D. L. Cowles (Ed.), *The critical experience: Literary reading, writing, and criticism* (pp. 1–6). Dubuque, Iowa: Kendall/Hunt.

Csikszentmihalyi, M. (1990). *Flow: The psychology of optimal experience*. New York: Harper & Row.

Csikszentmihalyi, M. (1993). *The evolving self: A psychology for the third millennium*. New York: HarperCollins.

Cusick, D. (2010). (Ed.). *Encyclopedia of contemporary Christian music*. Santa Barbara, CA: Greenwood Publishing.

Damasio, A. (1999). *The feeling of what happens: Body and emotion in the making of consciousness*. New York: Harcourt Brace and Company.

Davey, B. (Producer). Gibson, M. (Director). (2004). *The passion of Christ* [Motion picture]. USA: Newmarket Films.

Davidson, B. (1971). *African kingdoms*. New York: Time-Life Books. (Original work published 1966)

Davis, W. T., Blythe, T., Dreibelbis, G., Scalese, M., Winans–Winslea, E., & Ashburn, D. L. (2001). *Watching what we watch: Prime-time television through the lens of faith*. Louisville, KY: Geneva Press.

Dawson, L. L., & Cowan, D. E. (Eds.). (2004). *Religion online: Finding faith on the Internet*. New York: Routledge.

Demme, J. (Producer). Nunez, V. (Director). (1997). *Ulee's gold* [Motion picture]. USA: Orion Pictures.

Denisoff, R., & Plasketes, G. (1995). *True disbelievers: The Elvis contagion.* New Brunswick, NJ: Transaction.

Dershowitz, A. (1997). *The vanishing American Jew: In search of Jewish identity for the next century.* New York: Little, Brown.

Detweiler, R. (1989). *Breaking the fall: Religious readings of contemporary fiction.* Louisville, KY: Westminster John Knox Press.

Devine, D. (2000). *Simply devine: Memoirs of a hall of fame coach.* Champaign, IL: Sports.

De Fina, B., & Ulfland, H. (Producers). Scorcese, M. (Director). (1988). *The last temptation of Christ* [Motion picture]. USA: Universal Studios.

De Vries, H. (2001). In media res: Global religion, public spheres, and the task of contemporary comparative religious studies. In H. de Vries & S. Weber (Eds.), *Religion and media* (pp. 3–42). Stanford, CA: Stanford University Press.

De Vries, H., & S. Weber (Eds.) (2001). *Religion and media.* Stanford, CA: Stanford University Press.

Dobbelaere, K. (1989). The secularization of society? Some methodological suggestions. In J. Hadden & A. Shupe (Eds.), *Secularization and fundamentalism reconsidered: Vol. 3. Religion and political order* (pp. 27–43). New York: Praeger.

Doss, E. (1997, Summer). The power of Elvis. *American Art, 11*(2), 4–7.

Doss, E. (1999). *Elvis culture: Fans, faith, and image.* Lawrence: University Press of Kansas.

Douglas, A. (1977). *The feminization of American culture.* New York: Farrar, Straus, & Giroux.

Downey, J. (1968). *The music of American revivalism.* Ph.D. dissertation, Tulane University.

Duffett, M. (2001). Caught in a trap? Beyond pop theory's 'butch' construction of male Elvis fans. *Popular Music, 20*(3), 395–408.

Duffett, M. (2003). False faith or false comparison? A critique of religious interpretation of Elvis fan culture. *Popular music and culture, 6*(4), 513–532.

Duin, J. (2008, Sept. 5). Joel Osteen's still the name leaders' know. *The Washington Times.* Retrieved August 13, 2011, from http://www.washingtontimes.com/news/2008/sep/05/osteen-still-the-name-leaders-know/

Duncan, D. (2010). Entertainment. In D. A. Stout (Ed.), *The Routledge encyclopedia of religion, communication, and media* (pp. 144–152). New York: Routledge.

Durkheim, E. (1954). *The elementary forms of religious life.* London: Allen & Unwin (Original work published 1912).

Duveen, J., & Soloman, J. (1994). The great evolution trial: Use of role-play in the classroom. *Journal of Research in Science Training, 31*(5), 575–582.

Dwyer, R. (2006a). The saffron screen? Hindi movies and Hindu nationalism. In B. Meyer & A. Moors (Eds.), *Religion, media and the public sphere* (pp. 422–460). Bloomington: Indiana University Press.

Dwyer, R. (2006b). *Filming the gods: Religion and Indian cinema.* New York: Routledge.

Ehrenreich, B. (2006). *Dancing in the streets: A history of collective joy.* New York: Metropolitan.

Einstein, M. (2008). *Brands of faith: Marketing religion in a commercial age.* New York: Routledge.

Eisenstein, E.L. (1983). *The printing revolution in early modern Europe.* Cambridge: Cambridge University Press.

Eliade, M. (1959). *The sacred and the profane: The nature of religion.* Orlando, FL: Harcourt.

Ellul, J. (1964). *The technological society.* New York Vintage Books.

Ellwood, R. S. (1994). *The sixties spiritual awakening: American religion movement from modern to postmodern.* New Brunswick, NJ: Rutgers University Press.

el-Nawany, M. (2005). Law and the Middle East media: Between censorship and independence. In C. H. Badaracco (Ed.), *Quoting God: How media shape ideas about religion and culture* (pp. 59–67). Waco, TX: Baylor University Press.

Engle, Y., & Kasser, T. (2005). Why do adolescent girls idolize male celebrities? *Journal of Adolescent Research, 20*(2), 263–283.

Evans, C. H., & Herzog, W. R. (Eds.). (2002). *The faith of 50 million: Baseball, religion, and American culture.* Louisville, Kentucky: Westminster John Knox Press.

Evans-Pritchard, E. E. (1965). *The theories of primitive religion*. Oxford, England: Oxford University Press.

Evensen, B. J. (2000a). The evangelical origins of muckraking. In W. D. Sloan (Ed.), *Media and religion in American history* (pp. 186–205). Northport, AL: Vision Press.

Evensen, B. J. (2000b). The mass media and revivalism in the gilded age. In W. D. Sloan (Ed.), *Media and religion in American history* (pp. 119–133). Northport, AL: Vision Press.

Ewen, S. (1976). *Captains of consciousness: Advertising and the social roots of the consumer culture*. New York: McGraw-Hill.

Ferré, J. P. (Ed.). (1990). *Channels of belief: Religion and American commercial television*. Ames: Iowa State University Press.

Ferré, J. P. (2010). Mainline Protestantism. In D. A. Stout (Ed.), *Routledge encyclopedia of religion, communication, and media* (pp. 359–361). New York: Routledge.

Ferri, A. J. (2010). Emergence of the entertainment age? *Society, 47*, 403–409.

Fischer, C. S. (1982). *To dwell among friends: Personal networks in town and city*. Chicago: University of Chicago Press.

Fish, S. (1980). *Is there a text in this class*. Cambridge, MA: Harvard University Press.

Fleischer, R. (Director). (1980). *The jazz singer* [Motion picture]. USA: Associated Film.

Fletcher-Stack, P. (2010, July 16). LDS Church sees potential in proselytizing online. *The Salt Lake Tribune*. Retrieved from http://www.sltrib.com/sltrib/home/49942960-76/church-missionaries-online-lds.html.csp

Forbes, B. D., & Mahan, J. H. (Eds.). (2005). *Religion and popular culture in America*. Berkeley: University of California Press.

Freud, S. (1953). The uncanny. In J. Strachey (Ed. & Trans.), *The standard edition of the complete psychological works of Sigmund Freud* (Vol. 17, pp. 219–252). London: Hogarth (Original work published 1919)

Frykholm, A. J. (2005). The gender dynamics of the *Left Behind* series. In B. D. Forbes & J. H. Mahan (Eds.), *Religion and popular culture in America* (pp. 270–287). Berkeley: University of California Press.

Gabler, N. (2000). *Life: The movie: How entertainment conquered reality*. London: Vintage.

Gans, D. (1991). *Conversations with the Dead: The Grateful Dead interview book*. New York: Citadel Press.

Gay, P. (1969). *The enlightenment: An interpretation*. New York: Knopf.

Gerow, J. R. (1992). *Psychology: An introduction* (3rd ed.). New York: HarperCollins.

Gewehr, W. M. (1930). *The great awakening in Virginia, 1740-1790*. Durham, NC: Duke University Press.

Gibbs, E., & Bolger, R. K. (2005). *Emerging churches: Creating Christian community in postmodern cultures*. Grand Rapids, MI: Baker Academic.

Gibson, D. (2010a, January 8). Elvis, Michael, and other celebrity saints. *Politics Daily*. Retrieved from http://www.politicsdaily.com/...elvis-michael-and-other-celebrity-saints

Gibson, T. (2010b). Orality. In D. A. Stout (Ed.), *Routledge encyclopedia of religion, communication, and media* (pp. 301–304). New York: Routledge.

Goethals, G. T. (1981). *The TV ritual: Worship at the video altar*. Boston: Beacon Press.

Golan, G. J., & Kiousis, S. K. (2010). Religion, media credibility, and support for democracy in the Arab world. *Journal of Media and Religion, 9*, 84–98.

Golan, G. J. & Baker, S. (2011, August 12). *Perceptions of media trust and credibility amongst Mormon college students*. Paper presented at the annual meeting of the Association for Education for Journalism and Mass Communication (AEJMC). St. Louis, Missouri.

Golden, A. (2010). Material culture. In D. A. Stout (Ed.), *Encyclopedia of religion, communication, and media* (pp. 234–237). New York: Routledge.

Graf, H. J. (1995). Early modern literacies. In D. Crowley & P. Heyer (Eds.), *Communication in history: Technology, culture, society* (pp. 125–135). White Plains, NY: Longman.

Grazer, B. (Producer). Howard, R. (Director). (2006). *The Da Vinci Code* [Motion picture]. USA: Columbia Pictures.

Greenwald, J. (1998). *Future perfect: How Star Trek conquered planet earth*. New York: Penguin.

Griffiths, J. M. (2000, April/May). Back to the future: Information science for the new millennium. *Bulletin of the American Society for Information Science, 26*(4), 24–27.

Groening, M. (Producer). (2011). *The Simpsons* [TV series]. USA: Gracie Films.

Gruzd, A., Wellman, B., & Takhteyev, Y. (2011). Imagining Twitter as an imagined community [Special issue]. *American Behavioral Scientist.*

Hadden, J. (1987). Toward desacralizing secularization theory. *Social Forces, 65,* 581–611.

Hagstrom, A. (n.d.). The Catholic Church and censorship in literature, books, drama, and film. *Analytical Teaching, 23*(2), 147–156.

Hale, J. R. (1965). *Renaissance*. New York: Time-Life Books.

Haley, E., White, C., & Cunningham, A. (2001). Branding religion: Christian consumers' understandings of Christian products. In D. A. Stout & J. M. Buddenbaum (Eds.), *Religion and popular culture: Studies on the interaction of worldviews* (pp. 269–288). Ames: Iowa State University Press.

Hall, B. (Producer). (2005). *Joan of Arcadia* [TV series]. USA: CBS.

Hamberg, E. M., & Pettersson, T. (2002). Religious markets: Supply, demand, and rational choices. In T. G. Jelen (Ed.), *Sacred markets, sacred canopies: Essays on religious markets and religious pluralism* (pp. 91–114). Lanham, MD: Rowman & Littlefield.

Hammann, L. J., & Buck, H. M. (1988). *Religious traditions and the limits of tolerance.* Chambersburg, PA: Anima.

Hangen, T. (2002). *Redeeming the dial: Radio, religion, and popular culture in America*. Chapel Hill: University of North Carolina Press.

Hankins, B. (2003). Reformation, early modern Europe. In C. Crookson (Ed.), *Encyclopedia of religious freedom* (pp. 361–366). New York: Routledge.

Hart, K. R., & Holba, A. M. (Eds.). (2009). *Media and the apocalypse*. New York: Peter Lang.

Hatcher, A. (2010). Magazines. In D. A. Stout (Ed.), *The Routledge encyclopedia of religion, communication, and media* (pp. 229–232). New York: Routledge.

Havelock, E. (1963). *Preface to Plato*. Cambridge, MA: Harvard University Press.

Hedgepeth-Williams, J. (2000). Puritans and freedom of expression. In W. D. Sloan (Ed.), *Media and religion in American history* (pp. 17–31). Charlottesville: University of Virginia Press.

Heer, J. (2009). Updike's death is hard not to take personally. *National Post*. Retrieved from http://network.nationalpost.com/np/blogs/fullcomment/archive/2009/01/28/jeet-heer-updike-s-death-is-hard-not-to-take-personally.aspx

Hendershot, H. (2004). *Shaking the world for Jesus: Media and conservative Evangelical culture.* Chicago: University of Chicago Press.

Herskovitz, M., & Zwick, E. (1991). *Thirtysomething* [TV series]. USA: ABC.

Hess, M. E. (2001). Media literacy as a support for the development of a responsible imagination in religious community. In D. A. Stout & J. M. Buddenbaum (Eds.), *Religion and popular culture: Studies on the interaction of worldviews* (pp. 289–311). Ames: Iowa State University Press.

Hess, M. E. (2010). Media literacy. In D. A. Stout (Ed.), *Encyclopedia of religion, communication, and media* (pp. 245–250). New York: Routledge.

Hiatt, B. (2011, June 9). Monster Goddess. *Rolling Stone, 1132,* 40–47.

Hindus petition to boycott "Love Guru." (2008, June 18). *Saja Forum*. Retrieved from http://www.sajaforum.org/2008/06/movies-love-gur.html

Hitchcock, J. (1979). We speak that we do know: Religion as mass communication. In R. W. Budd & B. D. Ruben (Eds.), *Beyond media: New approaches to mass communication* (pp. 178–193). Rochelle Park, NJ: Hayden.

Hjarvard, S. (Ed.). (2008). The mediatization of religion. In *Northern lights: Film & media studies yearbook* (Vol. 6). Bristol, England: Intellect.

Hmelo-Silver, C. E. (2004). Problem-based learning: What and how do students learn? *Educational Psychology Review, 16*, 235–266.

Hobel, P. (Producer). Beresford, B. (Director). (1983). *Tender Mercies* [Motion picture]. USA: Universal Pictures.

Hollander, B. (2010a). Persistence in the perception of Barack Obama as a Muslim in the 2008 presidential campaign. *Journal of Media and Religion, 9*, 55–66.

Hollander, P. (2010b). Why the celebrity cult? *Society, 47*, 388–391.

Holmes, C. (2010a). Buddhism. In D. A. Stout (Ed.), *Routledge encyclopedia of religion, communication, and media* (pp. 53–55). New York: Routledge.

Holmes, C. (2010b). Newspapers. In D. A. Stout (Ed.), *Routledge encyclopedia of religion, communication, and media* (pp. 291–293). New York: Routledge.

Hood, R. W. (2005). Mystical, spiritual, and religious experiences. In R. F. Paloutzian & C. L. Park (Eds.), *Handbook of psychology of religion and spirituality*. New York: Guilford Press.

Hoover, S. M. (1998). *Religion in the news: Faith and journalism in American public discourse*. Newbury Park, CA: Sage.

Hoover, S. M. (2001). Religion, media and the cultural center of gravity. In D. A. Stout & J. M. Buddenbaum (Eds.), *Religion and popular culture: Studies on the interaction of worldviews* (pp. 49–60). Ames: Iowa State University Press.

Hoover, S. M. (2006). *Religion in the media age*. New York: Routledge.

Hoover, S. M., Abdollahyan, H., & Yeganeh, M. R. J. (Eds.). (2008). Media and religion in Iran [Special issue]. *Journal of Media and Religion, 7*(1, 2).

Hoover, S. M., & Clark, L. S. (Eds.). (2002). *Practicing religion in the age of media: Explorations in media religion and culture*. New York: Columbia University Press.

Hoover, S. M., Clark, L. S., & Rainie, L. (2004). 64% of wired Americans have used the Internet for spiritual or religious purposes. *The Internet and American Life Project*. Washington, DC: Pew Institute.

Hoover, S. M., & Lundby, K. (Eds.). (1997). *Rethinking media, religion, and culture*. Thousand Oaks, CA: Sage.

Huff, R. (2010, February 8). Super bowl ratings: Saints victory over Colts was most watched program of all time, beating "MASH." *New York Daily News*. Retrieved from http://www.nydailynews.com/entertainment/tv/2010/02/08/2010-02-08_super_bowl_ratings_preliminary_numbers_show_highest_viewership_in_20plus_years.html

Hunter, J. D. (1992). *Culture wars: The struggle to define America*. New York: HarperCollins.

Hymnowitz, K. (2008, June 13). Among the 'Rentheads.' *The Wall Street Journal*. Retrieved August 2011 from http://online.wsj.com/article/SB121331730861070229.html

Imber, J. B. (Ed.). (2010, September/October). Celebrity in America today [Special issue]. *Society, 7*(5).

Ingersoll, J. J. (2001). The thin line between Saturday night and Sunday morning: Meaning and community among Jimmy Buffett's Parrotheads. In E. M. Mazur & K. McCarthy (Eds.), *God in the details: American religion in popular culture* (pp. 253–266). New York: Routledge.

Innis, H.A. (1950). *Empire and communication*. Toronto: University of Toronto.

Innis, H. A. (1951). *The bias of communication*. Toronto, Canada: University of Toronto Press.

Jameson, F. (1991). *Postmodernism, or, the cultural logic of late capitalism*. Durham, NC: Duke University Press.

Jelen, T. G. (1996). Catholicism, conscience, and censorship. In D. A. Stout & J. M. Buddenbaum (Eds.), *Religion and mass media: Audiences and adaptations* (pp. 39–50). Thousand Oaks, CA: Sage.

John Paul II. (1987a, January 21). 21st *WCD*. Social communications at the service of justice and peace. *Insegnamenti di Giovanni Paolo II, 11*, 185–190.

John Paul II. (1987b, December 4). *Duodecimum saeculum*. Apostolic Letter.

Johnson, M. (Producer). Levinson, B. (Director). (1984). *The natural* [Motion picture]. USA: TriStar Pictures.

Johnstone, R. L. (2001). *Religion in society: A sociology of religion.* Upper Saddle River, NJ: Prentice Hall.

Joyce, J. (1916). *A portrait of the artist as a young man.* London: The Egoist LTD.

Kagan, J. P. (Director). (1981). *The chosen* [Motion picture]. USA: Analysis Film.

Katz, E. (1996). And deliver us from segmentation. *Annals of the American Academy of Political and Social Science, 546,* 22–33.

Katz, E., & Dayan, D. (1985). Media events: On the experience of not being there. *Religion, 15,* 305–314.

Kerr, P. A. (2003). The framing of Fundamentalist Christians: Network television news, 1980–2000. *Journal of Media and Religion, 2*(4), 203–235.

Kenny, J. (Writer). (2006). *The Book of Daniel* [TV series]. USA: NBC.

Kitzerow, P. (1990). Active learning in the classroom: The use of group role plays. *Teaching Sociology, 18,* 223–225.

Klausen, J. (2009). *The cartoons that shook the world.* New Haven, CT: Yale University Press.

Kramer, R. (Producer). (1997). *Nothing sacred* [TV series]. USA: ABC.

Kripalani, J. B., & Grover, V. (2002, December 2). Bollywood: Can new money create a world-class film industry in India? *Business Week.* Retrieved from http://www.businessweek.com/magazine/content/02_48/b3810013.htm

Kubey, R. (1991, March 6). The case for media education. *Education Week, 10*(1), 27.

Kubey, R., & Csikszentmihalyi, M. (1990). *Television and the quality of life: How viewing shapes everyday experience.* Mahwah, NJ: Erlbaum.

Kuhn, T. S. (1996). *The structure of scientific revolutions* (3rd ed.). Chicago: University of Chicago Press.

Laderman, G. (2009). *Sacred matters: Celebrity worship, sexual ecstasies, the living dead, and other signs of religious life in the United States.* New York: New Press.

Larsen, E. (2004). Cyberfaith: How Americans pursue religion online. In L. L. Dawson & D. E. Cowan (Eds.), *Religion online: Finding faith on the Internet* (pp. 17–22). New York: Routledge.

Latham, K. F. (2007). The poetry of the museum: A holistic model of numinous museum experiences. *Museum Management and Curatorship, 22*(3), 247–263.

Lattin, D. (2003). *Following our bliss: How the spiritual ideals of the sixties shape our lives today.* San Francisco: HarperCollins.

Lauterer, J. (2006). *Community journalism: Relentlessly local.* Chapel Hill: University of North Carolina Press.

Lee, J. (2009). Cultivating the self in cyberspace: The use of personal blogs among Buddhist priests. *Journal of Media and Religion, 8*(2), 97–114.

Leonard, B. J. (1999). The Bible and serpent-handling. In P. W. Williams (Ed.), *Perspectives on American religion and culture* (pp. 228–240). Malden, MA: Blackwell.

Lepter, J., & Lindlof, T. (2001). Coming out of abstinence: A root-metaphor study of Nazarenes' relation to movies and media. In D. A. Stout & J. M. Buddenbaum (Eds.), *Religion and popular culture: Studies on the interaction of worldviews* (pp. 217–234). Ames: Iowa State University Press.

LeRoy, M. (Producer). Fleming, V. (Director). (1939). *The Wizard of Oz* [Motion picture]. USA: Metro-Goldwyn-Meyer.

Lewis, C. S. (2001). *Mere Christianity.* San Francisco: HarperCollins. Originally pub. New York: Macmillan Publishers, 1952.

Lewis, T. (2010). Entertainment. In D. A. Stout (Ed.), *The Routledge encyclopedia of religion, communication, and media* (pp. 128–131). New York: Routledge.

Linderman, A. (1997). Making sense of religion in television. In S. M. Hoover & K. Lundby (Eds.), *Rethinking media, religion, and culture* (pp. 263–282). Thousand Oaks, CA: Sage.

Linderman, A., & Lövheim, M. (2003). Internet and religion. The making of meaning, identity and community through computer mediated communication. In S. Marriage & J. Mitchell

(Eds.), *Mediating religion: Conversations in media, culture and religion* (pp. 229–240) Edinburgh, Scotland: T & T Clark/Continuum.

Lindlof, T. (1988). Media audiences as interpretive communities. In J. A. Anderson (Ed.), *Communication Yearbook 11* (pp. 81–107). Newbury Park, CA: Sage.

Lindlof, T. (2010). Interpretive community. In D. A. Stout (Ed.), *The Routledge encyclopedia of religion, communication, and media* (pp. 182–185). New York: Routledge.

Lindlof, T. (2002). Interpretive community: An approach to media and religion. *Journal of Media and Religion, 1*(1), 61–74.

Lindsey, U. (2006, May 2). The new Muslim TV: Media-savvy, modern, and moderate. *Christian Science Monitor.* Retrieved from http://www.csmonitor.com/2006/0502/p01s04-wome. html?s=u2

Lindval, T. (2007). *Sanctuary cinema: Origins of the Christian film industry.* New York: New York University Press.

Lipner, J. (2001). A remaking of Hinduism? Or, taking the mickey out of valmiki. In H. de Vries & S. Weber (Eds.), *Religion and media* (pp. 320–338). Stanford, CA: Stanford University Press.

Lippy, C. H. (1996). *Modern American popular religion: A critical assessment and annotated bibliography.* Westport, CT: Greenwood.

Lippy, C. H. (1999). Pluralism and American religious life in the later twentieth century. In P. W. Williams (Ed.), *Perspectives on American religion and culture* (pp. 48–60). Malden, MA: Blackwell.

Littlejohn, S. W. (1982). An overview of contributions to human communication theory from other disciplines. In F. E. X. Dance (Ed.), *Human communication theory: Comparative essays.* New York: Harper & Row.

Lohrey, A. (2010). *Speaking of the numinous: The meaning of meaning.* Tasmania, Australia: Rishi.

Loomis, K. D. (2004). Spiritual students and secular media. *Journal of Media and Religion, 3*(3), 151–164.

Lovejoy, D. S. (1969). *Religious enthusiasm and the great awakening.* Englewood Cliffs, NJ: Prentice Hall.

Lövheim, M. (2004). Young people, religious identity and the Internet. In L. Dawson & D. Cowan, (Eds.), *Religion online: Finding faith on the Internet* (pp. 59–74). New York: Routledge.

Luthra, R. (2001). The formation of interpretive communities in the Hindu diaspora. In D. Stout & J. Buddenbaum (Eds.), *Religion and popular culture: Studies on the interaction of worldviews* (pp. 125–139). Ames: Iowa State University Press.

Lyden, J. C. (2003). *Film as religion.* New York: New York University Press.

Lyon, J. K. (2001). Mormonism and Islam through the eyes of a "universal historian." In J. W. Welch (Ed.), *BYU studies (Special Issue): LDS scholars engage Islamic thought* (pp. 221–236). Salt Lake City, UT: Brigham Young University.

Lyotard, J. (1992). *The postmodern explained.* Minneapolis: University of Minnesota Press.

Machlup, F. (1979). Stocks and flows of knowledge. *Kyklos 32*(1-2), 400–411.

Machlup, F. (1993). Uses, value, and benefits of knowledge. *Science Communication, 14*, 448–466.

Machlup, F., & Mansfield, U. (1983). *The study of information: Interdisciplinary messages.* New York: Wiley.

MacLaine, S. (1983). *Out on a limb.* New York: Bantam Books.

MacQuarrie, B. (2005, October 9). Portraits in power. *Boston Globe*, pp. 1–5.

Maguire, B., & Weatherby, G. A. (1998). The secularization of religion and television commercials. *Sociology of Religion, 59*, 171–178.

Mallia, K. L. (2009). From the sacred to the profane: A critical analysis of the changing nature of religious imagery in advertising. *Journal of Media and Religion, 8*(3), 172–190.

Marrati, P. (2001). "The Catholicism of cinema": Gilles Deleuze on image and belief. In H.

de Vries & S. Weber (Eds.), *Religion and media* (pp. 227–240). Stanford, CA: Stanford University Press.

Marshack, A. (1995). The art and symbols of ice man. In D. Crowley & P. Heyer (Eds.), *Communication in history: Technology, culture, society* (2nd ed., pp. 10–20). White Plains, NY: Longman.

Martin, D., & Coons, D. (2010). *Media flight plan.* Provo, UT: Deer Creek.

Martìn-Barbero, J. (1997). Mass media as a site of resacralization of contemporary cultures. In S. M. Hoover & K. Lundby (Eds.), *Rethinking media, religion, and culture* (pp. 102–116). Thousand Oaks, CA: Sage.

Marvin, C. (1997a). The communications revolution and the professional communicator. In E. S. Munson & C. A. Warren (Eds.), *James Carey: A critical reader* (pp. 128–143). Minneapolis: University of Minnesota Press.

Mazur, E. M., & Koda, T. K. (2001). The happiest place on earth. In E. M. Mazur & K. McCarthy (Eds.), *God in the details: American religion in popular culture* (pp. 299–320). New York: Routledge.

Mazur, E. M., & McCarthy, K. (Eds.). (2001). *God in the details: American religion in popular culture.* New York: Routledge.

McBride, J. (2001). Symptomatic expression of male neuroses. In E. M. Mazur & K. McCarthy (Eds.), *God in the details: American religion and popular culture* (pp. 123–138). New York: Routledge.

McCalib, P. T. (1968). Intensifying the literary experience through role playing, *The English Journal, 57*(1), 41–46.

McCormick, J., & MacInnes, M. (1962). *Versions of censorship.* Chicago: Aldine.

McCray-Pattacini, (2000). Deadheads yesterday and today: An audience study. *Popular Music and Society, 24*(1), 1–14.

McCune, C. (2003). Framing Reality: Shaping the news coverage of the 1996 Tennessee debate on teaching evolution. *Journal of Media and Religion, 2*(1), 5–28.

McInerny, R. (Creator). (1991). *Father Dowling Mysteries* [TV series]. USA: ABC.

McLuhan, M. (1964). *Understanding media: The extensions of man.* New York: Signet.

McMaster, J.C. (1998). "Doing" literature: Using drama to build literacy classrooms: The segue for a few struggling readers. *Reading Teacher, 51*(7), 574–584.

McNamara, A. (2001). The Aboriginal medium: Negotiating the caesura of exchange. In H. de Vries & S. Weber (Eds.), *Religion and media* (pp. 487–513). Stanford, CA: Stanford University Press.

Medved, M. (1992). *Hollywood vs. America: Popular culture and the war on traditional values.* New York: HarperCollins.

Meer, N., Dwyer, C., & Modood, T. (2010). Beyond "Angry Muslims"? Reporting Muslim voices in the British press. *Journal of Media and Religion, 9*, 216–231.

Mega-churches offer prayer, play, shopping. (2005, March 27). Retrieved from http://abcnews.go.com/GMA/Business/Story?id=617341&page=1

Mendieta, E. (2006). The enlightenment. In D. Stout (Ed.), *Encyclopedia of religion, communication, and media* (pp. 123–128). New York: Routledge.

Mercer, S. Rudin, S., & Shyamalan, M. N. (Producers). (2004). *The Village* [Motion picture]. USA: Touchstone Pictures.

Meyer, B., & Moors, A. (Eds.). (2006). *Religion, media, and the public sphere.* Bloomington: Indiana University Press.

Meyrowitz, (1985). *No sense of place: The impact of electronic media on social behavior.* New York: Oxford University Press.

Milhelich, J., & Papineau, J. (2005). Parrotheads in Margaritaville: Fan practice, oppositional culture and embedded cultural resistance in Buffett fandom. *Journal of Popular Music Studies, 17*(2), 175–202.

Milton, J. (2000). *Paradise lost.* London: Penguin Books. Originally pub. London: S. Simmons, 1674.

Miller, D. (1989). *Lewis Mumford: A life.* New York: Weidenfeld & Nicolson.

Miracle wheat scandal. (1913, January 1). *Brooklyn Daily Eagle,* pp. 1–2.

Mitchell, J. (2010). Radio. In D. A. Stout (Ed.), *The Routledge encyclopedia of religion, communication, and media* (pp. 371–374). New York: Routledge.

Moore, R. C. (2003). Religion and topoi in the news: An analysis of the "unsecular media" hypothesis. *Journal of Media and Religion, 2*(1), 49–64.

Moore, R. C. (2008). Secular spirituality/Mundane media: One newspaper's in-depth coverage of Buddhism. *Journal of Media and Religion, 7*(4), 231–255.

Moore, R. L. (1994). *Selling God: American religion in the marketplace of culture.* New York: Oxford University Press.

Moore, R. L. (2003). *Touchdown Jesus: The mixing of sacred and secular in American history.* Louisville, KY: Westminster John Knox Press.

Moses, P. (2005). The First Amendment and the Falun Gong. In C. H. Badaracco (Ed.), *Quoting God: How media shape ideas about religion and culture* (pp. 67–78). Waco, TX: Baylor University Press.

Moran, J. (2010). *Interdisciplinarity* (2nd ed.). New York: Routledge.

Morgan, D. (2010). Pamphlets. In D. A. Stout (Ed.), *The Routledge encyclopedia of religion, communication, and media* (pp. 315–317). New York: Routledge.

Morgan, D. (1998). *Visual piety: A history and theory of popular religious images.* Berkeley: University of California Press.

Mumford, L. (1963). *Technics and civilization.* New York: Harcourt, Brace. (Original work published 1934)

Mumford, L. (1986). The monastery and the clock. In D. Miller (Ed.), *The Lewis Mumford reader.* New York: Pantheon Books.

Murdock, G. (1997). The re-enchantment of the world: Religion and the transformation of modernity. In S. M. Hoover & K. Lundby (Eds.), *Rethinking media, religion, and culture* (pp. 85–101). Thousand Oaks, CA: Sage.

National Opinion Research Center. (2006–2007). *National congregations study.* Chicago: Author. Retrieved from http://www.soc.duke.edu/natcong/wave_2.html

Nelson, M. Z. (2005). *The gospel according to Oprah.* Louisville, KY: Westminster John Knox Press.

Nichols, M. (Director). (2003). *Angels in America* [TV miniseries]. USA: HBO.

Nord, D. P. (2000). The evangelical origins of mass media in America. In W. D. Sloan (Ed.), *Media and religion in American history* (pp. 68–93). Northport, AL: Vision Press.

Nygard, R. (Director). (1999). *Trekkies* [Motion picture]. USA: Neo Motion Pictures/Paramount Classics.

O'Connor, F. (1952). *Wise blood.* New York: Harcourt, Brace & company.

O'Hara, M. (1984). Drama in education: A curriculum dilemma. *Theory Into Practice, 13*(4), 314–320.

Olasky, M. N. (1988). *Prodigal press: The anti-Christian bias of the American news media.* Wheaton, IL: Crossway Books.

Olsen, M., & Scheffer, W. (Producers). (2011). *Big Love* [Miniseries]. USA: HBO.

Oncu, A. (2006). Becoming "secular Muslims": Yasar Nuri Ozturk as a super-subject on Turkish television. In B. Meyer & A. Moors (Eds.), *Religion, media, and the public sphere* (pp. 227–250). Bloomington: Indiana University Press.

Ott, S. (2002). Ad campaign aims to increase Jewish family size. *ScrappleFace.* Retrieved September 5, 2011, from http://www.scrappleface.com/?p=160

Otto, R. (1958). *The idea of the holy. An inquiry into the nonrational factor in the idea of the divine and its relation to the rational* (J. H. Harvey, Trans). New York: Oxford University Press.

Oubre, A. Y. (1997). *Instinct and revelation: Reflections on the origins of numinous perception.* Newark, NJ: Gordon & Breach.

Palmer, A. W., & Gallab, A. A. (2001). Islam and western culture: Navigating terra incognita. In D. A. Stout & J. M. Buddenbaum (Eds.), *Religion and popular culture: Studies on the interaction of worldviews* (pp. 109–124). Ames: Iowa University Press.

Paradis, (2002). The political economy of theme development in small urban places: The case of Roswell, New Mexico. *Tourism Geographies, 4*(1), 22–43.

Patterson, P., & Wilkins, L. (2011). *Media ethics: Issues and cases* (7th ed.). New York: McGraw-Hill.

Pauly, J. (1997). The Chicago school and the history of mass communication research. In E. S. Munson & C. A. Warren (Eds.), *James Carey: A critical reader* (pp. 14–33). Minneapolis: University of Minnesota Press.

Perry, S. D., & Wolfe, A. S. (2001). Branding religion: Christian consumers' understandings of Christian products. In D. A. Stout & J. M. Buddenbaum (Eds.), *Religion and popular culture: Studies on the interaction of worldviews* (pp. 251–268). Ames: Iowa State University Press..

Peters, J. D. (1999). *Speaking into the air: A history of the idea of communication.* Chicago: University of Chicago Press.

Petersen, T. R. (2010). Novels. In D. A. Stout (Ed.), *The Routledge encyclopedia of religion, communication, and media.* New York: Routledge.

Peterson, D. C. (2001). *The language of God: Understanding the Qur'an.* In J. W. Welch (Ed.), *BYU studies: LDS scholars engage Islamic thought* (pp. 51–68). Salt Lake City, UT: Brigham Young University.

Peterson, G. (2005). The Internet and Christian and Muslim communities. In B. D. Forbes & J. H. Mahan (Eds.), *Religion and popular culture in America* (pp. 123–138). Berkeley: University of California Press..

Pontifical Council for Social Communications. (1989, May 7). *Pornography and violence in the communications media: A pastoral response.* Vatican City: LEV.

Pontifical Council for Social Communications. (1997, February 22). *Ethics in advertising. Origins, 26*(38; March 13, 1997), 627–632.

Pontifical Council for Social Communications. Ethics in Internet (2002, February 22). *Origins, 31*(40; March 21, 2002), 672–676.

Pool, I. de Sola. (1984). *Technologies of freedom.* Cambridge, MA: Harvard University Press.

Postman, N. (1985). *Amusing ourselves to death: Public discourse in the age of show business.* New York: Penguin.

Postman, N. (1992). *Technopoly: The surrender of culture to technology.* New York: Vintage.

Postman, N. (1999). *Building a bridge to the eighteenth century; How the past can improve our feature.* New York: Alfred A. Knopf.

Potok, C. (1972). *My name is Asher Lev.* New York: Michael Mordechai.

Potter, W. J. (1998). *Media literacy.* Thousand Oaks, CA: Sage.

Prebish, C. S. (1993). *Religion and sport: The meeting of sacred and profane.* Westport, CT: Greenwood Press.

Primiano, L. N. (2001). Oprah, Phil, Geraldo, Barbara, and things that go bump in the night. In E. M. Mazur & K. McCarthy (Eds.), *God in the details: American religion in popular culture* (pp. 47–64). New York: Routledge.

Prothero, S. (2007). *Religious illiteracy.* San Francisco: HarperSanFrancisco.

Qualman, E. (2009, Aug. 11). Statistics show social media is bigger than you think. *Socialnomics.* Retrieved August 26, 2011, from http://www.socialnomics.net/2009/08/11/statistics-show-social-media-is-bigger-than-you-think/

Radway, J. (1984). *Reading the romance.* Chapel Hill: University of North Carolina Press.

Rafferty, K. (2003). Possession states across the world: An anthropological approach. In K. Rafferty & D. C. Ukaegbu (Eds.), *Faces of anthropology: A reader for the 21st century* (pp. 257–272). Boston: Pearson.

Ramo, J. C. (1996, Dec. 16). Finding God on the web. *Newsweek (148)*, 27.

Redmond, S., & Holmes, S. (Eds.). (2007). *Stardom and celebrity: A reader*. Los Angeles, CA: Sage.

Religion in the news: 2009. (2010, March 25). *Pew forum on religion and public life*. Retrieved from http://pewforum.org/Politics-and-Elections/Religion-in-the-News-2009.aspx

Reporting on religion: A primary on journalism's best beat. (2008). Retrieved August 31, 2001, from http://www.rna.org/

Reynolds, D. S. (1996). *Walt Whitman's America: A cultural biography*. New York: Vintage Press.

Reynolds, V., & Tanner, E. S. (1983). *The biology of religion*. New York: Longman.

Robinson, S. (2007). Spirituality: A story so far. In J. Parry, M. Nesti, S. Robinson, & N. Watson (Eds.), *Sport and spirituality: An introduction* (pp. 7–21). New York: Routledge.

Rodman, G. (1996). *Elvis after Elvis: The posthumous career of a living legend*. London: Routledge.

Rojek, C. (2007). Celebrity and religion. In S. Redmond & S. Holmes (Eds.), *Stardom and celebrity: A reader* (pp. 171–180). Los Angeles, CA: Sage.

Roof, W. C. (1993). *A generation of seekers: The spiritual journeys of the baby boom generation*. New York: HarperCollins.

Roof, W. C. (1999). *Spiritual marketplace: Baby boomers and the remaking of American religion*. Princeton, NJ: Princeton University Press.

Rothenbuhler, E. W. (1998). *Ritual communication: From everyday conversation to mediated ceremony*. Thousand Oaks, CA: Sage.

Rouget, G. (1985). *Music and trance: A theory of the relations between music and possession*. Chicago: University of Chicago Press.

Rushdie, S. (1988). *The satanic verses*. New York: Viking Penguin Press.

Samuelsen, E. (2010). Drama. In D. A. Stout (Ed.), *The Routledge encyclopedia of religion, communication, and media* (pp. 116–118). New York: Routledge.

Sayre, S., & King, C. (2010). *Entertainment and society: Influences, impacts, and innovations* (2nd ed.). New York: Routledge.

Sheldon, C. M. (1896). *In his steps*. Chicago: Chicago Advance.

Schement, J., & Stephenson, H. (1996). Religion and the information society. In D. Stout & M. Buddenbaum (Eds.), *Religion and mass media: Audiences and adaptations* (pp. 261–289). Thousand Oaks, CA: Sage.

Schippert, C. (2007). Saint Mychal: Virtual saint. *Journal of Media and Religion, 6*(2), 109–132.

Schmandt–Besserat, D. (1995). The earliest precursor of writing. In D. Crowley & P. Heyer (Eds.), *Communication in history: Technology, culture, society* (2nd ed., 21–29). White Plains, NY: Longman.

Schofield Clark, L. (2003). *From angels to aliens: Teenagers, the media, and the supernatural*. New York: Oxford University Press.

Schofield Clark, L. (2007). *Religion, media, and the marketplace*. New Brunswick, NJ: Rutgers University Press.

Schofield Clark, L., & Hoover, S. M. (1997). At the intersection of media, culture, and religion: A bibliographic essay. In S. M. Hoover & K. Lundby (Eds.), *Rethinking media, religion, and culture* (pp. 15–36). Thousand Oaks, CA: Sage.

Schultze, Q. J. (2008). Following pilgrims into cyberspace. In Q. J. Schultze & R. H. Woods (Eds.), *Understanding evangelical media: The changing face of Christian communication* (pp. 137–148). Downers Grove, IL: IVP Academic.

Schultze, Q. J. (1996). Evangelicals' uneasy alliance with the media. In D. A. Stout & J. M. Buddenbaum (Eds.), *Religion and mass media: Audiences and adaptations* (pp. 61–73). Thousand Oaks, CA: Sage.

Schultze, Q. J. (2002). *Habits of the high-tech heart: Living virtuously in the information age*. Grand Rapids, MI: Baker Academic.

Schultze, Q. J. (2003). *Christianity and the mass media in America*. East Lansing: Michigan State University Press.

Schultze, Q. J., & Woods, R. H. (Eds.). (2008). *Understanding evangelical media: The changing face of Christian communication.* Downers Grove, IL: IVP Academic.

Scorsese, M. (Director). (2000). *The last temptation of Christ* [Motion Picture]. United States: Criterion Collection.

Shank, G., & Simon, E. J. (2000). The grammar of the Grateful Dead. In R. G. Adams & R. Sardiello (Eds.), *Deadhead social science: You ain't gonna learn what you don't want to know* (pp. 51–74). Lanham, MD: AltaMira Press.

Sifrey, M. L. (2010, July 27). Religious identity and Internet use in America. *techPresident.* Blog reporting Pew Internet and American Life Project survey conducted January 14–27, 2010. Retrieved from http://techpresident.com/blog-entry/religious-identity-and-internet-use-america

Silk, M. (1995). *Unsecular media: Making news of religion in America.* Urbana: University of Illinois Press.

Silverblatt, A. (2001). *Media literacy: Keys to interpreting media messages.* Westport, CT: Praeger.

Simon, R. (1966). *The reformation.* New York: Time-Life Books.

Sitney, P. A. (2002). *Visionary film: The American avant-garde, 1943–2000* (3rd ed.). Oxford, England: Oxford University Press.

Skinner, A. C., & Millett, R. L. (1999). *C. S. Lewis: The man and his message, a Latter-Day Saint perspective.* Salt Lake City, UT: Bookcraft.

Sloan, W. D. (2000). The origins of the American newspaper. In W. D. Sloan (Ed.), *Media and religion in American history* (pp. 32–53). Northport, AL: Vision Press.

Smith, K. (Producer & Director). (1999). *Dogma* [Motion picture]. USA: Lions Gate Entertainment.

Sobel, D. (1999). *Galileo's daughter: An historical memoir of science, faith, and love.* New York: Walker & Company.

Soukup, P. (2006). Contexts of faith: The religious foundation of Walter Ong's literacy and orality. *The Journal of Media and Religion, 5*(3), 175–188.

Spielberg, S., Molen, G., & Lusting, B. (Producers). Spielberg, S. (Director). (1993). *Schindler's list* [Motion picture]. USA: Amblin Entertainment.

Spilka, B., Hood, R. W., Hunsberger, B., & Gorsuch, R. (2003). *The psychology of religion: An empirical approach* (3rd ed.). New York: Guilford Press.

Stark, R., & Finke, R. (2002). Beyond church and sect: Dynamics and stability in religious economics. In T. G. Jelen (Ed.), *Sacred markets, sacred canopies: Essays on religious markets and religious pluralism* (pp. 31–62). Lanham, MD: Rowman & Littlefield.

Steinbeck, J. (1939). *The grapes of wrath.* New York: The Viking Press.

Steinberg, S. R., & Kincheloe, J. L. (Eds.). (2009). *Christotainment: Selling Jesus through popular culture.* Boulder, CO: Westview Press.

Stolow, J. (2006). Communicating authority, consuming tradition: Jewish Orthodox outreach literature and its reading public. In B. Meter & A. Moors (Eds.), *Religion, media, and the public sphere* (pp. 73–90). Bloomington: Indiana University Press.

Stout, D. A. (1996). Protecting the family: Mormon teachings about mass media. In D. A. Stout & J. M. Buddenbaum (Eds.), *Religion and mass media: Audiences and* adaptations (pp. 85–99). Thousand Oaks, CA: Sage.

Stout, D. A. (2001). Beyond culture wars: An Introduction to the Study of Religion and Popular Culture. In D. A. Stout & J. M. Buddenbaum (Eds.), *Religion and mass media: Audiences and adaptations* (pp. 3–18). Thousand Oaks, CA: Sage.

Stout, D. A. (2002). Religious media literacy: Toward a research agenda. *Journal of Media and Religion, 1*(1), 49–60.

Stout, D. A. (2004). Secularization and the religious audience: A study of Mormons and Las Vegas media. *Mass Communication and Society, 7*(1), 61–75.

Stout, D. A., & Buddenbaum, J. M. (Eds.). (1996). *Religion and mass media: Audiences and adaptations.* Thousand Oaks, CA: Sage.

Stout, D. A., & Buddenbaum, J. M. (Eds.). (2001). *Religion and popular culture: Studies on the interaction of worldviews.* Ames: Iowa State University Press.

Stout, D. A., & Buddenbaum, J. M. (2002a). Genealogy of an emerging field: Foundations for the study of media and religion [Special issue]. *Journal of Media and Religion, 1*(1), 5–12.

Stout, D. A., & Buddenbaum, J. M. (Eds.). (2002b). Religion and television [Special issue]. *Journal of Media and Religion, 1*(3), 61–74.

Stout, D. A., Martin, D. W., & Scott, D. W. (1996). In D. A. Stout & J. M. Buddenbaum (Eds.), *Religion and mass media: Audiences and* adaptations (pp. 243–260). Thousand Oaks, CA: Sage.

Stout, D. A., & Scott, D. (2003, August). *Religious community on the Internet: An exploratory analysis of Mormon websites.* Paper presented at the annual meeting of the Association for Education in Journalism and Mass Communication (AEJMC). Kansas City, Missouri.

Stout, D. A., Straubhaar, J., & Newbold, G. (2001). Critics as audience: Perceptions of Mormons in Reviews of Tony Kushner's *Angels in America.* In D. A. Stout & J. M. Buddenbaum (Eds.), *Religion and popular culture: Studies on the interaction of worldviews* (pp. 187–215). Ames: Iowa State University Press.

Strate, L. (2006a). *Echoes and reflections: On media ecology as a field of study.* Cresskill, NJ: Hampton Press.

Strate, L. (2006b). The Judaic roots of Neil Postman's cultural commentary. *The Journal of Media and Religion 5*(3), 189–208.

Strayer, K .L. (2010). Anabaptists. In D. A. Stout (Ed.), *Encyclopedia of religion, communication, and media* (pp. 8–11). New York: Routledge.

Streisand, B. (Director). (1983). *Yentl* [Motion picture]. USA: Metro-Goldwyn-Mayer.

Study of Online Consumer Segmentation Uncovers "Occasionalization" as Next Step to reviving marketing and retailing on the Web. (2001). *Booz-Allen & Hamilton and Nielsen Net ratings study.* Retrieved August 26, 2011, from http://findarticles.com/p/articles/mi_m0EIN/is_2001_April_2/ai_72585138/

Sturgill, A. (2004). Scope and purposes of church web sites. *Journal of Media and Religion, 3*(3), 165–176.

Stipe, M. (Producer). (2004). *Saved* [Motion picture]. USA: United Artists.

Sylvan, R. (2001). Rap music, hip–hop culture, and "the future religion of the world." In E. M. Mazur & K. McCarthy (Eds.), *God in the details: American religion in popular culture* (pp. 281–298). New York: Routledge.

Sylvan, R. (2002). *Traces of the spirit: The religious dimensions of popular music.* New York: New York University Press.

Sylvan, R. (2005). *Trance formation: The spiritual and religious dimensions of global rave culture.* Boston: Routledge.

Tanner, R., & Reynolds, V. (1983). *Biology of religion.* Upper Saddle River, NJ: Addison-Wesley.

Tart, C. T. (1983). Altered states of consciousness. In R. Harre & R. Lamb (Eds.), *The encyclopedic dictionary of psychology* (pp. 19–20). Cambridge, MA: MIT Press.

Telushkin, J. (1994). *Jewish wisdom: Ethical, spiritual, and historical lessons from the great works and thinkers.* New York: Morrow.

The Cyberchurch Is Coming: National Survey of Teenagers Shows Expectation of Substituting Internet for Corner Church. (1998). Oxnard, CA: Barna Research Group. Retrieved May 23, 2009, from http://www.barna.org/PressCyberChurch.htm

Thigpen, D. E. (1995, May 22). Leaving little to chants. *Time, 45*(21), 72.

Thompson, J. B. (1990). *Ideology and modern culture.* Stanford, CA: Stanford University Press.

Tilson, D. J. (2000, June). *Devotional-promotional communication and Santiago: A thousand-year public relations campaign for Saint James and Spain.* Paper presented at the 2000 International Invited Seminar, University of Stirling, Stirling Media Research Institute, Stirling, Scotland.

Tilson, D. J., & Chao, Y. Y. (2002). Saintly campaigning: Devotional-promotional communication and the U.S. tour of St. Thérèse's relics. *Journal of Media and Religion, 1*(2), 81–104.

Todorov, T. (1975). *The fantastic: A structural approach to a literary genre.* Ithaca, NY: Cornell University Press.

Tolkein, J. R. R. (1954). *The lord of the rings.* London: Geo, Allen & Unwin.

Toronto, J. A. (2001). Many voices, one Umma: Sociopolitical debate in the Muslim community. In J. W. Welch (Ed.), *BYU studies: LDS scholars engage Islamic thought* (pp. 29–50). Salt Lake City, UT: Brigham Young University.

Toronto, J. A., & Finlayson, C. (2001). Islam: An introduction and bibliography. In J. W. Welch (Ed.), *BYU studies: LDS scholars engage Islamic thought* (pp. 8–28). Salt Lake City, UT: Brigham Young University.

Trumbill, C. G. (1913). *Anthony Comstock, fighter.* New York: Fleming H. Revell.

Turner, V. (1974). *Dramas, fields, and metaphors: Symbolic action in human society.* Ithaca, NY: Cornell University Press.

Turow, J. T. (1992). *Media systems and society: Understanding industries, strategies, and power.* New York: Longman.

Tuzin, D. (1984). Miraculous voices: The auditory experience of numinous objects. *Current Anthropology, 25*(5), 579–596.

Underwood, D. (2006). The problem with Paul: Seeds of the culture wars and the dilemma of journalists. *Journal of Media and Religion, 5*(2), 71–90.

Updike, J. (1960). *Rabbit run.* New York: Alfred A. Knopf.

Updike, J. (1999). *More matter: Essays and criticism.* New York: Knopf.

Valenzano, J. M., & Menegatos, L. (2008). Benedict the bifurcated: Secular and sacred framing of the Pope and Turkey. *Journal of Media and Religion, 7,* 207–230.

Valenti, J., & Stout, D. A. (1996). Diversity from within: An analysis of the impact of religious culture on media use and effective communication to women. In D. A. Stout & J. M. Buddenbaum (Eds.), *Religion and mass media: Audiences and* adaptations (pp. 183–196). Thousand Oaks, CA: Sage.

Valiunis, A. (Jan., 2006). Spirit in the abstract. *First Things.* Retrieved from http://www.firstthings.com/article/2007/01/spirit-in-the-abstract

Vance-Trembath, S. (2006). Catholicism. In D. A. Stout (Ed.), *Encyclopedia of religion, communication, and media* (pp. 196–203). New York: Routledge.

Veysey, L. R. (1965). *The emergence of the American university.* Chicago: University of Chicago Press.

Voltaire, (1759). *Candide.* Paris: Kramer.

Vultee, F., Craft, S., & Velker (2010). Faith and values: Journalism and the critique of religion coverage of the 1990's. *Journal of Media and Religion, 9,* 150–164.

Warren, H. (2010). Television. In D. A. Stout (Ed.), *The Routledge encyclopedia of religion, communication, and media* (pp. 428–430). New York: Routledge.

Warren, H. (2001). Southern Baptists as audience and public: A cultural analysis of the Disney boycott. In D. A. Stout & J. M. Buddenbaum (Eds.), *Religion and popular culture: Studies on the interaction of worldviews* (pp. 169–186). Ames: Iowa State University Press.

Warren, H. (2005). *There's never been a show like Veggie tales: Sacred messages in a secular market.* Lanham, MD: AltaMira Press.

Waters, K. (2008). Pursuing periodicals in print and online. In Q. J. Schultze & R. H. Woods (Eds.), *Understanding evangelical media: The changing face of Christian communication* (pp. 71–84). Downers Grove, IL: IVP Academic.

Webster, R. W. (1990). *A brief history of blasphemy: Liberalism, censorship, and "The Satanic Verses."* Ipswich, UK: Orwell Press.

Weisberger, B. A. (1958). *They gathered at the river: The story of the great revivalists and their impact among religion in America.* Boston and Toronto: Little, Brown.

Wellman, B. (1999). The network community. In B. Wellman (Ed.), *Networks in the global village*. Boulder, CO: Westview Press.

Wellman, B., & Gulia, M. (1999). Virtual communities as communities: Net surfers don't ride alone. In M. A. Smith & P. Kollock (Eds.), *Communities in cyberspace* (pp. 167–194). New York: Routledge.

Whitaker J., & Atkinson, K. (Producers). Atkinson, K. (Director). (1974). *Cipher in the snow* [Motion picture]. USA: Brigham Young University.

Whitemen, V. L., & Nielsen, M. (1986). An experiment to evaluate drama as a method for teaching social work research. *Journal of Social Work Education, 3*, 31–42.

Whitfield, S. J. (2000). The Jewish contribution to American journalism. In W. D. Sloan (Ed.), *Media and religion in American history* (pp. 166–185). Northport, AL: Vision Press.

Wiener, N. (1948). *Cybernetics, or control and communication in the animal and machine*. Cambridge, MA: MIT Press.

Wigoder, G. (2002). *The new encyclopedia of Judaism*. New York: New York University Press.

Williamson, M. (Producer). (2003). *Touched by an angel* [TV series]. USA: Moon Water Productions.

Woods, C. (Producer). Anspaugh, D. (Director). (1993). *Rudy* [Motion picture]. USA: TriStar Pictures.

Woods, R. H., & Patton, P. (2010). *Prophetically incorrect: A Christian introduction to media criticism*. Grand Rapids, MI: Brazos Press.

Wright, C. (1986). *Mass communication: A sociological perspective* (3d ed.). New York: Random House.

Wuthnow, R. (1988). *The restructuring of American religion*. Princeton, NJ: Princeton University Press.

Wuthnow, R. (1994). *Producing the sacred: An essay on public religion*. Urbana: University of Illinois Press.

Wuthnow, R. (2003). *All in sync: How music and art is revitalizing American religion*. Berkeley: University of California Press.

Yerkes, J. (Ed). (1999). *John Updike and religion: The sense of the sacred and the motions of grace*. Grand Rapids, MI: Eerdmans.

Young, B. (1977). *Discourses of Brigham Young*. (J. A. Widstoe, Ed.). Salt Lake City, UT: Deseret.

Young, B. W. (1994). Moral and philosophical criticism. In D. L. Cowles (Ed.), *The critical experience: Literary reading, writing, and criticism* (pp. 22–47). Dubuque, Iowa: Kendall/Hunt.

Zaleski, J. (1997). *The soul of cyberspace: How technology is changing our spiritual lives*. New York: HarperEdge.

Index

A

Abdul Aziz, 42

Access to Insight Web site, 44

accuracy and religion reporting, 106–107

activism: media activism, 110–111;
  theologically based activism, 108–110

advertising. *See* strategic communication

affect and the numinous, 6

age of information, 19–20

AHAD (American Hindus against
  Defamation), 43–44, 64–65, 118

AIDS crisis, 68–69, 101

Aken society, 27

Akron Buddhist Cyber Temple, 45

Al Risala ("The Message"), 42

almsgiving, 41, 46

Altar to Elvis (Doss), 50

the Amish, 38–39

Anabaptists, 38–39

ancient Egypt, 14–15, 98

ancient Greece, 15–16, 27

Angel Network, 49

Angels in America (television movie), 41,
  68–71

Angley, Ernest, 28

Anna Karenina (Tolstoy), 49

anthropology and religion, 3, 21, 23

anti-Semitism, 40–41, 118

ARDA (Association of Religion Data
  Archives), 81

Aristotle, 64

art, Christian, 35–36

audience response criticism, 62–63, 71

authority and the Internet, 76

Ayat Ayat Cinta (film), 42

Aztec dancers, 27

B

baby boomers, 48, 117

Bakker, Jim, 19, 64, 91, 101

Bakker, Tammy Faye, 19, 64, 91, 101

Barnum, P. T., 17, 100

barriers to religious media criticism, 3–6,
  67–68

baseball fans, 7

belief and the numinous, 6

Bellow, Saul, 41

Bennett, James Gordon, 99–100

Berava caste, 27

Bhagavad Gita, 29, 43

Bharata Natyam dancers, 27

bias: and religion news coverage, 103–105;
  and Western self, 27–28

the Bible, 29, 38

Big Love (television miniseries), 101–102

blasphemy and media criticism, 119–120, 121

blogs, religious, 80, 82, 93, 103, 111

Bodhi Magazine, 44

The Book of Mormon (Broadway show), 114

Boston Red Sox, 54

brain processes, 11, 26–27

branding, religious, 18, 114–115, 121

Brigham Young University, 40

Brooklyn Daily Eagle, 64

Buddhism, 44–45, 105, 108
Buffett, Jimmy, 52–53
Building a Bridge to the Eighteenth Century (Postman), 109–110
Burning Man festival, 31

C
Campbell, Heidi, 73–74
catechism, 22, 46
Catholic rock mass, 28, 36, 86
Catholicism, 35–37, 78–79, 102, 120
Cayce, Edgar, 18
celebrity and religion, 94–95, 96
censorship, 35–36, 46, 67–68, 110–111
charismatic megachurches, 1, 25, 31, 57–58
The Chosen (film), 41
Christian paradox of the world, 34
Christian Science Monitor, 100
Christianity as media audience, 34–40
Church of Fools, 80
Cipher in the Snow (Sheldon), 62
civil religion, 12
classroom learning activities: overview, 123–124; *Redeeming Value* play, 125–164; *Redeeming Value* synopsis, 124; using the play in the classroom, 124–125
closed system of religious journalism, 109, 112
cocooning, 76–77, 82
commercialism and religion, 93–94, 114, 116–117
communications evolution, 2
communitas rituals, 58
communities: and the Internet, 74–75, 101–102; interpretive, 33–34; and journalism, 101–102, 111, 112; and mainline Protestantism, 38; and media–religion studies, 11–12; and the numinous, 6; and popular media, 47–48; Satsanghi textual communities, 43
compatibility argument, 87–88, 96
Comstock, Anthony, 67–68
congregations. *See* communities
conservative Protestants, 37, 102, 106
consumer culture, 114, 117, 121
conventions, Star Trek, 51
conversion, demonstrative, 27
Cook, James, 27
correlation as mass media function, 20
critical studies, 65–66
criticism. *See* media criticism
crossover entertainment, 93–94, 96
Crystal Cathedral, 57

cultural conflict and media–religion dualism, 5
cultural religion: overview, 47–48, 58; charismatic megachurches, 57–58; Deadheads and Parrotheads, 52–54; defined, 8; described, 12; Elvis fandom and worship, 50–51; emergent churches, 56–57; and mediazation of shared culture, 15; and the numinous, 58; Oprah Winfrey, 49; questions to ponder, 59; Rothko Chapel community, 55–56; sports fans, 54–55; Trekkies, 51
culture war, 8
The Curious Case of Benjamin Button (film), 36
Cyber Temple of Shaolin Zen, 45
cyberchurches, 79–80, 82

D
Da Vinci, Leonardo, 35, 119
Dalai Lama, 94, 105
dance raves, 7, 13–14, 25
database proselytizing, 78, 82
Dawkins, Richard, 4
Deadheads, 7, 52–54
decision-making and new media technology, 74
deep listening, 11, 26, 32
defamation, 43–44, 64, 103, 112, 118, 121
definitions of religion, 3–4
demonstrative conversions, 27
denominational religion: defined, 8; and Internet strategies, 77–79; and the numinous, 45
Devil's Playground (film), 39
Devine, Dan, 65
Dhamma media, 44
didactic criticism, 62, 71
Disney products, 5, 12
Dobson, James, 4, 37, 89
dogma, 46
drummer caste, 27
dualism, 4–5, 8, 62

E
early religious cultures and entertainment, 85–86
ecstatic states, 11, 13–14, 17
Eddy, Mary Baker, 100
education and religion reporting, 105–106
Egypy, ancient, 14–15, 98
Eliade, Mircea, 3
Elvis fandom, 4, 7, 50–51, 95

emergent churches, 56–57
enlightenment, 44–45
entertainment media: overview, 85;
    compatibility argument, 87–88; and
    emergent churches, 56–58; entertainment
    media, 88–93; films, 90; incompatibility
    argument, 87; as mass media function,
    20; new forms of religious entertainment,
    93–94; and the numinous, 95; online
    entertainment, 92–93; popular fiction,
    88; questions to ponder, 96; radio, 89–90;
    religion and celebrity, 94–95; and religion
    fusion, 85–87; television, 91–92
ethical criticism, 63–65
Evangelical Christians, 18–19, 37, 102, 106,
    116

F

Facebook, 19
faith and religious entertainment, 87–88
Falun Gong, 110–111
Falwell, Jerry, 19
the fantastic, 6
fatwah, 42, 46, 68
Fenway Park, 54
fiction, religious, 88
films and religious entertainment, 33, 39,
    44, 90
"Fins" and Jimmy Buffett concerts, 53
Fischer, C. S., 75
Five Pillars of Islam, 41–42, 46
flow, 28–30, 32
Focus on the Family radio program, 4, 37,
    89–90, 108
formalism, 63
fourth estate, 108, 112
Freud, Sigmund, 6
Frey, James, 49
Fuller, Charles, 101
Fundamentalists, 102, 104, 106

G

Ga society, 27
Garcia, Jerry, 52–53
genetics and religion, 25
genre communities, 21, 33–34
Gilded Age, 100
glossolalia, 27, 32
God's Army (film), 39
Godspell (musical), 17
Goodman, Elayne, 50
The Gospel According to Oprah (Nelson), 49
Graceland, 50

Graham, Billy, 18, 54
Grapes of Wrath (Steinbeck), 63, 88
Grateful Dead band, 52
the Great Awakening, 28

H

Habits of the High-Tech Heart (Schultze), 74
Haredi orthodox Jews, 40
Harris, Sam, 4
Haskalah (enlightenment), 41
Hebrew Bible, 40
hierarchy maintenance and denominational
    Internet use, 78–79
Hinduism, 42–44, 64–65, 86
Hinn, Benny, 28
Hitchens, Christopher, 4
Homer, 15
The Hour of Power, 57
Hutterites, 38–39, 79
hybrid genres, 42, 71, 89–90, 96, 111
hypothalamus, 32

I

iconography, nondenominational, 55–56
Idaho Statesman, 105
The Idea of the Holy (Otto), 7
identity and the Internet, 75–76
idolatry and celebrity worship, 95
IMC (integrated marketing communication),
    118, 121
In His Steps (Sheldon), 62
inclusiveness and religion reporting, 107
incompatibility argument, 87, 96
Index of Forbidden Books, 36
indirect censorship, 68
Industrial Revolution, 114, 117, 121
information age, 19–20
information society, 23
informationism, 87
integrated marketing, 118
interactivity, 92
interdisciplinary studies, 166–167
International Church of Las Vegas, 57
the Internet: age of information and
    networks, 20–21; authority questions, 76;
    Catholic Web sites, 36–37; community
    issues, 74–75; and flow, 29–30; full-
    experience occasions, 79–80; hierarchy
    maintenance, 78–79; identity questions,
    75–76; information boundaries, 79;
    institutional strategies, 77–79; the
    Internet and the numinous, 74; Internet
    neutrality myth, 81–82;

the Internet (*continued*) and media activism,
  43–44; media vs. message, 13; and
  numinous media, 31; occasionalization,
  79–81; proselytizing, 78; questions to
  ponder, 83; and religious entertainment,
  92–93; social network occasions, 80–81;
  user perspectives, 76–77
interpretive communities, 11–12, 21, 23,
  33–34, 43–45, 46
Iranian Muslims, 42
Islam, 41–42, 76, 110

J
Jackson, Michael, 95
jam bands, 54
The Jazz Singer (film), 41
Jesus Christ Superstar (musical), 17
John Paul II, Pope, 35
journalism and religion: overview, 97–98;
  demands of the news media, 102–103;
  Gilded Age revivalism, 99–100; and the
  information age, 101–102; journalism and
  the numinous, 111–112; media activism,
  110–111; in New England, 98–99; the
  printing press, 98; questions to ponder,
  112; religion in the news, 103–105;
  reporting principles, 105–107; sacred-
  secular divide of modern era, 100–101;
  theologically based journalism, 107–110
Judaism, 33, 40–41

K
Kant, Emmanuel, 64
Karma, 43
Krishna, 43–44, 46, 64–65
Kushner, Tony, 68–70

L
Lady Gaga, 54
Lakewood Church, 12, 57
Las Vegas, Nevada, 40, 93–94
Last Judgement (painting), 36
The Last Supper (painting), 35, 119
The Last Temptation of Christ, 4, 90
Leaves of Grass (Whitman), 67
Legion of Decency, 36
leisure and religious entertainment, 86–87, 9
  6
Lennon, John, 94
liminality, 53, 58, 59
literacy: media, 61, 67–68, 71, 91; religious,
  106
literary criticism, 22–23

literature: and flow mental state, 29; and
  genre communities, 33; and Hinduism,
  43; and Judaism, 40–41; Mormon, 39
little ones concept, 36
Love Guru (film), 64
Luther, Martin, 16, 115

M
MacLaine, Shirley, 18
mainline Protestants, 37–38, 102
Malamud, Bernard, 41
Man and Superman (play), 63
Margaritaville, 53
marketing. *See* strategic communication
marketplace of ideas, 38, 46, 112
Marxist analysis, 65–66
masala films, 44
mass media functions, 20
material culture and religion, 93–94, 114,
  116–117
materialism, 66
media activism, 110–111, 112
media as religion, 9–10, 23, 33
media-centric community, 58
media convergence, 32
media criticism: overview, 61–62; audience
  response criticism, 62–63; barriers
  to, 3–6, 67–68; didactic criticism, 62;
  ethical criticism, 63–65; formalism, 63;
  Marxist and critical analysis, 65–66; and
  the numinous, 66–67, 71; questions to
  ponder, 72; sample critique of *Angels in
  America*, 68–71
media ecology, 22, 23
media history: the 1960s, 17; age of
  information and networks, 19–20; ancient
  Egypt, 14–15; ancient Greece and oral
  tradition, 15–16; ecstatic states, 13–14;
  nineteenth-century revivalism, 16–17; the
  Reformation, 16; televangelism, 18–19;
  twentieth-century New Age religion, 18
media literacy, 61, 67–68, 71, 91
media message communities, 11–12
media rejection, 21, 34, 38–39
media–religion interface: barriers to media
  and religion studies, 3–6; depictions
  of religions and public relations, 1; and
  interdisciplinary studies, 166–167; levels
  of analysis, 11–12; and popular culture,
  2; questions to ponder, 8; religion and
  the numinous, 6–7; religion as broad
  analytical concept, 2–3; varied types of,
  1–2

media–religion studies: the 1960s, 17; age of information and networks, 19–20; and ancient Egypt, 14–15; ancient Greece and the oral tradition, 15–16; and anthropology, 22; current day synthesis, 20; historical insights, 13–20; interdisciplinary, 5, 20–21, 166–167; levels of analysis, 11–12; and literary criticism, 22–23; media as religion, 9–10; and media ecology, 22; medium vs. message, 13; need for common analysis terminology, 5–6; nineteenth-century revivalism, 16–17; personalized religion, 11; and psychology, 21; questions to ponder, 24; the Reformation, 16; secularization, 12–13; and sociology, 21; televangelism, 18–19, 64, 71, 92, 96; trance behavior and ecstatic states, 13–14; twentieth-century New Age religion, 18
mediated religion, 8
mediazation, 15, 23
meditation, 30, 32, 56
medium vs. message, 13
Medved, Michael, 4
megachurches, 1, 25, 31, 57–58
Mennonites, 38–39
mental states: defined, 32; emotional states and the brain, 26–27; flow, 28–30; meditation, 30; and numinous media, 31; trance, 30–31, *See also* physiology and mental states
merchandising and New Age religion, 18
Mere Christianity (Lewis), 29
Michelangelo, 35, 36
Midway to Heaven (film), 39
Mill, John Stuart, 64
Moody, Dwight L., 87, 100
moral engagement and media rituals, 10
Mormons: and *Angels in America*, 69–71; and *Big Love*, 101–102; and the Internet, 76, 78; as media audience, 39–40; media coverage of, 104, 106, 108–109; and media rejection, 21, 34; Mormon film, 33, 39; Mormon literature, 88; and religious branding, 114; and secularization, 12
Morrison, Jim, 17
Muhammed, Prophet, 41, 42
music festivals, 17
Muslims, 21, 76, 104

N

National Catholic Reporter, 2
The National Catholic Reporter, 36

The Natural (film), 63
Nazarenes, 34, 68
neurophysiology, 32
neutrality myth, 81–82
New Age religion, 18, 30, 48
New England and religion journalism, 98–99
New York Herald, 99–100
the news. *See* journalism and religion
Newsweek, 73, 101
NFL (National Football League), 55
the 1960s, 17, 28
nineteenth-century revivalism, 16–17, 87, 99–100
Nirvana, 45
Nixon, Richard, 17
NPR (National Public Radio), 102
the numinous: and advertising, 120; and cultural religion, 58; and denominational audiences, 45; described, 6–7; and entertainment, 95; and journalism, 111–112; numinous media and mental states, 31; and semantics of "religion", 4

O

O magazine, 49
occasionalization and Internet usage, 79–82
Old Fashioned Revival Hour, 101
oral tradition, 15–16
Osteen, Joel, 12, 19, 57, 94
Otto, Rudolph, 7
Out on a Limb (MacLaine), 18

P

pamphlets and religious advertising, 115
Paradise Lost (Milton), 29
parishioners. *See* communities
Parrotheads, 7, 52–53
The Passion of Christ (film), 25, 80, 90, 117
Pentecostal songs, 28
People of the Book, 40
permission marketing, 78, 82
personal identity and the Internet, 75–76
personal media environments, 32
personalized religion, 11, 24
physiology and mental states: overview, 25–26; brain processes and media–religion studies, 11; and current day numinous media, 31; emotional states and the brain, 26–27; flow, 28–30; meditation, 30; questions to ponder, 32; religion and mental states through time, 27–28; trance, 30–31; types of mental states, 28–31

The Pietà (statue), 35
pilgrimage, 46
Pilgrim's Progress (Bunyan), 29
Pizzo, Angelo, 65
pluralism, religious, 16, 48, 58, 107, 116, 121
Pontifical Council for Social
    Communications, 36
popular fiction and religious entertainment,
    88
popular media and flow, 29
postmodern religion, 49
Potok, Chaim, 41, 88
Potter, Ralph, 64
preaching and social media, 40, 78
Presley, Elvis, 4, 7, 50–51, 95
Prestonwood Baptist Church, 57, 93
primary ties, 80, 82
printing as numinous medium, 16
printing press and religion journalism, 98
privatized religious experience, 10, 19
problem-based learning. *See* classroom
    learning activities
Prophetically Incorrect (Wood and Patton), 22
proselytizing and the Internet, 40, 78
Protestants, 37–39, 102
psychology and religion, 21, 24
public relations. *See* strategic communication
pulpit as stage, 17
Puritanism, 27, 28, 108

Q

"questers", 1–2, 83, 87–88
the Quran, 29, 42

R

R-rated movies, 21, 34, 39, 68
radio: and religious entertainment, 89–90;
    and religious journalism, 100–101, 102,
    108, 111
Radio Islam, 2, 42
rave events, 31
Real Life Singles Ward (film), 39
reciprocal relationships, 114, 115, 121
the Reformation, 16, 46
Reformed Church in America, 57
reincarnation, 43
religion: as analytical concept, 2–3, 165–166;
    as commodity, 48; and semantics, 3–4
religion–marketing paradox, 115–116
religious attitude and the numinous, 6
religious branding, 18, 114–115, 121
religious cultural shifts, 7
religious literacy, 106

religious news publications, 63–64, 71
religious pluralism, 16, 48, 58, 107, 116, 121
religious theater, 17
Rent (musical), 6–7
revivalism, nineteenth century, 16–17, 87,
    99–100
ritual behavior: anthropological study of,
    22; communitas rituals, 58; defined, 8;
    and Elvis fandom, 4, 7, 50–51, 95; and the
    Internet, 77, 82; and media as religion, 10,
    22; and the numinous, 6; ritual healing,
    27
ritual view of communication, 10
RNA (Religion Newswriters Association),
    101, 106, 107
Robertson, Pat, 19, 101
Roman Catholicism, 35–37, 78–79, 102, 120
Romney, Mitt, 104
Roth, Philip, 41
Rothko Community Chapel, 55–56
Rothko, Mark, 55
Rudy (film), 65
rumspringa, 38–39
Rushdie, Salman, 4, 42, 68
Russell, Charles Taze, 64

S

sacred-secular divide and journalism,
    100–101
Satanic Verses (Rushdie), 4, 42, 68
Satsanghi textual communities, 43
Schindler's List (film), 67
Second Life, 80
secondary ties, 80, 82
secularism: advertising and religion,
    119–120; sacred-secular divide and
    journalism, 100–101
secularization: defined, 8; and media-
    religion studies, 12–13; overlap with
    religious entertainment, 93–94; theory, 24
Seinfeld (television program), 41
Shakers, 25
Shambhala Sun, 44
Shankar, Ravi, 17
Shaw, George Bernard, 63
Sheen, Fulton J., 18, 91
Show Me!, 64
Simon Birch (film), 63, 90
The Simpsons (television show), 91
Slumdog Millionaire (film), 36
Smith, Joseph, 39
social networks: age of, 19–20; and religious
    Internet usage, 80–81; and religious news,

101–102; social media and religiosity, 77, 82

socialization, 20

societal religion, 12

sociology and religion, 21, 24

Southern Baptist Convention, 5, 12

"The Space" and Grateful Dead concerts, 52–53

speaking in tongues, 27, 32

the Spinners, 53

spiritual marketplace, 117, 121

spiritualism, 17, 28

spirituality and Oprah Winfrey, 49

sports fans, 7, 54–55

St. Thérèse relics, 120

Star Trek (television program), 51, 63

Staubach, Roger, 54

stone architecture, 14

storytelling analysis, 63

strategic communication: overview, 113–115; advertising and the numinous, 120; growth of religious advertising, 116–118; integrated marketing, 118; material culture and religion, 93–94, 114, 116–117; public relations, 118; questions to ponder, 122; religion in secular advertising, 119–120; religion–marketing paradox, 115–116; and religious branding, 18, 114–115, 121; and religious pluralism, 116; spiritual marketplace, 117

Super Bowl Sunday, 55

surveillance, 20

Swaggert, Jimmy, 19

Swidan, Sheik Tarek, 42

symbol flattening, 119, 121

T

televangelism, 18–19, 64, 71, 92, 96

television: and Mormonism, 39–40; religion in secular advertising, 119–120; and religious entertainment, 91–92; and religious journalism, 111

Tennent, Gilbert, 99

the news. *See* journalism and religion

the numinous: and denominational audiences, 45; and the Internet, 74; and media criticism, 66–67, 71

Thebes, 14

theologically based activism, 108–110

Thirtysomething (television program), 41, 92

Torah, 29, 40

trance behaviors: and brain processes, 11, 25–27; described, 30–31, 32; and media

history, 13–14; and music concerts, 52–53

Trekkies, 51

Tricycle, 44, 108

Trinity United Church of Christ, 49

truth in art, 65

Turkle, Sherry, 73

Tutu, Desmond (Archbishop), 94

twentieth-century New Age religion, 18

Twitter, 75, 80–81

U

UFO enthusiasts, 7, 18

Ulee's Gold (Demme), 63

the uncanny, 6

Unitarianism, 79

Universal Ethician Church, 56

Universal Life Church On-Line, 77

Unsecular Media (Silk), 22

Unshackled! radio drama, 89

Updike, John, 63, 88

user perspectives and the Internet, 76–77

V

valuing process, 81, 82

vani (text) interpretations, 43

the Vatican, 36–37, 80

video games, religious, 29–30

Vietnam War, 17, 28

The Village (film), 63

virtual communities, 43–44

W

Watchtower (magazine), 64, 109

Western self and ecstatic states, 27–28

Whitefield, George, 99

Whitman, Walt, 67

Widespread Panic, 54

Wilson, Ron, 78

Winfrey, Oprah, 2, 7, 49

The Wizard of Oz (film), 65–66

Woodstock music festival, 17

world religions and denominations: overview, 33, 45; Anabaptists, 38–39; Buddhism, 44–45; Christian audiences, 34–40; from congregation to interpretive community, 33–34; conservative Protestants, 37; Hinduism, 42–44; Islam, 41–42; Judaism, 40–41; mainline Protestants, 37–38; Mormons, 39–40; Protestants, 37–39; questions to ponder, 46; religious organizations and the media, 34–45; Roman Catholics, 35–37

X

Xena, Warrior Princess (television program), 43–44

Y

Yentl (film), 41
young adults and cultural religion, 48
Young, Brigham, 39